D1744565

WOMEN'S WRITING AND MUSLIM SOCIETIES

Women's Writing and Muslim Societies

THE SEARCH FOR DIALOGUE, 1920–PRESENT

Sharif Gemie

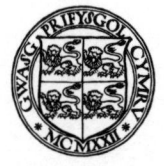

UNIVERSITY OF WALES PRESS
CARDIFF
2012

British Library Cataloguing-in-Publication Data
A catalogue record for this book is available from the British Library.

ISBN   978-0-7083-2539-1 (hardback)
        978-0-7083-2540-7 (paperback)
e-ISBN 978-0-7083-2541-4

Typeset by Mark Heslington Ltd, Scarborough, North Yorkshire
Printed by CPI Antony Rowe, Chippenham, Wiltshire

SMILE

From S to A and back again: the most important return journey in the world

Contents

Acknowledgements

This is the first work I have written without Pat. This was a difficult task, made a little easier by help and assistance from a range of people. In no particular order, I would like to thank Catherine Phelps, for her detailed criticism of the manuscript; Sarah Lewis of University of Wales Press, for her guidance; Hannah Perlin, Heather Parnell, Tim Jones, Diana Wallace and Ali Wardak for their advice on particular points; Miss Rutherly Stanshore and the Invisible Brethren (and sistren) for support and encouragement; Roz and Tim, as ever.

Note on Citations

Within this work there are many quotations from a range of works. These are all short: most of them are less than 60 words long, and none is longer than 180 words. All of these are properly referenced. After some consultation, we consider that these come under the Fair Use provision, and do not constitute a commercial exploitation of author's work. Permission to cite short extracts has been received from the following publishers:

Pages 39 and 52 from *Selected Writings*, Mai Ghoussoub, edited by Rebecca O'Connor, Saqi Books, London, 2008.

Extracts from *The Butterfly Mosque: A Young Woman's Journey to Love and Islam* by Wilson, G. Willow reproduced by permission of Atlantic Books.

Extracts from *In Search of Fatima: A Palestinian Story* by Karmi, Ghada, reproduced by permission of Verso.

List of citations

Qanta A. Ahmed, MD, *In the Land of Invisible Women: a Female Doctor's Journey in the Saudi Kingdom* (Naperville, Ill.: Sourcebooks, 2008). Four citations of 68 words, 148 words, 71 words and 83 words.

Fadia Basrawi, *Brownies and Kalashnikovs: a Saudi Woman's Memoir of American Arabia and Wartime Beirut* (Reading: South Street Press, 2009). One citation of 40 words.

Rania al-Baz, *Défigurée: quand un crime passionnel devient affaire d'Etat* (Paris: Michel Lafon, 2005). One translated citation of 117 words.

Hélé Béji, *Islam Pride: Derrière le voile* (Paris: Gallimard, 2011). Two translated citations of 75 words and 48 words.

Carmen Bin Ladin, *The Veiled Kingdom* (London: Virago, 2004). Two citations of 22 words and 69 words.

Laura Blumenfeld, *Revenge: a Story of Hope* (London: Picador, 2002). One citation of 38 words.

Dounia Bouzar and Saïda Kada, *L'une voilée, l'autre pas: le témoignage de deux musulmanes françaises* (Paris: Albin Michel, 2003). One translated citation of 47 words.

Pamela Bright, *A Poor Man's Riches* (Liverpool: MacGibbon and Kee, 1966). One citation of 46 words.

Anne Brunswic, *Bienvenue en Palestine: Chroniques d'une saison à Ramallah* nouvelle édition (Arles: Actes Sud, 2004). One translated citation of 94 words.

Lady Evelyn Cobbold, *Pilgrimage to Mecca* (1934; London: Arabian Publishing, 2009). One citation of 137 words.

Pauline Cutting, *Children of the Siege* (London: Heinemann, 1988). One citation of 126 words.

Waris Dirie and Cathleen Miller, *Desert Flower: the Extraordinary Life of a Desert Nomad* (London: Virago, 1998). One citation of 36 words.

Hadani Ditmars, *Dancing in the No-fly Zone: a Woman's Journey through Iraq* (Adlestrop: Arris Books, 2006). One citation of 42 words.

Veronica Doubleday, *Three Women of Herat* (London: Jonathan Cape, 1988). One citation of 65 words.

Oriana Fallaci, *The Rage and the Pride* (New York: Rizzoli, 2001). Two citations of 11 words and 24 words.

Zlata Filipović, *Zlata's Diary*, trans. Christina Pribichevicj-Zorić (London: Viking, 1994). One citation of 62 words.

Marguerite van Geldermalsen, *Married to a Bedouin* (London: Virago, 2006). One citation of 71 words.

Mai Ghoussoub, *Selected Writings*, ed. Rebecca O'Connor (London: Saqi, 2008). Two citations of 62 words and 55 words.

Joumana Haddad, *I Killed Scheherazade: Confessions of an Angry Arab Woman* (London: Saqi Books, 2010). Three citations of 54 words, 22 words and 27 words.

Lesley Hamilton, *Where the Mountains Roar: In Search of the Sinai Desert* (London: Victor Gollancz, 1980). One citation of 47 words.

Sarah Hobson, *Through Persia in Disguise* (London: John Murray, 1973). Two citations of 65 words and 66 words.

Hala Jaber, *The Flying Carpet to Baghdad: One Woman's Fight for Two Orphans of War* (London: Pan, 2010). Three citations of 117 words, 50 words and 35 words.

Shelina Zahra Janmohamed, *Love in a Headscarf: Muslim Woman Seeks the One* (London: Aurum, 2009). Five citations of 26 words, 47 words, 58 words, 63 words and 90 words.

Ghada Karmi, *In Search of Fatima: a Palestinian Story* (London: Verso, 2002). Six citations of 127 words, 116 words, 55 words, 99 words, 56 words and 92 words.

Shappi Khorsandi, *A Beginner's Guide to Acting English* (n.p.: Ebury Press, 2009). One citation of 40 words.

Norma Khouri, *Forbidden Love: Love and Betrayal in Modern-day Jordan* (London: Doubleday, 2003). One citation of 96 words.

Christina Lamb, *The Sewing Circles of Herat: My Afghan Years* (London: HarperCollins, 2002). Two citations of 129 words and 54 words.

Afschineh Latifi with Pablo F. Fenjives, *Even After All This Time: a Story of Love, Revolution, and Leaving Iran* (London: Fusion, 2005). Three citations of 81 words, 63 words and 51 words.

Pardis Mahdavi, *Passionate Uprisings: Iran's Sexual Revolution* (Stanford California: Stanford University Press: 2009). One citation of 98 words.

Ella K. Maillart, *The Cruel Way* (1947; London: Virago Press, 1986). Three citations of 25 words, 54 words and 97 words.

Zaiba Malik, *We are a Muslim, Please* (London: Windmill Books, 2011). Two citations of 47 words and 112 words.

Azadeh Moaveni, *Lipstick Jihad: a Memoir of Growing Up Iranian in America and American in Iran* (New York: Public Affairs, 2005). Two citations of 46 words and 13 words.

Colette Modiano, *Turkish Coffee and the Fertile Crescent: Wanderings through the Lebanon, Mesopotamia, Israel, Jordan and Syria* (London: Michael Joseph, 1974). One citation of 31 words.

Dervla Murphy, *Full Tilt: Ireland to India with a Bicycle* (London: Eland, 1965). Three citations of 42 words, 27 words and 40 words; *Tales from Two Cities: Travel of Another Sort* (London: John Murray, 1987). Two citations of 49 words and 81 words.

Azar Nafisi, *Reading Lolita in Tehran: a Memoir in Books* (New York: Random House, 2003). Two citations of 71 words and 34 words.

Susan Nathan, *The Other Side of Israel: My Journey Across the Jewish-Arab Divide* (New York: Doubleday, 2005). Two citations of 36 words and 136 words.

Asra Q. Nomani, *Standing Alone in Mecca: an American Woman's Struggle for the Soul of Islam* (San Francisco: HarperSanFrancisco, 2005). Five citations of 3 words, 26 words, 36 words, 75 words and 74 words.

Daniela Norris and Shireen Anabtawi, *Crossing Qalandiya: Exchanges across the Israeli/Palestinian Divide* (London: Reportage, 2010). Two citations of 29 words and 43 words.

Melanie Phillips, *Londonistan: How Britain is Creating a Terror State Within* (London: Gibson Square, 2006). One citation of 41 words.

Rona Randall, *Jordan and the Holy Land* (London: Frederick Muller, 1968). Two citations of 57 words and 72 words

Deborah Rodriguez, *The Kabul Beauty School: the Art of Friendship and Freedom* (London: Hodder & Stoughton, 2008). Five citations of 29 words, 54 words, 27 words, 54 words and 59 words.

Nawal El Saadawi, *The Hidden Face of Eve: Women in the Arab World*, trans. Dr Sherif Hetata (London: Zed Books, 1980). Three citations of 50 words, 100 words and 35 words.

Jehan Sadat, *A Woman of Egypt* (London: Bloomsbury, 1987). Four citations of 26 words, 176 words, 67 words and 151 words.

Zainab Salbi with Laurie Beckland, *Between Two Worlds: Escape into Tyranny; Growing Up in the Shadow of Saddam* (New York: Gotham, 2005). Three citations of 96 words, 65 words and 52 words.

Åsne Seierstad, *The Bookseller of Kabul*, trans. Ingrid Christophersen (London: Little, Brown, 2003). Two citations of 86 words and 70 words.

Freya Stark, *A Winter in Arabia* (1940; London: Arrow Books, 1991). Three citations of 50 words, 134 words and 25 words.

Allegra Stratton, *Muhajababes* (London: Constable, 2006). One citation of 142 words.

Nahal Tajadod, *Passeport à l'iranienne* (Paris: JC Lattès, 2007). One translated citation of 59 words.

Raymonda Hawa Tawil, *My Home, My Prison* (New York: Holt, Rinehart and Winston, 1979). One citation of 97 words.

Suzy Wighton, *One Day at a Time: Diaries from a Palestinian Camp* (London: Hutchinson, 1990). One citation of 88 words.

Emma Williams, *It's Easier to Reach Heaven than the End of the Street: a Jerusalem Memoir* (London: Bloomsbury, 2006). One citation of 134 words.

G. Willow Wilson, *The Butterfly Mosque: a Young Woman's Journey to Love and Islam* (London: Atlantic Books, 2010). Four citations of 66 words, 138 words, 85 words and 90 words.

A Party with a Hundred Women: On Dialogue, Orientalism and Women's Writing

This book is about journeys and about people who travel between cultures. Sometimes making such journeys can seem so simple. Take, for example, a musician like the Moroccan oud player Anouar Brahem. His elegant, precise playing leads assorted trios and quartets, including pianos, oboes, saxophones, accordions and various types of percussion, creating a form of fusion of musical traditions of the Arab world with the improvisatory qualities of jazz and the precision of Western classical music. It's possible to object that these forms and techniques are not really 'Arab', and that – in reality – his discs represent a type of dilution of Arab musical traditions into the forms of the Western world. Brahem would just smile in response. Ask him to include bagpipes, a German oompah band, a bass'n'drums beat, and his smile would grow broader: these would be there on his next album, not sounding exactly as you might expect, but washed into his soaring melodies.

Brahem's work is not a unique example of cross-cultural transfer. Alongside him there are singers such as Iness Mezel, who has made three albums. She was born in Paris, with an Algerian-Berber father and a French-Italian mother. Her family moved to Algiers when she was seven. There she encountered many different forms of musical culture. 'You absorb everything you see and hear and you're happy to discover new things', she recalls. When her family then returned to France, she discovered something else. She gradually became aware of French racism, of the troubled legacy of the bloody struggles of the Algerian war of independence (1954–62) and her father's ambivalence towards France. She's proud of her mixed background: she studied piano at the Conservatoire, and Kabyle, Arab, Algerian, French and Auvergnat cultural forms have also inspired her. She sings in French and Berber. On her latest CD, *Beyond the Trance*, she's assisted by Justin Adams, a type of super-session-musician/multi-instrumentalist/producer, whose growing body of music has spearheaded a style often referred to as 'desert blues'. Here, Tuareg ex-guerrillas and refugees pick up electric guitars and drums and fabricate a droning, repetitive, shuffling, hypnotic beat, quite unlike anything else. Mezel and Adams have successfully worked together to produce a wonderful example of cultural fusion. One reviewer described *Beyond the Trance* as

> a swirling mix of rock and pop and blues and jazz and soul and funk and traditional Berber music. Just when you decide it might be one thing, it turns out to be another, so you cannot make assumptions about the music, you just have to sit and enjoy the ride.[1]

These initiatives are inspiring, suggesting a sort of trans-national, trans-linguistic, cosmopolitan, multi-ethnic zone, a 'Third Space' in the words of Homi Bhabha, a place of exchange, fusion and transformation, independent of the cultural domination of either East or West, created by a new generation of itinerant, multi-talented, poly-cultural artists.[2] They certainly suggest that cultural structures are more plastic than many might think, and point to a cheerfully diverse, libertarian alternative to the threatening global cultural monolith of the McWorld.

Not Without My Daughter

At first sight, the hundred works analysed in this book might well be expected to provide some further examples of 'Third Space' cultures. Each work has been written by someone who is deeply concerned with relations between East and West. In most cases, the authors are humanitarian, thoughtful, caring women, providing clear evidence of their concerns for their immediate family and for the wider world. Their works often appear to be based on an unspoken premise: that women, in particular, have something of value to bring to discussions concerning the evaluation of Muslim societies and cultures. These books usually describe types of journeys, sometimes in the most literal sense of a physical voyage to a different land, but often also in more metaphorical or political senses: perhaps as a passage from a settled, confident community to a more itinerant, uncertain condition. Most of them suggest a quite pessimistic vision of global cultures. Rather than an assured, cosmopolitan mixing of cultures, one finds instead the creation of camps, a desperate, nervous quest for belonging, the construction of walls rather than the building of bridges. The most recent of these books suggest disturbing and threatening visions of the immediate future: few of them suggest any clear hope. These latest authors write with an obvious sense of urgency, appealing for community, solidarity and continuity between particular groups of women.

Betty Mahmoody's *Not Without My Daughter* (1988) is one of the most celebrated of these works (it was the basis for a film script with the same name). The title's four words – with no subtitle – reveal something of the nature and the potential importance of these works: they are written by women in a language which speaks to women's lives; they address the themes of the centrality of family, the preservation of generational continuity and the construction of a female-centred unity in the face of adversity.

In a world where little positive credit is given to women's voices, this is a sphere of exchange and debate which has been largely created by women's initiatives. It is almost certain that because this is such a solidly feminine culture, it has therefore been largely ignored by critical opinion, easily dismissed as some form of sub-anthropological chick lit. I believe that these works teach an important lesson: they tell us something vital about the manner in which globalisation has really been constructed over the past century.

The contrast between the polarised dilemmas suggested by these works and the easy fusion suggested by Brahem's and Mezel's music is clear. Possibly, this is simply a difference in genres. Maybe it is easier for those who practise a non-verbal art to borrow, adapt, transform and re-create; perhaps, despite the examples of postcolonial novels, it remains true that languages and literary forms are too rooted in national or religious cultures to permit any easy crossing of the frontiers. But there remains another dimension to such comparisons: while a relatively wide audience may enjoy Brahem's and Mezel's music, it is to the written word that we turn for clear, hard information about the state of the world. The troubled, uneasy works to be analysed in this book are surprisingly popular: they are commercially viable; they are seized, with alacrity, by major publishing houses, and new titles are appearing each week. Their substantial educational function is one good reason for studying them.

It is difficult to give a precise date for the origins of this form of women's writing. Its probable beginnings lie in the early eighteenth-century development of orientalism. Billie Melman's authoritative study of this topic cites the publication in 1718 of Lady Mary Wortley Montagu's letters concerning Turkey as an important pioneering text.[3] It was followed by a steady stream of publications, running parallel to the rather better-known male writing on the Orient. From its beginnings, this form of women's writing suggested a different approach from that taken by men. 'The women's experience of the Orient was private rather than "civic" or public, individual rather than institutionalised and finally it was a-political', notes

Melman.[4] On occasion, women's works on the Orient were positively valued: women were judged to be capable of forms of empathy and sensitivity which men lacked. In particular, women writers had something specific to say about the structures of the harem, an institution to which foreign men were usually denied access. Often nineteenth-century women writers attempted to de-sensationalise and de-eroticise the harem, producing more realistic pictures of Muslim women's daily lives. At times, their consideration of women's space in the Orient could even lead to critical reflections on women's lives in the West.[5] In literary terms, these women writers followed male writers in taking the older model of the pilgrimage and transforming it into something more secular and modern, contributing to the development of modern travel-writing.

The subsequent development of nineteenth-century orientalism has been studied and evaluated by a number of writers. However, very frequently, these studies stop in 1914, as if the First World War and the subsequent collapse of so many empires ended these literary forms and the questions that they raised. This attitude certainly contrasts with the work of Edward Said, the writer who transformed our understanding of orientalism, and who was always alert to continuities stretching from the eighteenth century to the contemporary period in which he was writing.[6] One key purpose of the present work is to examine the decades after 1918, and to evaluate the extent to which the older forms have survived and developed into the twenty-first century.

Placing East–West exchanges in this different chronological context changes the frame of reference in several important ways. These issues will be explored at greater length in the next chapter: here, I will give a brief summary of the most significant issues. First, the travellers themselves change. The eighteenth-century and nineteenth-century forms of writing were dominated by a group who I will term, possibly with some exaggeration, 'aristocratic-orientalists', who produced forms of travel-writing. These older types of travel lingered well into the twentieth century: the hippy trail out to Morocco, Afghanistan and other points East is probably the last, great example of this travelling culture. In the twentieth century the aristocratic-orientalists were then joined by two quite different types of female writer: professional women – doctors, nurses, aid workers, archaeologists, sociologists, academics, journalists and anthropologists – travelled eastwards, and they wrote of their experiences; sometimes they were then followed by Western tourists, whose writing tends to follow the lead set by the professional women. These women, the professionals and tourists, have a more muted, less admiring analysis of the Orient. The third and most significant change is that Muslim women began to write. In the sample of texts to be considered for this book, about half the works consulted were either written by Muslim women or by women who had been brought up as Muslims but had renounced their faith. Their substantial presence transforms the nature of the debate: it is no longer appropriate to ask, in the words of Gayatri Spivak, 'Can the subaltern speak?'[7] There is no doubt that the subalterns are speaking, and that their words are finding some commercial success within the West. The more pertinent questions are: are they being heard? Are they being understood? How are they interpreted? Lastly, another type of writing began to develop in the late twentieth century: more polemical, this is not structured around travel within Muslim countries, although it may involve travel to, or at least observation of, Muslim communities based in the West. Frequently the concern of such writers is the new, long-term presence of substantial Muslim communities in Western towns and cities.

The new, prominent presence of Muslim writers within this literary sub-sphere does not, of itself, make the zone necessarily more egalitarian or tolerant. The dominant language of the zone remains English; the principal publishers are American or British; the main audience is Western. Without any doubt, this sphere of debate is based in the West, and it seems clear that there is no 'equal but opposite' sphere of debate created by Muslim women, writing in Arabic or another Eastern language, concerning the West. Muslim writers entering this sphere have to play by the West's rules; at times, this can result in Muslim writers adopting even more rigid forms of Islamophobia and pro-Western idealisation than Western writers. But, having made these qualifications, it has to be acknowledged that the simple presence of this new generation of Muslim writers has undoubtedly changed the nature of the zone: a point to be explored in later chapters.

Given how firmly this literary sub-sphere is rooted in the West and its cultures, it is therefore difficult for it to function as a place of successful dialogue between cultures, because for dialogue to be fruitful it has to be based on some approximate form of equality and mutual respect. Instead, we find continuities with the intellectual and cultural structures identified by Said in his *Orientalism*. One frequently notes the same unchecked confidence in the ability of Western observers to make accurate generalisations about Muslim societies, the same unthinking assumption of Western superiority, the same naive teleology according to which the West represents the future, the East the past. Rather than building bridges, many of these works seem instead to function as walls or dams. In a sense, this book analyses a series of mistakes and failures. In making this observation, I make no claim concerning my ability to correct these errors or to be able to provide any easy solution for them: the problem faced by these writers is, without doubt, overwhelmingly difficult, far more difficult than it may appear at first sight. The key question remains that set by Said over thirty years ago: 'to ask how one can study other cultures and peoples from a libertarian, or a nonrepressive and nonmanipulative, perspective'.[8] My hope is that through studying this series of errors, we may be a little wiser; more able to understand the limits of our understanding and – perhaps – more open to new ideas concerning how dialogue might be constructed. In a world which is growing dangerously polarised, such a process is needed more than ever. Within the overall impression of failure and limitation, there are some sparks of hope in these works which are worth considering, and to which we will return in the conclusion.

A hundred women

Almost by definition, it is difficult to delineate strict borders for this study. After a few moments of consideration, one realises that the topic of 'women's writing and Muslim societies' is potentially enormous, even if one limits the study to the decades following 1920. The problem is made more serious by the lack of previous studies which directly concern the topic: this means that there is little sense of a canon of key works that must be read. (Indeed, it is almost certain that any reader with more than a passing acquaintance with the topic will be able to identify works which I have not consulted: given the potential size of the topic, I make no apology for their absence.) However, it seems reasonably certain that there is 'a zone', already established in literary practice, which is waiting for its formal acknowledgement. One clear sign of this are the occasional explicit examples of women reading each other's works. Thus Azar Nafisi publishes her *Reading Lolita in Tehran* in 2003; when Bee Rowlatt edits her e-mail exchanges with May Witwit, she entitles her collection *Talking about Jane Austen in Baghdad* (2010), and Joumana Haddad then responds by including a chapter on 'An Arab woman reading the Marquis de Sade' in her iconoclastic *I Killed Scheherazade* (2010).[9] Carol Anway, shocked by her American daughter's conversion to Islam, notes how influential the film *Not Without My Daughter* has been in shaping American attitudes to Islam.[10] Willow Wilson also notes the influence of the same film: having arrived in Cairo, and met Omar, she became aware of the lesson that she had drawn from the film, namely that there was 'the honour-killing wife-imprisoning fundamentalist' within every Muslim male.[11] Further indirect evidence comes from some accidental similarities: thus Raymonda Hawa Tawil's autobiographical account of growing up in Jordan and the occupied West Bank is entitled *My Home, My Prison* (1979), and Haleh Esfandiari entitles her account of her arrest and imprisonment in Tehran *My Prison, My Home* (2009).[12] As will be seen, it is also relatively simple to identify some structural continuities in these works, stretching from Edith Wharton's *In Morocco* (1920) to Hala Jaber's *The Flying Carpet to Baghdad* (2010).[13] There is also a certain continuity in packaging and presentation: publicity for these works also suggests a family resemblance within a reasonably clear literary zone.

The argument to be presented in the chapters that follow is not that these works constitute a single ideological bloc, but that together they have created a cultural zone, a female-authored and orientated literary sub-sphere, in which some consistent concerns and themes have developed, alongside some important differences. Perhaps the most obvious common feature of these works, which is expressed in a variety of very different ways, is a concern for the 'condition of Muslim society question' (a point to be explored in the next chapter).

After some consideration, I decided to impose some necessary limits on my research, always with the aim of following the contours of this literary sub-sphere, rather than attempting to cut a cross-section through it. I decided to concentrate on first-person narratives, thus eliminating many academic works on the Middle East written by female specialists. I decided to concentrate on non-fiction, for two reasons: while there have been many finely written novels concerning Muslim societies which have the capacity to move and inspire readers, the key quality of the books in which I am interested is their truth-claim, and no novel can have the same truth-claim as these apparently authentic autobiographical works. Secondly, the majority of the authors to be considered are non-professional writers: the typical itinerary of their works is the path from the diary, or the collection of letters, to an edited text; non-fiction is clearly their preferred medium.

The 'Muslim societies' referred to in the title is deliberately intended to be a broad, flexible category, referring at once to whole societies in which Islam is the dominant religion, but also to sub-cultures (such as the Muslim Palestinians who are also Israeli citizens), small communities (like the Muslim presence in Bradford) and even geographically dispersed families and individuals in the USA and Europe with few direct connections to other Muslim cultures. A further qualification is that readers should remember that the term 'Muslim' can signify a number of different forms of identity: first, a person who defines their life according to the five criteria outlined in the Koran; secondly, a cultural Muslim, a person who perhaps has no clear, confident faith in the Koranic principles, but continues to live alongside Muslims and to follow some of the precepts (such as Ramadan); thirdly, 'Muslim' can function as an ideological term. Thus, in 2005, riots broke out in the poorer quarters of many French cities. Many commentators rushed to label these 'Muslim' riots, although there is no evidence that Muslims were more prominently involved in these riots than Catholics, Jews or agnostics, and certainly no proof that the riots were organised by Muslim groups. In order to identify this literary zone more clearly, I accepted some geographical limitations, which has produced some awkward results. The Muslim-majority nations that feature in this book stretch from Afghanistan to Morocco.

I also decided to concentrate on reasonably commercially successful works that met these criteria, although on occasion dissident works published by small-scale alternative publishers have been included, usually because of the contrast that they can suggest with the more successful works. While I have reviewed works dating from 1920 to the present, I have concentrated on the more recent decades, which have clearly seen an ever-increasing number of relevant works. The inclusion of the older works allows a clearer sense about what is 'new' about the newer works. Many literary scholars might have accepted all the above parameters, and then chosen to study a relatively small number of texts in detail, using each text as an example of some wider trend. After consideration, I have deliberately chosen not to follow this method: I am less interested in the detailed, structural analysis of a small number of texts than in the development of some valid generalisations concerning a wider literary sub-sphere. For this reason, I have set myself the goal of consulting a hundred relevant books and other texts: while I will not claim that this is a rigorously selected scientific sample, I consider that it is sufficient to be the basis for valid generalisation. (If there are readers who consider that this sample is faulty, then the answer is obvious: construct your own sample, and then go to your word processor.) In the final analysis, however, this book must be considered as a preliminary 'mapping' of a new, unrecognised zone, which may well be subject to revision.

A note on generalisation

'No one in their senses would say "I have spent ten years in Holland and therefore I know all about Bulgaria"', observed Freya Stark, 'but it is a fact that seven out of ten people will assume that a visit to Morocco opens the secret of Samarkand. The East is just East in their minds, a homogeneous lump.'[14] This observation rings true today: how can one possibly generalise about the lives of Waris Dirie (who lived in a family of nomadic farmers in rural Somalia), Jehan Sadat (the wife of the Egyptian president) and Qanta Ahmed (a Western Muslim and a qualified doctor, who briefly lived in Saudi Arabia)? While each could be described as a 'Muslim woman', the differences between them are so great that it would seem impossible to cite them all in the same paragraph. There are such a wide variety of different types of Muslim women: believers living in Muslim-majority countries;

believers in Western countries; Western converts, and then also groups such as the many Iranian-Americans, who often seem to have a semi-detached relation to Islam, and people from a Christian background such as Lebanese Arabs or some Palestinians, who can also have a lifelong familiarity with forms of Islam. Unfortunately, however, having recognised these variants, a degree of generalisation is essential for this study. The strongest justification for this is a pragmatic one: these women themselves will very frequently draw simple comparisons between East and West, and even make crucial decisions based on such thinking. While making some necessary qualifications, this work will follow them, and will even use the term 'Middle East' as a simple, if geographically inaccurate, term to describe the Muslim-majority countries I am discussing.

The hundred-women party

But it's time to talk about something else. This is the big one: the Party at the End of the Universe, the Great Dinner Party, the celebration of the marriage of Heaven and Hell, of East and West. What children will result from this outrageous union? Some handsome, luminous, turquoise-eyed, olive-skinned beauty, with a smile for every living being? Or some horrific hybrid, a fanatical hard-core fundamentalist pornographer?

The hundred women are arriving, in limousines, taxis, minibuses, in coaches and on foot. There's still so much to get ready. In they come, in miniskirts and hijabs, in black robes and high-heels, in trouser suits and gypsy skirts, with veils, long hair, contoured perms and punk spikes, giggling, cackling, smiling and laughing. Oh boy, this lot are going to be difficult. They speak English, Arabic (in 365 different variants), French, Hebrew and Farsi: will they ever be able to talk to each other? Their books pile up on the shelves, and spill over the tables. Falluci eyes up Haddad; the political punch-up of the century is going to start here in a few minutes. Ayman takes Rodriguez aside, and in her slow, patient mid-Western voice begins to explain how Muslims and Christians worship the same God. Chahdortt screams against the veil as a small group of Saudis spread out a prayer mat. The room is getting hotter, and voices grow louder. And then, there, in the corner, it's a little girl, her head wrapped in a black scarf, her face screwed up, her eyes full of tears. She is bawling her heart out, with all the agony that only a 7-year-old can feel: who is she? Where did she come from?

CHAPTER ONE

Travellers' Tales: a Typology

'This was never meant to be a book.'
Bee Rowlatt[1]

The theme of the journey is present in all these hundred works. Sometimes it is there in the most obvious form, as a physical transition from A to B. But nearly always these hundred women are more interested in other aspects of travel: for them, the most important point of the journey is not tangible movement through space, but the more troubling, intangible changes that take place within the traveller; a process that can take a few days or last a whole lifetime. The manner in which these women use the image of the journey even in the titles of their works makes this clear. Sattareh Farmaian subtitles her autobiography 'A woman's journey from her father's harem through the Islamic revolution', and the title to Deborah Kanafani's work evokes how she 'found her way through politics, love and obedience in the Middle East'.[2] Some of the most important journeys can be extremely short: when Susan Nathan travelled from Tel Aviv to the Arab town of Tamra, a mere hour's train journey, she realised that she had nonetheless crossed 'a boundary, one that is real as well as psychological'.[3] Western polemicists such as Oriana Fallaci and Melanie Phillips do not travel, but their books concern migration and its effects: they are therefore still writing about travel, even if they are not travel-writers. In fact, only two of our authors are genuinely static. Shirin Ebadi's *Iran Awakening* is a political autobiography.[4] Ebadi wrote her book while still living in Iran; she went into exile to Canada in 2009, and thus one could claim that her work was a 'chronicle of a journey foretold'. Nawal El Saadawi's *The Hidden Face of Eve* is a collection of essays written by an Egyptian doctor living in Egypt.[5] There is no obvious journey here, but in an indirect, metaphorical manner, it could be said that her arguments have travelled from Egypt to the West; certainly, she discusses how Western readers will receive her arguments.

Most of the accounts of journeys in these works fall into one of three categories. There are the reasonably clear-cut examples of day-by-day travel writing written by the older orientalists; the more extended accounts of exile and migration, sometimes stretching over decades, produced by some of the Muslim writers; finally, the provocative idea of undertaking a journey to the other while staying within one's own country. Dervla Murphy wrote of 'travel of another sort' when she visited Bradford in 1986, and Sadek Hajji and Stéphanie Marteau undertook a 'Journey into Muslim France'.[6]

This chapter will present a preliminary typology of these travellers' tales. In examining these hundred works we face a constant challenge: are these authors simply too different to permit any easy comparison? In this chapter I will address this question by exploring several means by which their works can be classified: by literary genres; by types of author; as different types of women's writing; as rather unusual forms of political commentary. As this book is not principally a work of literary criticism or analysis, the discussion of forms and structures will be brief. My intention here is not to establish one single, correct classification; like a pack of cards, these texts can be arranged and categorised in diverse ways. By considering different methods of classification, we can reach a clearer understanding of the nature of these books. Some important political issues will be introduced in this chapter, and then discussed at greater length in the chapters that follow.

Forms of writing

With a few important qualifications, this book is primarily concerned with three literary genres: travel writing, semi-autobiographical memoirs and polemics. These genres can be presented chronologically, as evolving forms but – in truth – they stretch over each other, across the decades, like irregular archaeological strata. Travel writing is undoubtedly the oldest form, and seemed to come almost instinctively to the first generation of twentieth-century women writers on Muslim societies. These colonists, colonists' wives and colonial civil servants refer back to the landmark works of T. E. Lawrence and – to a lesser extent – to the *Thousand and One Nights* and to Kipling. They write in the first person, and they date their entries, day by day, reasonably precisely: in such works one immediately gains a sense of the author's close emotional presence, and we share in their journeys as they move across new landscapes. Obviously, there is no fixed date for the final end of this genre: it remained the favoured form well into the 1960s, but Anne Brunswic was still using it to record her stay in Ramallah in 2004.

The reports by professionally trained women, such as those written by the sociologist Ruth Woodsmall or the archaeologist Kathleen Kenyon, suggest a shift away from this established format.[7] As political issues and social debates grew more important, the simplicity of the day-by-day record no longer seemed so attractive or useful; it actually prevents longer discursions on substantial points, and often reduces the author's thoughts to a constant recital of first impressions. By the 1980s and 1990s the memoir – or the semi-autobiographical memoir – had become the norm. In part, this may simply be because the nature of the journey changed: when the surgeon Pauline Cutting was posted to the Bourj al-Brajneh Palestinian refugee camp in Beirut, she arrived in a plane in 1985 and flew out in 1987: such speedy journeys provide little material for the type of mock-heroic recitals of extended odysseys that the older orientalists liked to tell. Between those two dates, she made some journeys to different bases for Palestinian refugees in Lebanon, but it was clear that the substance of Cutting's experience could not be expressed through a series of vignettes concerning the different places that she had seen, for the most important aspect of her work was her long period of enforced immobility in a refugee camp under siege.[8] Furthermore, the important new authors of the 1990s, the many Muslim women who began to publish their works with increasing frequency, never make use of the travel-writing format. For these new generations of writers, a reflexive dimension was an essential component of their works, and this could not be expressed through the older format. However, similarities remain: these memoirs are always first-person works, and they are often still structured around journeys.

Finally, some writers turn to a form that is less obviously rooted in the revelation of self and accounts of travel: the polemic. Chahdortt Djavann's *Bas les voiles!* (Down with the Veil!), published in 2003, could be cited as marking an important turning point.[9] These writers wish to distance themselves from the established traditions of personal and confessional literature, and to claim a wider viewpoint. They are no longer merely witnesses or participants; they are accusers and judges. Their works are more explicitly angry; indeed, as will be seen, they frequently offer the raw emotion of their words as a guarantee of their authenticity. Sometimes – as in the case of Melanie Phillips's *Londonistan* – they move from the first person to the more impersonal third person, but in most cases, despite the claim to a wider viewpoint, these authors still write as 'I', and their works often retain a substantial autobiographical dimension.[10] Thus, Ayaan Hirsi Ali writes that 'I used to be a Muslim; I know what I am talking about.'[11] Furthermore, their works often make comparisons between diverse places and regions and thus retain a similarity with the older forms of travel writing.

The majority of the works to be considered in this book can be fitted reasonably easily into one of these three formats. This is not to say that no other formats are used. Several female authors have edited collections of interviews.[12] This format is nearly always justified by the author with a statement along the lines of 'I wished to give speech to those who have none',[13] or that the author aims to present 'a personal history of the Palestinians, in their words, to provide a more humanist understanding of what it means to be Palestinian in the twenty-first century'.[14] The results are often disappointing. Inevitably, a collection of different 'speeches' lacks consistency, and once the author has given these texts the high status of the 'speech of the speechless', it then becomes almost impossible to criticise them. Paradoxically, it is often the author's or editor's interventions, introductions and conclusions that are more revealing than their painstakingly gathered interviews. Only an extremely well-edited collection, such as that presented by Bouzar and Kada, or a more synthetic approach, such as that taken by Pardis Mahdavi, escape this contradiction.[15]

Other formats are available. *Zlata's Diary* is a simple, unadorned diary by a teenage girl from Sarajevo: an effective and moving account of a tragic experience.[16] Laura Blumenfeld's *Revenge: a Story of Hope* is constructed as a type of extended meditation on the ethics of revenge, caused by the shock she felt after a terrorist attack on her father.[17] In practice, the work takes the form of a series of journeys to different sources of opinion and evidence. British comedian Shappi Khorsandi has attempted to tell a migrant's story as comedy in *A Beginner's Guide to Acting English*.[18] While one can hear her distinctive, resonant voice reaching the punchlines at the end of the paragraphs, the final result is not impressive: neither particularly amusing nor genuinely observant. Two other contemporary British writers – Zaiba Malik and Shelina Janmohamed – frequently adopt a semi-comic tone; Malik's *We Are a Muslim* (2011) is particularly striking, for humour and tragedy run parallel in her work, giving it a distinctive, edgy feel.[19] A couple of French-language works have – apparently – pioneered the female Muslim erotic confessional, one of which is presented as 'the audacious and sensual confession of a modern Sheherazade'.[20] Here it is noticeable how hard the publishers work to exploit an apparently exotic coupling. Imagine – a Muslim woman with a sex life! Who would have thought it possible? Obviously, Muslim women have as much right to produce pornography/erotica as anyone else, but these works seem to say more about French obsessions with a mysterious, sensual Orient than about women's self-discovery. One or two of our hundred works stray into the less-than-attractive format of the semi-ghost-written celebrity autobiography, but even here there are some surprises. Waris Dirie's *Desert Flower* tells her extraordinary story, from desert nomad to supermodel, and while some passages seem to celebrate the glamorous lifestyle of the permanently gorgeous, the narrative is laced with sufficient self-deprecating humour to avoid vanity, and the work ends with a moving, heart-felt plea against the practice of female genital mutilation.[21] Jehan Sadat's autobiography does follow some easily recognisable clichés of the

rags-to-riches story, but also includes some extended passages of perceptive observation concerning the state of Egypt.[22] The last minority genre
worth noting are works that are constructed as dialogues, of which I have
only found a few examples: Bee Rowlatt and May Witwit, *Talking about
Jane Austen in Baghdad* and Daniela Norris and Shireen Anabtawi, *Crossing
Qalandiya*, to which Bouzar and Kada's distinctively edited collection of
interviews could be added.[23] These works raise questions about power,
politics and the nature of dialogue to which I will return in the
conclusion.

Women writing to women

In a possibly over-schematic manner, one can identify five principal types
of author among the sample of a hundred works. These can be listed in an
approximately chronological fashion.

Orientalists

Women of leisure but, more often in the decades after the Second World
War, women freely adopting travel as a means to discover new experiences,
and even to search for the exotic. This category eventually blurs with the
'intrepids', those who took the hippy trail out to the East in the 1960s and
1970s, and with some rather ambitious tourists.

Professional women

Whether sociologists, anthropologists, reporters, surgeons, nurses or aid
workers, these are women whose journeys are structured by the demands
of their profession. As trained, professional people they often possess a
certain set of standards by which to judge the societies they visit: their
attitudes are therefore often more critical, more judgemental than those of
the orientalists.

Migrant Muslims

This is a complex category, for often their migration is not a simple
process. For example, Afschineh Latifi was born in Iran in 1969. She left
with her mother in 1980, and then followed a complex, difficult route
across Europe before finally reaching the USA in 1982. She then finally
travelled, briefly, to Iran in 1995. If we consider her at that point, should
we classify her as an Iranian returning to Iran, or as an American visiting
Iran? While this category of author is clearly the one which is growing
fastest, and has produced some memorable and striking works, it is significant that rather than producing a simple narrative which asserts a clear
Muslim identity, their works describe a far more tortuous process.

Western Muslims, converts

This, too, is a complex category. For example, Qanta Ahmed is an American-trained doctor and a Muslim. She applied to work in Saudi Arabia in about 1999. She considered that she 'knew' Islam, but she was often bewildered and sometimes alienated by what she found in Saudi Arabia – and yet, on visiting Mecca, she then experienced a type of spiritual re-awakening. We face the same question as in the previous category: should we see this as her 'return' to a Muslim country, or as her first visit?

Polemicists

To date, these have largely been Western women writing about the presence of Muslims in Western countries, and often expressing radical antipathy to aspects of Muslim culture. Their narratives are less autobiographical and less travel-orientated than the previous works, but it is noticeable that often they still write in the first person. Recently, some Arab women have adopted this form of the essay in a manner that seems to counter the Western narratives: the work by Joumana Haddad is particularly noteworthy in this respect.[24]

Having recognised these different types of writing, we can now consider some similarities and contrasts within the texts.

Mary Louise Pratt distinguished two types of colonial travel writing: a bureaucratic, information-gathering form, and a sentimental form, more concerned with desire, sex, spirituality and individual experience.[25] Among these hundred works, there is no doubt that the second is clearly the most common. An observation by Vita Sackville-West illustrates this point. In 1926, she reminded herself of the following advice concerning how a writer should construct a memoir: 'let him write to his public as to a familiar friend'.[26] Something of this ethic seems to run through all these works. Frequently, there is a type of rough-and-ready, amateur quality to them: one basic point that cannot be overstressed here is the variety of the authors' experience and competence. On the one hand, there are authors such as Sackville-West, Dervla Murphy, Melanie Phillips, Mai Ghoussoub and Azar Nafisi, each of whom could be described as professional writers, who are fully capable of writing clear, elegant, expressive prose. On the other hand, the majority of these hundred women are amateur authors, whose works are often their first publications. In many cases they write because they feel they have to. Their texts begin as diaries, letters and blogs, and the final manuscripts retain the immediacy of such personal writing.[27] These are formats that are suitable for the part-time, non-professional writer but also – it must be noted – they are formats that can be flawed by repetitiveness, shallowness and obsessional qualities. The meeting of amateur author and serious dilemma leads to some unusual and distinctive results. For example, consider the manner in which Carol Anway, an American Christian, describes the most desperate spiritual and familial crisis in her life, when she feared that her recently converted daughter was leaving her for Islam. Anway explains her feelings by referring to songs by the Beatles: 'Yesterday', a time when she was happy and felt reasonably confident in herself, and 'Hey Jude', a moment when she needed to take stock of her life, and face the future.[28] The final impression from these pages is confused: certainly, one sees an inexperienced writer trying her hardest to describe some impossibly difficult feelings; one senses her anguish, but there is also something almost too intimate in the simple naivety of her writing. Similar issues arise in other texts. 'BAM!' is the term that Na'ima Roberts chooses to evoke her first step towards her conversion to Islam, a conversation with an Egyptian woman.[29] 'Why?!!!' cries Betty Mahmoody when she learns that an American woman has voluntarily chosen to live in the Islamic Republic of Iran.[30] One has to be clear here: this is not bad, stupid or incompetent writing; it is not writing that deserves to be dismissed; it is often writing that has a significant documentary value, which can be thought-provoking, perceptive, gripping and hard-hitting; equally this is not sophisticated, professional writing, and its commercial success raises the question of why this form of informal, semi-autobiographical amateur memoir has grown increasingly popular.

While none of these writers explicitly address the issues raised by being a female author in a cross-cultural setting, it is noticeable how frequently they assume or invoke a female audience. Dirie dedicates her book to her mother; Wassyla Tamzali dedicates hers to her grandmother; Carmen Bin Ladin tells her daughters 'this book is for you'; Hanan El-Cheikh's *Toute une histoire* (Quite a Story) is actually a biography of her mother; in her introduction, Latifa thinks of 'all those Afghani girls who have kept their dignity until their last breath' and of her mother; Woodsmall hoped that 'this study should lead to more mutual appreciation and more effective cooperation between the women of the East and the women of the West'.[31] Within this near consensus, Tehmina Durrani seems unusual: almost alone, her dedication is not exclusively to women but to all 'the people of my country'.[32] Often the female identity of author and (assumed) reader is echoed by the books' titles: *In the Land of Invisible Women*; *Défigurée* (A Disfigured Woman); *Une femme en colère* (An Angry Woman); *Daughters of Another Path*; *A Saudi Woman's Memoir*; *Les filles voilées parlent* (The Veiled Girls Speak); *Three Women of Herat*.[33] The covers often follow this theme: predictably, veils predominate, and a variety of stolid, miserable, good-looking or radiant female faces stare out from underneath them.

Some of these works are set in a political or bureaucratic context. Pamela Bright refers frequently to the work of the United Nations Relief and Works Agency (UNRWA), the organisation created to care for Palestinian refugees; Pauline Cutting and Suzy Wighton include some sustained reflections on the politics within the Palestinian refugee camps; the tale told by Deborah Rodriguez is set among the various relief agencies and non-governmental organisations active in post 9/11 Afghanistan; Hala Jaber, a war correspondent, describes in detail her work relationship with the *Mail on Sunday* and the *Sunday Telegraph*.[34] In a small way, these works suggest the progressive broadening of women's experiences: where Virginia Woolf noted that the female novelist's main source of material was necessarily limited to the middle-class drawing room, these women draw on far wider sources of inspiration.[35] But these are the exceptions: the archetype in these works remains that of the journey by the independent female observer, unattached to any political or bureaucratic institution and, therefore, authentic. Colette Modiano's words in her introduction sketch out an ethic to which many of these authors seem to aspire: 'Seeking whatever truth is hidden among the tangled passions and hatreds, prejudices and traditions, I have stifled my opinions and set aside preconceptions. I believe that I have been unbiased.'[36] The cover blurb to Dervla Murphy's *Tales from Two Cities* makes a similar point: 'Dervla Murphy has no religious affiliations and belongs to no political party, pressure group or "race relations" organisation.' Given that Murphy is – in part – studying Muslim political cultures, why should it be expected that her readers will immediately identify with her non-religious, non-political status and even accept her apparent ignorance about Islam as an advantage?[37]

This same point is neatly illustrated by Sadat's title, *A Woman of Egypt*, a choice of words which presents her not as the widow of the most powerful man in the country, not as a reasonably influential political figure in her own right, but as 'just' a woman. A similar pose is adopted by both Ayaan Hirsi Ali and Asra Nomani, despite their radically different political positions. The British edition of Hirsi Ali's *Caged Virgin* is subtitled 'A Muslim woman's cry for reason'; Nomani's book is entitled *Standing Alone in Mecca: an American Woman's Struggle for the Soul of Islam*.[38] These similar titles, by such different authors, suggest a common deep structure shared by many of our writers. They assume some distinctive, positive quality in being a woman, although this point is never properly explained. They also prioritise their individual identities: they are not representative members of communities or organisations but individuals, often working against the crowd. The terms used in the subtitles raise further questions. Why a 'cry', a 'struggle' and not – for example – a proposal, a campaign, an analysis, a manifesto or an account? These questions remain unanswered in these texts. One senses that the authors are deliberately attempting to de-politicise their works, to reduce them to a basic, unanswerable ethical case, and even relying on a certain emotional charge as a guarantee for their authenticity. Tamzali introduces herself as 'an angry woman' and, writing from quite different perspectives, both Fallaci and Ghoussoub compare their words to screams.[39] Certainly, in all these works there is a strong sense of deep passion, sometimes merely present in hints and implications, sometimes spelt out, even paraded by the author. Collectively, they downplay important political issues. While some adopt recognisably feminist stances, the majority seem to drift towards a more apolitical maternalism. 'Why must men involve me in their stupid war games?' asked Mahmoody. 'Why could they not just leave me alone to be a wife and a mother?'[40]

A story about an independent, isolated, non-political woman, however, would not be much of a story. What makes these works distinctive and – more crudely – sellable is that each, in different ways, attempts to trace lines of contact between East and West. Often it seems that this 'Eastern' dimension (for want of a better phrase) is sufficient to guarantee their success. Here, female authors seem to enjoy a certain privilege: there seems to be some sort of working assumption that female identity gives the author a particular insight into East/West relations. 'Ask anyone in the West about Islam or the Islamic revival', notes Fedwa Malti-Douglas, 'and women will enter the subject of the conversation immediately'.[41] The current state of the literary marketplace is nicely illustrated by the title of Marguerite van Geldermalsen's work, *Married to a Bedouin*, with no further explanatory subtitle.[42] The reader needs to check the author's name to confirm that we are examining a woman's account of her marriage to a male Bedouin. Why was this brief title judged to be sufficient for a commercial publication? If I wrote a work entitled 'Widower of a Newport girl', can we imagine publishers rushing to offer generous advances? Or Bedouin women gasping over their cappuccinos: 'A Newport girl?! I have got to read this!' This form of presentation links these works to a specifically Western obsession with Eastern societies and cultures; they circulate within a space that, whatever the wishes of the individual authors, has been constructed by decades, if not centuries, of orientalist writing and colonial political development. Often publishers are keen to make links with this older tradition. Fadia Faqir has made some pertinent observations about this point: a Jordanian-British novelist, she has experienced consistent pressure from her publishers to use images of veiled women on the covers of her works, even when they are completely unrelated to her subject matter. 'Bedouin Jordanian women are represented on the cover by Afghani women in burqas,' she complains. 'I could write about daleks in outer space and the designers and hordes of public relations teams would dress them in Afghani burqas.'[43] More interesting still, she has come under pressure to present her novels as non-fictional 'misery memoirs'.

Is there some 'opposite but equal' form of Eastern obsession with the West, an occidentalism developed by Muslim or Arab peoples? One can find some examples of a similar Muslim interest in other countries, sometimes even expressed in women's travel narratives.[44] And, certainly, prejudices and misconceptions about the nature of Western societies circulate freely in the Arab and Muslim worlds. But it is apparent that nothing resembles this growing torrent of Western-produced narratives about the East which now draws in the participation of Muslim women.

While it is clear that this torrent includes diverse streams and currents, the observations made in this section point to some shared similarities, even if only in the sense that often these works ask similar questions and address themselves to similar audiences.

The political in the apolitical

In general, these works downplay political issues and instead present women's narratives as somehow more honest, more authentic and perhaps even more humane than the more aggressively confrontational style associated with male authors discussing the politics of the Middle East. Yet, when one considers them as a bloc, the political pressures that have encouraged their production are obvious. Of the hundred works I have consulted, only two were originally written in Arabic, twenty in French, two in Spanish, one in Norwegian, one in German and one in Serbo-Croat. Over two-thirds were originally written in English. This linguistic profile suggests a basic inequality: while the Western world is hungry to read the words of Arab or Muslim women, the conditions of the market impose certain preliminary conditions on would-be authors. First, one must learn to write in English (or, at least, acquire the assistance of a translator and/or ghost-writer).

The presence of Muslim writers is double-edged. On the one hand, it gives access to the great cultural traditions of the West, and it enables the author, potentially, to reach an audience which is wider than the Arab-Muslim world. It marks a break with the characteristic silence of bewildered immigrant woman.[45] Given the difficulties of censorship and other forms of government pressure experienced by authors in many Middle Eastern countries, publishing in the West could well be a liberating experience.[46] On the other hand, publishing in the West also requires a type of conformity, and Fadia Faqir's irritation at being expected to package her novels as Muslim misery memoirs is a good example of how market pressures may well be distorting authors' intentions.

The languages in which these works were written and published clearly do not reflect the authors' experiences: eighteen write principally about Iran, seventeen about Israel, Palestine or the Holy Land, nine about Afghanistan, seven about Saudi Arabia, five about Morocco, four about Egypt, four about Iraq, three about Jordan, two about Algeria and one for both Somalia and Pakistan. This evidence suggests how these works straddle an awkward border: while their truth-claim is often based on their author's status as a reliable, neutral, apolitical woman, their coverage of the world is clearly structured by some of the most violent and bitter political struggles of the contemporary world. There is a similar mismatch when one considers the most obvious cultural connections: if British women simply want to find out about the Muslim world, then why do they not read about the Muslim societies with which Britain has been most strongly connected, principally Egypt and Pakistan? If French women wish to do the same, why do they not study Algeria? Instead, a strange geo-cultural distortion emerges from these works, with Iran clearly credited with some curious place of honour as the world's leading Muslim society, instead of being recognised for what it is: the only Shi'a Muslim government in the world, based on a unique blend of radicalism, incipient patriotism and an unusual interpretation of Muslim political thought. (To confuse matters further, Mahmoody twice identifies Iranians as 'Arabic', which constitutes a double error: 'Arabic' is a language, and therefore a person cannot be 'Arabic'; as the dominant language in Iran is Farsi, not Arabic, Iranians cannot be classified as Arabs.[47]) Equally, Egypt, which is by far the largest country in the Middle East, seems to suffer a curious under-representation within these works.

Alongside these studies of Muslim majority countries, some of our authors write of the West. Six speak principally of Muslims in France; seven of Britain; four more generally of Europe; another five describe their journeys from Muslim majority countries to the USA and three to Britain. It seems probable that more examples of this type of narrative, relating a journey to the West, not to the East, will appear in the years to come.

The conceptual vocabulary that they use evolves over the years. Here, once again, we find an important difference between the first generation of orientalists, and the subsequent generations of more professional women, migrant Muslim women, Western Muslims and polemicists. Indeed, one can almost date these works by the vocabulary that they use. In an approximate fashion, one finds that the oldest works describe journeys to the Orient (or the East); the subsequent generations are more likely to travel to the Middle East or the Holy Land, while the last generation often use 'Islam' or 'Muslim' as key conceptual terms.

For the older orientalists, their journey was almost a type of ultimate holiday, sometimes even a form of pilgrimage, and certainly recognised as a privilege. Edith Wharton visited Morocco in 1917: she hoped that her book would be of use to future 'happy wanderers' who visit a land that is 'too curious, too beautiful, too rich in landscape and architecture' not to attract travellers.[48] Waiting for her train in a cold Victoria Station, Sackville-West believed that she could still sense 'a far, faint aroma' of Persia, seemingly produced from the labels on her suitcases.[49] When they meet local people, these orientalists often express admiration. Rona Randall's words concerning Jordan sum up much of this older attitude.

> The Jordanian people – fascinating, courageous, diverse, contradictory, sometimes infuriating and inexplicable, but always charming and always kind; a people with a natural dignity, however poor they may be, and whose inherent pride prevents them from revealing the distaste they must often feel for Western casualness. This dignity stems from their tradition, their faith and their timeless background.[50]

Cycling through Afghanistan, Dervla Murphy is struck by 'another day of incredible, unforgettable and indescribable beauty'. She decides that, having met many Afghans, it is correct to equate the term 'Afghan' with 'gentleman'.[51] Visiting east Africa, Odette du Puigaudeau has time to admire 'the veiled grace of the women' and the harmony and peace of the bush; she feared the entry into this forgotten corner of a modern, Western civilisation 'which has made a wrong turning', for it was based on materialism, violence and arrogance.[52] One should not take Murphy's, Randall's and Puigaudeau's appreciations of Eastern societies too seriously – they are intended as thought experiments, as provocations, even as fantasies; they certainly are not intended to contradict the basic premise that the West is superior to the East. These passages are, however, revealing: the Orient for them was a space which allowed one to think comparatively, and this could include an element of provocative self-criticism.

The difference between these older images and the newer polemical works is blindingly obvious. Oriana Fallaci describes Muslims as having 'no accomplishment in the domain of science, of technology, of welfare' and warns that 'the mosques of Milan and Turin and Rome simply overflow with terrorists or candidate terrorists who dream of blowing up our bell-towers, our domes'.[53] Melanie Phillips evokes a 'deadly cultural meltdown' produced by the uncontrolled presence of Muslims in Britain: 'This book is a warning – to Britain, to America, and to all who care for freedom.'[54] Where once a Western description of the Orient spoke of grace, beauty and wisdom, now a description of Islam refers to violence, terrorism and fear. In fact, the differences between these two visions are not quite as incompatible as they may seem (a point to be explored later): yet our first impression, of a descent from wonder into hostility and panic, remains valid. Such changes can be related to the long, difficult adjustment of Western countries to a postcolonial, globalised world, which seems to have involved a loss of confidence and a rising sense of concern about the Other. Thus, the June 1948 British Nationality Act proposed a wide, generous interpretation of Britishness, open to all residents of the Empire and Commonwealth; this confidence and generosity was then narrowed by successive governments, to the point where the 1981 Act only recognised citizens of the UK as British. 'What had been a singular and universal national identity in 1948 was now a fractured and insular vision of Britishness', comments Kathleen Paul.[55] A similar decline can be observed in France, from a confidence, optimistic assertion of the universal values incarnated in the ideals of 1789 to a far more suspicious, hostile attitude to the presence of other cultures on French soil.[56]

The works to be analysed here provide examples of a similar shift, but also of something more: as reasonably influential texts that have circulated widely, they have also educated a large section of the Western reading public, providing them with the concepts and ideas by which to understand and to interpret some complex and important historical processes. These books refer to an extremely wide range of issues, from the most tragic and serious, through the mundane, the comic, to the most uplifting and delightful. However, there is a common thread running through them, apparent once one ignores the difference in the vocabulary used. Whether they speak of Orient, Middle East or Islam, these works assume that there is something special about these societies which merits study and consideration. Searching for a term to express this point more clearly, I am tempted to borrow a phrase from Thomas Carlyle who, in 1840, argued that alongside all the important social issues that were being debated in British Parliament, there was one single, overriding issue that was yet more pressing: 'The Condition of England Question' which was the 'alpha and omega of all'.[57] These hundred women, collectively, seem to be discussing 'The Condition of Muslim Society Question', and even the most apparently innocent, playful piece of touristic reportage can be presented as a contribution to this more serious topic. As will be seen, the exact meaning of the question is inherently unclear: it has been understood in quite contrasting ways.

Writing about women's writing

This work refers to some extremely important issues: female liberation and oppression; the development of global political cultures; terrorism and war; Islam and Islamophobia; orientalism and colonialism. Yet, surprisingly, it is hard to find direct precedents for this study.

Since the 1980s, there has been a continuing and welcome development of interest in women's writing. Often led by academics in literature departments, this has tended to focus on women's fiction, and to concentrate on novels, seeing these as – arguably – the most demanding or the most telling form of writing. Following the publication of Edward Said's iconoclastic *Orientalism*, which devised a convincing analytic framework with which to understand the Western obsession with Eastern societies, some researchers turned to consider what Billie Melman neatly termed 'Women's Orients'.[58] This in turn required a necessary reassessment and critique of Said's sometimes incomplete thinking.[59] One of the most memorable contributions to this was Sara Mills's *Discourses of Difference*, published in 1991, which presented a provocative and thoughtful consideration of women's travel writing in a colonial setting.[60]

I have found works by authors such as Mills and Melman to be more than useful, alerting me to some issues in the interpretation of this type of material.[61] But, in many important ways, the issues discussed here are quite different from those analysed by Melman and Mills. In part, the difference is simply chronological: Melman's sample of works ends in 1918, Mills's in 1930; this work extends into the present day. This different chronology leads to three extremely important issues. First, women's writing on Muslim societies has become mainstream. Laura Bush rated Azar Nafisi's *Reading Lolita in Tehran* as nineteenth in her list of 'twenty-five works to read before you're twenty-five'.[62] These works can no longer be dismissed as odd works written by women who are – in Mills's colourful summary – 'indomitable, eccentric and mostly rather crazy'.[63] Secondly, the zone has changed significantly since the mass entry of Muslim writers, which arguably can be dated back to Nawal El Saadawi's *The Hidden Face of Eve*. Neither Melman nor Mills consider this form of possible counter-discourse, yet in recent decades it has become more and more prominent.[64] In my sample of a hundred works, forty-three are written by Muslim women, a further seven by ex-Muslim women, forty-five by non-Muslims, and there remain five whose religious affiliations are unclear. Thirdly, there is the question of the changes within Western cultural forms since 9/11. As will be seen, I am sceptical of arguments that present this date as the dramatic turning-point in world history; instead, it seems more realistic to argue that this was a moment when existing tendencies were radicalised and strengthened. While the tragedy of 9/11 may have encouraged Western readers to find out more about Muslim cultures, the more significant dates in women's writing about Muslim societies are probably the Iranian Revolution of 1978–9, which marked the end of a long cycle of secular nationalist protest in Muslim societies, and then a curious interim period in the late 1990s, defined by the Oslo Accords of 1993 between Palestinian and Israeli forces and the election of the reformist Mohammad Khatami as president of Iran in 1997. The importance of this period is that both events suggested political liberalisation, and seemed to promise peace and stability, thus encouraging travellers to visit the respective zones. Many of the works written in succeeding years can be dated to journeys, projects and other experiences in this period. In both cases, the promises of liberalisation and reconciliation were unfulfilled: the liberal Khatami was replaced by the authoritarian Ahmadinejad in 2005; the hopes of the Oslo Accords were destroyed by Israeli intransigence and rising social and political tensions, which finally exploded in the second Palestinian intifada in September 2000. These stories of lost hopes from the 1990s were then circulated to a post-9/11 Western audience: an illustration of the old observation that history does not move along a straight line; instead, the narrative of history is produced as irregular, unpredictable spirals smash into each other.

Very little has been written directly about this literary sub-sphere. Farsaneh Milani wrote a short essay in 2008 which I found extremely useful, and which could be cited as a direct inspiration for this work.[65] Alongside this, there have been some book reviews of particular works which hint at some more general lines of enquiry and analysis.[66] Rather than directly following the themes and issues raised by previous literary scholars, I have preferred to consider some of the ideas presented in the course of an extended debate concerning the nature of identity and multi-culturalism within the context of a globalised world.

Multiculturalism is a potentially confusing term, and can mean different things in different contexts. Arguably, its first coherent use was in a Canadian context in the 1980s and 1990s, when a protracted political debate about the presence and future of the French-speaking minority in Quebec led to some extended comparisons between French speakers and other minority groups in Canada, such as Native Americans. This led to the philosophical conceptualisation of group rights to identity.[67] In Britain, the term has become a type of scapegoat for various strands of ultra-secular and conservative thinkers: in denouncing multiculturalism, their aim is often to criticise the nature of the new permanent or long-term Muslim presence in British towns.[68] These interventions have since provoked a series of replies, which have often produced more subtle and nuanced ideas than some of the original concepts produced in the Canadian context.[69] This debate forms the principal conceptual context for my study.

Conclusion

Despite decades of talk about the emancipation of women in Western society, there are still very few public situations in which women's participation is genuinely, fully appreciated and validated, and this strange literary sub-sphere is one of the rare examples where this comes close to being the case. From Vita Sackville-West to Carol Anway, women have constructed, if not one method for describing Muslim societies, then a set of methods, concerns and techniques which seem to be shared by a range of different writers. It is certain that one reason why their works have developed with such little analysis or acknowledgement is simply because they are women writers: while women can be accepted as witnesses, they are rarely applauded as analysts. I have tried to express a measured appreciation of their texts, which certainly possess great positive qualities as well as significant flaws. What can easily appear as awkwardness, naivety or even incompetence can also be read as sincerity, honesty and authenticity. However, such judgements on their quality are of limited value. The key point is that these works are one of the main forms in which a large section of the Western reading public has learnt about Muslim societies; these texts form the basis of their judgements. For this reason alone they merit study.

CHAPTER TWO

Author and Self

'You've no idea how strange I feel lately – almost as if I've started
seeing things differently – through your eyes.'

Daniela Norris[1]

Sometimes travel challenges people in unexpected ways. I encountered an
interesting example of this a couple of years ago, when I helped an Arab
student with a patchy knowledge of English to fill out a form. We finished
the main part, and then got to the obligatory 'Ethnic identity monitoring'
section. My student glanced at this for a second, and then immediately
ticked the box labelled 'white'. Reader, I could not stop myself: I looked at
her dark brown eyes, her almost-black hair, her high cheekbones and her
coffee-coloured skin, and I asked her why she had ticked that box. 'Because
I'm not black' she replied immediately, as if explaining an obvious point to
a stubborn, slow-witted child.[2] Perhaps she was right. But, without any
doubt, her self-identification as a 'white' person was challenged by her stay
in Britain.

In this chapter we will explore how our hundred authors present their
identities to their readers. A key theme to consider is whether the act of
writing functions as a form of liberation for them.

Travelling with an orientalist writer

The older generation of orientalists nearly always chose to present their
accounts in the form of travel writing: a form of narrative organised by
date and place. This form of writing set a type of model for the generations
that followed, and is therefore worth considering in some detail.

Travel writing is an odd way of presenting one's personality: indeed,
sometimes it seems to function better as a means of hiding rather than
revealing oneself. After reading a piece of travel writing, one often gets the
same impression that can arise if you sit next to a stranger during a long
train journey. Having being so physically close for several hours, you can
make some accurate observations about the other person: whether they are
nervous or calm, what they like to read, even how they read, perhaps
whether or not they are familiar with the journey. But, unless you fall into
a long conversation with them, you will still lack some of the most basic

information: who are they? Why are they travelling? What is their final destination? It is almost as if because you have sat so close together, you cannot see the whole person, but only certain detailed fragments of their personality.

The presentation of the self in travel writing often seems like this. We see the world through the author's eyes as they describe what they see through the train window. At first sight, these images can seem almost like the opposite of a more personal form of writing, such as a diary: Annemarie Schwarzenbach joked that she ought to term her account of her travels in Persia 'an impersonal journal', for nothing seemed more anonymous than writing a description of a valley.[3] But as we follow the journey, we usually come to appreciate that the most interesting points are not what the writer sees through the window, but what the writer says about what she sees through the window; the writer is not a fixed camera which mechanically records views, but also a commentator and an editor. The information about the author herself then emerges, bit by bit, apparently almost at random. This focus leads to a distinctive form of narration: one aspect of which is that because these authors want to explore their own identities, they rarely tell stories concerning their fellow travellers. Ella Maillart's *Cruel Way*, in which there is some interplay between herself and her fellow traveller 'Christina' is actually rather unusual; more typical is Vita Sackville-West's *Passenger to Teheran*, in which there is no reference at all to her real-life travelling companion Dorothy Wellesley, who accompanied her for a large section of her journey.[4] This point illustrates a larger tendency, present in most of these works: whether the orientalists travel in groups or not, they wish to write about themselves as individuals.

A second aspect of the travel-writing format used by this selection of writers is a downplaying of the physical, geographical description of the landscape. This can be done quite subtly so that sometimes the reader does not even notice a shift in focus from external sights to internal, personal feelings. However, this shift can be made quite explicitly. Sackville-West asked: 'What more odious than the informative book of travel?'[5] In these works the internal journey of personal development is almost always the most important aspect, and this point remains surprisingly true from Vita Sackville-West to Azar Nafisi.[6] While many of these hundred works do include long context-setting descriptions concerning Middle Eastern history, politics and geography, these are never the most memorable sections and – indeed – a problem with works such as Evelyn Cobbold's *Pilgrimage to Mecca* and Na'ima Roberts's *From My Sisters' Lips* is their relentlessly factual, didactic tone.[7]

This type of travel-writing narrative often leads to a type of hide-and-seek game in which the author is revealed and then hidden, almost a type

of teasing with the reader: whether deliberate or not, this features prominently in Anne Brunswic's *Bienvenue en Palestine* (Welcome to Palestine).[8]
We realise straight away that she is not Palestinian: but it takes a few
hundred pages to work out that Brunswic is Jewish and French, and that
she has chosen to travel to Palestine because of her doubts concerning the
nature of the Israeli state. The older travel writers make this confusion
more entangled by frequently adopting a self-deprecating, mock-heroic
tone, thus leaving the reader unclear about their true feelings.

For the writers themselves, such features could be an advantage or even
a pleasure: just as their journeys allowed them to play games with their
identities, so their narratives include a similar playful dimension. When
pilgrims in Mecca mistook Cobbold for a Turk, she did not correct them.[9]
When Saudi tribesmen greeted Freya Stark as a representative of the
British government, she laughed to herself: they did not know that she had
deliberately travelled without seeking official permission, knowing that it
would have been refused to her.[10] The orientalists enjoyed these challenges
and unexpected dilemmas that travel presented them. 'Travelling is questioning!', Maillart happily observed.[11]

Usually the older generation of orientalist travellers saw a significant
difference between their 'free', non-regulated, open-minded travel and
the planned excursions of the tourists. When Maillart came across an old
mosque in Afghanistan, she was delighted 'to have found something we
enjoyed because it was our own discovery: no sense of duty towards a
guide book had made us visit it'.[12] Lesley Hamilton was infuriated to
meet a group of thirty-five European tourists at the top of Mount
Sinai: 'How dare they come up onto *my* mountain.'[13] Dervla Murphy
expresses a similar scorn towards the comfort-seeking tourists: 'I'm afraid
I've very little patience with people who complain indignantly about
places like Afghanistan being primitive. Why didn't they . . . find that out
before coming here?'[14] The orientalists sought an intense personal pleasure
in their journeys; this could not be shared with a vulgar crowd of
tourists.[15]

Other voices: ghost-writers

Before considering what these texts tell us about the writer's identity, there
are some other issues that we must discuss. To what extent are we hearing
the author's authentic voice? One significant feature of a number of these
texts is the manner in which the opening chapter takes the form of 'flash-
forward' to a crisis moment – the assassination of President Sadat in 1981
for Jehan Sadat, the suspicious 'robbery' suffered in 2000 by Iranian-
American academic Haleh Esfandiari – and then the succeeding chapters

'flashback' to the decades, years or months before the crisis.[16] To a certain extent, the device works well in establishing the author as a significant figure with a story to tell, and raises a certain anticipation in the reader. A common structure emerges, rather like the narrative of a detective novel: an incident, then an explanation of 'how I got there' and finally an extended section explaining how the incident was resolved or – more often – normalised. But the structure also breaks up what could have been a simpler, clearer narrative of personal development and, sometimes, it provokes a collision of the personal and political, a feature that limits many of these works. Lastly, when one sees its frequent use, one begins to suspect that something else is in play here: the 'flash-forward' begins to look more like a journalistic trick designed to grab the reader's attention, and so suggests the heavy hand of the ghost-writer. One starts to wonder: who defined the 'defining moment'? Was this really the free choice of the writer?

There are some moments where one comes to doubt the authenticity of the narrative. *Moi Nojoud, 10 ans, divorcée* (I, Nojoud, ten years old and a divorcee) is the autobiography of a Yemeni girl who reluctantly accepted marriage to an older man, and then undertook a protracted legal battle to gain a divorce. At one point she stares across a market place at a crowd of black-veiled women 'who all look alike. Black shadows, more frightening than attractive.'[17] Is this really how a Yemeni girl would see a crowd of veiled women? Isn't it more likely that she would have learnt a trick like that taught by the Saudi-based crime writer Zoë Ferraris: 'remember . . . when you approach a [veiled] woman on the street, look at the *handbag*'.[18] It seems at least possible that this description is a contribution of a ghost-writer or an editor. A similar doubt arises in Latifa's *My Forbidden Face*. Her life was ruined by the Taliban victory in Kabul: Latifa was forced to hide indoors for years. In her book, she comments on the visit by a Taliban minister to France: 'A Taliban in Paris, home of the rights of man!'[19] Again, is the ascription of a unique political identity to Paris really a spontaneous comment by a young Afghan woman? Would she automatically think of Paris as the home of the rights of man? Or does this phrase come from her French ghost-writer?

Such points do not imply that therefore these texts are worthless. Anyone who has ever written any book will concede that a text is always a compromise between what you want to write, what you can write and what you have to write. The fact that there may be some outside interference in some of these works merely signals a warning to us: be cautious. Some of these authors are inexperienced and relatively powerless. If they are new to the West, then they are also easily manipulated or – more kindly – a little too willing to accept well-meaning advice. And these works, ghost-written or not, remain one of the most important means by which Western readers have formed judgements on Muslim societies: they are therefore still worth considering.

Other voices: women walking in Lawrence's footsteps

Another more-or-less unanswerable question is the extent to which these works constitute a distinctive woman's voice or whether they merely run parallel to the paths created by the more professional, more prestigious works of male authors. The question is ultimately unanswerable because of the sheer volume and range of material. Are we comparing Carol Anway with François Chateaubriand? Azar Nafisi with T. E. Lawrence? Tentatively, there seems quite a strong argument that in terms of content, these works are noticeably different from men's writing. For example, even in the brief review of women's orientalist writing in the previous chapter, one feature that emerged was the tendency of many of the older writers to use extremely positive language when considering Oriental societies: as a generalisation, their words were probably more positive than the tone usually adopted by male writers. This may be because, for these women, the journey was an exceptional privilege, which therefore had to be celebrated. But – as will be seen in the next chapter – this is nothing more than a tendency.

The one point that can be discussed with some certainty is the extent to which these women writers cite male authors as inspirations or guides. Here the pattern is clear: the vast majority do not cite any precedents; the mode of writing they adopt is that of a free individual almost spontaneously choosing to write a book, apparently ignoring all precedents and pioneers, and normally not situating herself within a larger historical or cultural tendency. The occasional obvious signs that these books have drawn inspiration from previous works is usually not noted: thus Bee Rowlatt and May Witwit, authors of *Talking about Jane Austen in Baghdad* make no explicit reference to Azar Nafisi's *Reading Lolita in Tehran*.[20] However, among the minority who do cite previous authors, there is a surprise: the long shadow of T. E. Lawrence. Ten works refer to him explicitly, sometimes in the most incongruous circumstances. Christine Lamb, travelling in Afghanistan in 2001, considers it necessary to inform her readers that the Afghan deserts are not 'the majestic sands of T. E. Lawrence': she assumes, without question, that her readers will be familiar with Lawrence's vision of the desert.[21] Lesley Hamilton cites four great imperial travellers as inspirations: E. H. Palmer, C. M. Doughty, Major Jarvis and Lawrence.[22] Sometimes, casual reference is made in passing. Adina Hoffman drives past Azraq, 'the town where T.E. Lawrence set up headquarters'.[23] Predictably, the Muslim writers usually do not refer to Lawrence. Shelina Janmohamed makes a reference that is so cursory that it is almost meaningless.[24] Sadat's reference to him is clearly negative: 'Many Westerners think of us still as riding camels, hidden behind veils. But that is the story of Lawrence of Arabia, not of modern Egypt.'[25]

Alongside Lawrence, eight of our authors refer to *The Arabian Nights*. This second source is often referred to in passing by the Western authors, as a means of contextualisation. When Colette Modiano saw the mosque at Khadimain, she was impressed with its beauty and colourful mosaics. 'It is like stepping into the pages of the *Arabian Nights*.'[26] Murphy visited an Afghan chief's house in Mukur. 'It's all deliciously like the *Arabian Nights*.'[27] Nafisi refers to the work quite differently, considering it as an important guide. She asked her private reading group to consider how such 'great works of literature could help us in our present trapped situation as women'.[28] Muslim writers refer to it in another way, contesting its status. Nawal El Saadawi notes the work's popularity in the West, where it is considered to give an authoritative insight into the Arab character, and then vigorously challenges this interpretation.

> Anyone with the slightest knowledge of Arab literature knows that the stories related in *A Thousand and One Nights* are only a partial and one-sided reflection of a very narrow section of Arab society, as it lived and dreamed, loved and fornicated, intrigued and plundered, more than ten centuries ago.[29]

Joumana Haddad, from a Lebanese Christian background, refers to the work in a manner that is as wildly negative as possible. 'I killed Scheherazade', she boasts.

> I killed her in me. And I am quite determined to kill everything and everyone that even remotely looks or behaves like her in my unconscious, imagination and mind. So her sisters, daughters, grand-daughters and all her descendants had better close down the concessions business, or stay away, far away from me.[30]

Last on our list of literary references is *Kim*, who is referred to by two Western women, one of whom is Stella Rimington, who cites the work as a reason for her trip from India to Afghanistan. 'I had been reading Kipling's *Kim*, and I wanted to see something of the area where the Great Game had begun.'[31]

This evidence shows the range of opinions and implicit differences between the works. While for some the status of Lawrence or *The Arabian*

Nights seems so obvious as to be beyond discussion, others are openly contemptuous of the worth of such sources. But, to return to the original question, these scattered references certainly suggest that these women writers usually do not consciously aim to imitate male writers, and their occasional, sometimes apparently accidental, similarities suggest instead that these hundred works are quite separate from the more prestigious works written by men on similar topics.

Motivations

Why did these women write their books? A wide variety of different reasons are given. Sometimes these are innocent, almost pastoral in tone: a wish to record an exceptional sight or to note a particular beauty. Juliette de Baïracli Levy speaks of her love of water. 'Always I have tried to live close to water, by seas or lakes or rivers. This lifelong love for water brought me to Galilee in the summer time.'[32] Lesley Hamilton adopts something of the same tone with reference to the desert: 'I imagined that I would go into the desert and write of it as an observer.'[33] Dervla Murphy's account begins with a similar record: 'On my tenth birthday a bicycle and an atlas coincided as presents and a few days later I decided to cycle to India.'[34] Twenty-two years later she set off. These references suggest the extent to which the literature here is sometimes travel writing in the most basic sense of the term: these are authors who wish to travel to see new things. Such simple reasoning grows less and less common over the decades. In general, the writers' attention turns from mountains and deserts, from mosques and palaces, to people.

Sometimes the journey, and the effects of the place on the person, is presented almost in medical terms – as a cure. Maillart comes very close to saying this explicitly: she was concerned about the effects of a chronic disease (and associated problems of drug dependency) on her friend 'Christina' (actually Annemarie Schwarzenbach). Maillart's hope was that a long journey, far away from Western society might assist Christina's recovery.[35] In a sense, Maillart was also looking for her own cure. She saw Europe in 1939 as a society threatened by war, militaristic values, and she remembered her answer to a question that Carl Jung had asked her: 'Why do you travel?' She had answered: 'To meet those who know how to live peacefully.'[36] Veronica Doubleday could positively enjoy living in Tehran in 1973, for it was 'free from the ugly accoutrements of twentieth-century life that I was so glad to escape'.[37] For these writers, the East seemed to contain a solution or an escape that was not available in the West. One of the strangest aspects of the moving story told in Hala Jaber's *Flying Carpet* is how closely it echoes these older themes. She describes the anguish that her infertility caused her, and her narrative then turns on how she, a childless woman, met a motherless Iraqi child in a Baghdad hospital.[38]

For others, the treasure contained by the East is quite different: it is religion. Elizabeth Hamilton was drawn to Jerusalem, 'the city of castellated walls known to me in childhood from Bible pictures . . . The city that Christ wept over.'[39] Rona Randall found that 'there is no better guide than the Old and New Testaments to accompany the traveller in Jordan'.[40] There is even a distant echo of these arguments in Melanie Phillips's *Londonistan*, where the author criticises the apparent domination of the values of the Bible by concepts of human rights.[41]

In recent years this narrative has been turned on its head. Some Muslim women now seek a cure, a prize or a solution in the West. This is expressed in its most desperate and anguished form by May Witwit's e-mail from war-ravaged Baghdad to Bee Rowlatt: 'WHAT DO YOU ADVISE ME TO DO, BEE?? HELP, I'M GOING MAD.'[42] Ayaan Hirsi Ali sounds a similar note in a calmer tone: 'We will need the help of the liberal West.'[43] Sometimes one can even detect a cult of the wonderful West which seems to echo the orientalists' observations about the mysterious East. 'London! I didn't know anything about it, but I liked the sound of it', recalls Waris Dirie. 'I didn't know where it was, but I knew it was far away. And far away was where I wanted to be.'[44]

These references suggest two forms of journeys of expectation. Participants from both East and West look for cures, solutions and forms of escape: both carry with them misconceptions, exaggerated hopes and even prejudices. But there are important differences between the two. While the problems raised by the orientalists are certainly serious – who could dismiss the threat of world war in 1939 as trivial? – there is little sense of personal anguish in their dreams and expectations. The Muslim migrants are often in a different situation: as we will see, their desperation is immediate, personal and even physical in character. The contrast between the two voices points to a power relationship: these are not 'opposite but equal' discourses. Their exchanges do not form a dialogue between equals, but something more like an arena of irregular, ricocheting calls, echoing over chasms of power, prejudice and incomprehension.

The appeal for comprehension forms one of the most common motives for writing among the more recent authors, particularly those who are most distant from the older model of travel writing. This marks a significant shift in the intellectual basis of their work: beneath the apparent continuity in styles and structures from the older examples of orientalist travel writing to the more modern forms of autobiography, this new role that has been ascribed to this form of women's writing transforms it. The

texts which result from this are quite different from the established forms
of Western autobiography, which can be summarised as:

1. classic autobiography: the celebration of an individual's success,
   sometimes despite serious obstacles;
2. misery memoir: the story of an individual's survival, despite serious
   obstacles;
3. testimonio: the story of an individual's participation in a wider
   process which endangers a whole community.[45]

Of the three, it is the third that seems closest to many of the more recent
works. Wighton's diary from the Bourj al-Brajneh refugee camp provides a
neat example of this: it seems – at first sight – to be simply her own work.
But she notes in her preface that once the Palestinians became aware that
she was writing this journal, they would ask her to record incidents, until
she felt that the text had become 'a journal of our collective experience'.[46]
She was not asking the reader to admire her, but to consider the wider
experience of the Palestinian refugees. However, the *testimonio* is not the
only autobiographical form that these texts resemble: one can also find
examples that are closer to the classic autobiography and the misery
memoir. In conclusion, it seems legitimate to argue that these women have
pioneered a new type of autobiographical writing, a point to which we will
return in this chapter's conclusion.

Western women venturing into the Middle East sometimes refer explicitly to their role of representing a collective group. Thus, war journalist
Anne Nivat explains that she seeks to listen to those who cannot speak.[47]
But this new task carries with it a set of problems, of incongruities which
can appear quite intractable. Jaber comments: 'For a moment, I wondered
whether anyone at the office in London understood what it meant to drive
through Baghdad, with all its shooting and looting, on a mission to select
and reject injured children with inconsolable families for a slot on the
inside pages of our newspaper.'[48]

Like the older examples of orientalist travel writing, the newer, more
autobiographical works still present an image of the author as 'only' a
single, apolitical woman: this often appears to readers as a type of reassur-
ance about the nature of the text. Yet, by raising the issues of who gets
heard and who gets ignored, who speaks, who writes and who listens, these
women are also raising highly politicised questions about power and
communication in a globalised world, in a form which still achieves some
noticeable commercial success. Sometimes these awkward questions are
side-stepped by the authors themselves, with the apparently optimistic
assumption that everyone who hears the story will therefore accept their

case, and so the problem will be solved. Norma Khouri, exposing forced marriage, sexual violence and domestic abuse in Jordan, writes that Jordanian 'women still pray that their silent cries will be heard'.[49] May Witwit first started writing to Bee Rowlatt because she wanted 'to expose my country's misery'.[50] Unfortunately, 'being heard' is rarely sufficient to solve a problem. Aside from serious issues concerning power structures and authorities, such naive comments assume a transparent, equitable public sphere, in which all voices are treated fairly. Others write with a far greater scepticism, noting the existence of prejudice and misinterpretation which prevents voices from being heard. Pauline Cutting speaks of a 'veil of untruths' distorting news of the Bourj al-Brajneh camp, and Emma Williams of a 'maze of lies' surrounding the situation of Palestinians living in the occupied territories.[51] 'The more we assemble to make our voices heard,' notes Haddad, 'the more our discourse is misunderstood.'[52] Sayeeda Warsi argues that Islamophobia has become part of respectable middle-class culture in today's Britain.[53] Often the problems raised in these works cannot be solved by simply speaking to the world. Muslim women are increasingly aware that even relatively innocent autobiographical stories, sometimes semi-humorous in tone, still carry a political edge in the current context. 'Stories like mine have remained unheard,' argues Janmohamed, 'as they do not fit neatly with prevailing stereotypes which tell tales of Islam's oppression or of those rejecting Islam.'[54] At times, one can sense the sort of frustration with prejudice and blind power that drove Frantz Fanon to fury: 'When I speak irrationally, they present a rational case. When I speak rationally, they present "the truly rational". At each round in the game, I lose.'[55] A number of works by dissident thinkers within France aim to address a similar issue: the particular manner in which veil wearing has been portrayed. Dounia Bouzar and Saïda Kada set themselves the goal of speaking about veils without forgetting the women who wear them.[56] Ismahane Chouder, Malika Latrèche and Pierre Tevanian see their edited work as giving back the right to speak to veiled women.[57] Houria Boutelja explains that she decided to talk because of the contempt that was being shown to a whole people.[58] This project is often linked to a deep frustration, even anger, that not one person has been ignored, but a larger group.

At first sight, it seems that this more collective, more (despite appearances) politicised approach to writing is particularly suitable for Muslim women. However, there are indications that Western women, writing about Muslim societies, are also growing more concerned about the politics of comprehension, and are thinking in more collective terms. Curiously, while Anway's writing is relatively simple, her appeal is quite sophisticated and original: as an American Christian woman, she asks

Christians and other non-Muslim women to make a greater effort to understand Muslim women. 'May this book be an opportunity to cross over for a brief time to understand their approach and commitment to another path.'[59] Hélé Béji makes a similar effort – with noticeably less success – to understand the motives of veil-wearing women in modern France and Tunisia.[60]

Lastly, the urge to voice that which has not been heard can also lead to the circulation of forms of prejudice: sometimes things are not heard for good reason. Thus Oriana Fallaci feels 'an obligation to speak', to unleash a waterfall of ideas, to cry 'a scream of rage and pride'.[61] The emotional excitement that runs through her books comes from the release offered by taboo-breaking: at last, she permits herself to say what she really thinks about Muslims, without the self-imposed constraints of fairness or respect for others. Like the release felt by a crowd laughing at a racist joke, the emotions provoked by her writing can be cathartic and collective; they do not and cannot aid a process of dialogue.

Dangerous words: violence and writing

The older orientalists were having fun: a point that has often been ignored by previous studies on their writing. They were confident; they enjoyed the sights that they saw; they could laugh at a poorly organised journey; they could relish letting people make mistakes about their identities; they could even feel that their voyages were teaching them something profound about the nature of the world. Freya Stark produced an eloquent, joyful celebration of her journey through the Saudi Arabian desert in 1937–8:

> Perhaps it is some echo of the days when we too, unburdened with possessions, wandered lightly on the surface of the world, that give the unexpressible delight to the sight of a road that vanishes, a road that winds into the distance, the landscape of tomorrow melting into the landscape of today. Some books, like the *Pilgrim's Progress*, give this feeling and, recognizing it, we know that the charm of the horizon is the charm of the pilgrimage, the eternal invitation to the spirit of man. To travel from fortress to fortress, over the high $j\bar{o}l$ [hills] where men still walk with guns upon their shoulders, and at the end of days to see before you land that is yet unknown – what enchantment in this world, I should like to know, is comparable to this?[62]

They rarely felt in any real danger. When Murphy cycled along icy roads outside Belgrade, she was attacked by wolves, and responded by promptly shooting one in the skull. She adopts a similarly breezy, no-nonsense approach when considering the issue of sexual harassment in Afghanistan. When forced to sleep out in the open in the company of five male strangers, she commented: 'This is the only country I was ever in where not one single man of any type has made the slightest attempt to "get off" with me, so I feel no qualms about a night at the mercy of my five companions.'[63] The Orientalists' confidence, their sense of security about their selves and their positions is clear on every page: it is these qualities that allow them to make jokes and to enjoy themselves.

Some more recent works by Westerners evoke something quite different: a clear sense of acute danger. Betty Mahmoody was beaten up and imprisoned by her Iranian husband; Laura Blumenfeld tells of her quest to find the Palestinian man who tried to kill her father; Haleh Esfandiari of her imprisonment in an Iranian jail.[64] These are cautionary tales: they warn of the dangers at the borderline, of problems that cannot be resolved by a well-aimed shot from Murphy's pistol. For these women, the Orient is no longer a place of wonder and pleasure.

Many of the more modern Muslim writers speak of quite different journeys, in which danger, confusion and obstacles are the norm rather than the exception. For these writers, identity is a problem rather than a game. This can be seen even in the most basic of points: their names. Fadjyah becomes Fudgie, Ghada becomes Garda, Shaparack becomes Sharkattack or Shipwreck (and eventually Shappi), sisters Afsaneh and Afschineh desperately change their names to Janey and Julie, and then Amy and Ashley, in order to be accepted.[65] Of course, if cross-cultural encounters could be reduced to mere challenges of pronunciation, then all would be simple. This is not the case: these women's experiences concerning their names is merely their first step on a longer, more difficult journey concerning their place in Western society. This is one reason why it is far more difficult for these Muslim migrants to write good-humoured, self-deprecating narratives: their journeys do not take them through games with identity but through existential challenges and physical danger.

These women have faced some horrific problems. Ayaan Hirsi Ali, Nawad El Saadawi and Waris Dirie all speak of their personal experience of female genital mutilation: when one considers that Dirie's career in the West was based on her striking physical beauty, this was an exceptionally courageous step by her. (One qualification, however, here: while Hirsi Ali explicitly links genital mutilation with Islamic culture, Saadawi and Dirie make no such connection.) Others are not detached, external observers of violence, but immediate witnesses and even casualties. Norma Khouri learns of the death of her best friend, stabbed twelve times, after a secret affair: she suspects that this murder was carried out by her friend's brother.

Saudi TV personality Rania al-Baz was attacked by her estranged husband and left with her face horrifically disfigured.[66] Teenage Zlata Filipović records 'We've had too much horror. The days here are full of horror. Maybe we in Sarajevo could rename the day and call it horror, because that's what it's like . . . This isn't life, it's an imitation of life.' Most chillingly of all, she later realises that she is no longer recording shelling and bombing in her diary because 'I've become used to it'.[67] An e-mail from Witwit starts: 'I'm writing to you with the sound of bombs and guns roaring all over the area.'[68]

Others have suffered political persecution. Malika Oufkir went through a series of confinements in Morocco, including house arrest and imprisonment in a secret jail, that lasted over fifteen years.[69] Shappi Khorsandi's father faced death threats and police harassment for his writing: this was one reason why her family left pre-revolutionary Iran. Shirin Ebadi and Haleh Esfandiari were both arrested and held in Iranian jails.[70]

Their accounts of such experiences are disturbing and moving. The contrast between them and the older orientalist tales is clear, and provokes many questions. Were the older orientalists innocent romantics, while the newer generations of Muslim exiles tell us the awful truth about Muslim societies? Or does this difference between the two trace the development of the Middle East into a more barbaric, violent, despotic place in recent decades? The historical record challenges this second interpretation. Innocent, playful orientalist writing was still being produced after repeated outbreaks of colonial violence: after the 1919 Amritsar massacre in India, after the revolt and subsequent heavy-handed repression of Palestinian Arabs in 1936, after the Sétif massacre in Algeria of 1945 and after the expulsion of approximately two-thirds of a million Palestinians in 1948. It would be hard to demonstrate objectively that the Middle East is a significantly more violent region in 2010 than it was in 1920.

More importantly, the contrast between the two narratives is not necessarily one that outlines the border between illusion and truth. At approximately the same time that Khouri was writing her grim account of violence against women in Jordan, Marguerite van Geldermalsen was writing a gentle, hippy-ish account of her brief romance and subsequent long, loving marriage to Mohammad, a Jordanian Bedouin.[71] We have no right to assume that Khouri's gruesome story somehow 'trumps' or negates Geldermalsen's pastoral romance: both are true; both tell us something valid about the nature of Jordanian society. The narrative of violence is not inherently more representative, 'true' or 'real' than that of beauty, pleasure or play. The best accounts often include the most varied emotions, such as can be found in both Cuttings's and Wighton's accounts of the Bourj al-Brajneh refugee camp in Lebanon. Khorsandi and Malik both record in detail the racism and prejudice at work in contemporary Britain, but both also can see the incongruities, the comic absurdities inherent in the cultural collisions in which they have participated.[72]

It is often assumed that a modern memoir by a woman concerning Muslim societies must necessarily be an account of violence and extreme oppression. However, one can cite many examples of recent accounts by Muslim women which document essentially non-violent lives. Sattareh Farmaian, Fadia Basrawi, Shelina Janmohamed and Fatéma Hal could each be cited as examples of relatively straightforward, non-traumatic autobiographical accounts by modern Muslim women.[73] Each woman certainly faced problems and dilemmas, but these did not involve a personal confrontation with forms of extreme violence. It is significant that these works have been relatively sidelined, in favour of the more sensational works which resemble the 'misery memoir'. Instead of considering the new focus on extreme forms of violence as an objective indication of the nature of Muslim political culture, it seems more likely that they reveal a change in the nature of the literary market, which seems to have begun in the 1980s or 1990s. Arguably, Nawal El Saadawi could be seen as initiating this tendency, despite her clear intention to push critical public opinion in quite a different direction (this is discussed in more detail in the next chapter). The commercial success of Mahmoody's *Not Without My Daughter* certainly provided another impetus to this development, as did Djavann's contributions to the 2003–4 debate on the veil in France.[74] But it may well be the post-9/11 reactions that finally fixed the structures of reception. Today, the Muslim misery memoir sells: in place of the orientalist narrative of wonder, the market now demands a Muslim narrative of violence. The most curious point of all is that, in their respective times, both narratives have been accepted unquestionably as the correct way to represent the societies and cultures of the Middle East.

Alongside accounts of violence within Muslim-majority societies, modern Muslim writers also describe another form of violence: the psychological and cultural violence that they experience as migrants. This has received less attention in the Western media. As noted above, the process begins with the mangling of Arabic and Muslim names: a trivial point in itself, possibly, but which is indicative of a deeper and broader clash of experiences. Perhaps surprisingly, only a minority recall simple, outright, obvious racism. Fadia Basrawi grew up in a tiny American enclave in the Saudi Arabian desert, nicknamed Aramcoland, a company town for the oil industry: as odd a micro-society as can possibly be imagined. One day she confronted Bobby, the school bully and a white American. Having thrown a stone at him, she then taunted him: he couldn't hit her back because she was a girl. Her mistake. He threw a large stone which caught the back of her head. Unfortunately for Bobby, he also made the error of yelling 'Take that you dirty Arab!'[75] This insult became the basis for a mini-diplomatic incident in this micro-society. This was the last thing that Basrawi wanted: her intention had been to prove how tough she was, and instead she was the object of 'patronizing pity' from authorities, teachers and parents.

Malik's experience is more depressingly familiar. Waiting for a bus in Bradford, she listened to the conversation of two white women in front of her.

'Oh, just look at those Pakis,' one of them remarked. 'They breed like rats, don't they?'

'Oh, I know,' replied the other. 'It's disgusting, isn't it? They're disgusting, aren't they?'

I had to interject.

'It's better being a rat than fucking dead old cows like you two.'[76]

Such incidents record confrontations between a reasonably clearly self-identified Arab or Pakistani girl and a white person. Basrawi immediately understood why Bobby was using this language; Malik was familiar with this type of prejudice and even believed that she knew how to deal with it: 'I have to respond to abuse with abuse'.[77]

Other writers encounter specific prejudice against them as Muslims. Shelina Janmohamed even manages to turn this into a well-targeted joke. While travelling in Jordan, she meets Anne, a French student, who challenges Sara and Shelina first about their veils, and then about their religious values: 'You people are backwards, living in the Middle Ages, with a religion of ignorant Arabs . . . You Muslim women are oppressed, forced to cover up and not express yourselves. You have to stay at home and men run everything.' Janmohamed is quite capable of answering back. First, she offers to call her husband, so that Anne can check her facts, and then remembers that she has no husband. Sara goes through the same process. Finally, Sara pretends to call Shelina's father in order to confirm Anne's arguments.

Is that Shelina's father? Yes, yes. I was just calling to check. She is oppressed, isn't she? Yes, yes, understand. You forced her to suggest that she goes travelling on her own to show her how repressed and subjugated she is. Yes, yes, it makes complete sense.[78]

Janmohamed is clearly used to such incidents, and has even prepared tactics in order to deal with them. The clashes recorded by Basrawi, Malik and Janmohamed are clear-cut: in a sense, both sides know the script and understand the parts that they play. But many of the cases of prejudice cited by these authors suggest a different type of interaction.

The point which needs to be stressed here is that the apparently simple logic of popular racism – there is black and white or, in the more advanced model, black, brown, yellow and white – makes no obvious sense to many of these young women. Remember, as with the example of the Arab student at the beginning of this chapter, Muslim migrant writers do not necessarily think of themselves as inherently or biologically different from the white majority population. Rather than understanding racism immediately, they are mystified by it. Azadeh Moaveni was born in Iran, but grew up in the USA. She was confused about her place in America's racialised hierarchy. 'Was I brown? All the Iranians I knew seemed to consider themselves Europeans with a tan.' She was even confused about whether she counted as an immigrant. 'Immigrants came on boats. We came on planes.'[79] More touching and probably more typical is the nasty incident recorded by the Palestinian Ghada Karmi, concerning a lunch queue at her London school in the 1950s. She was queuing with a friend; two girls in front of them seemed to have stopped, so Karmi and her friend passed in front of them.

> As I did so, I heard one of the girls mutter something at me. I did not catch it, but noticed [my friend] Josie had gone red and was looking embarrassed. When I asked her what was wrong, she said, 'It's one of those girls we pushed past. She called you an FF.'
> 'What?' I asked mystified.
> 'Don't you know what that is?' said Josie disbelievingly.
> I shook my head.
> 'Filthy foreigner,' she said slowly, 'that's what it means.'
> I remember feeling astonished and hurt. Why would anyone want to say such a thing to me? It gave me a sickening feeling that I was somehow different, undesirable, contemptible. I could not reconcile this with my belief in my own assimilation and it preyed on my mind.[80]

Korsandi also captures the illogicality of racism. Arriving in London after a hurried departure from Iran in 1976, she, her sister and her mother are astonished by the appearance of a punk couple sitting opposite them on the underground. The couple laugh at the newly arrived refugees, shove past them, and on their way out shout 'Go home!' After they have left, the other people in the carriage express their disapproval. One says: 'You take no notice of people like that! It ain't your fault you're a Paki.' Predictably, the two girls are completely bewildered: 'But what were they saying, Maman? Why did they tell us to go home? Maman, what's a Paki?'[81]

Afshineh and Afsanah Latifi experience similar confusion when they go to high school in Virginia after a long, tortuous journey from Iran. They realise that there is a hierarchy among the pupils, but take some time to understand it. At the top of the hierarchy were the white 'preppies'. 'In our hearts we desperately wanted to be like them. We wanted to be white, rich and American.' What of the others?

> The black kids at school were definitely nicer to us. They were more open and sort of playful. I think they were curious about who we were. We weren't really white, not in the *Mayflower* sense of the word, anyway, but we certainly weren't black, either. Whatever we were, we were outsiders just like them, and I think they saw us as kindred spirits.

Afshineh thinks she's finally worked out the school hierarchy: there are poor black kids and rich white kids. Her sister corrects her. 'No. It's divided into three. The poor black kids, the rich white kids, and us.'[82] Oufkir even manages a joke, of sorts, on this theme. Having escaped fifteen years imprisonment in Morocco, she arrives in France. There she sees the movie *E.T.* She finds the film completely incomprehensible, but leaves with one clear impression. 'I think I'm the alien.'[83]

These accounts challenge the standard narrative of assimilation propounded by national authorities in Europe and the USA. According to these clichés, huddled Muslim masses arrive, fleeing despotism and thirsty for the freedoms promised them by the great tradition of Western liberal values. If they experience problems with assimilation, it is because Western liberalism is too heady a mixture, too strong a wine, for these poor outcasts. Of course Western liberal values are worthy of respect, but these writers are pointing to a quite different set of problems: the issue that they find difficult to understand is racism, not liberalism. Readers may be surprised by this point. Here, I am not arguing that Muslim-majority societies are havens of toleration and liberty: prejudice and xenophobia exist in these as well, and frequently Arab attitudes to black cultures resemble Western racism.[84] But – as a generalisation – racism in the Western model, which often seems as natural as fish and chips, is not substantially present in Muslim societies. Social and cultural prejudices are articulated in other forms.

One could read Betty Mahmoody's *Not Without My Daughter* as a bitter, Swift-ian satire on the strange, perverted assimilation process that our Muslim migrant writers confront. For a few months, Mahmoody finds herself in an exceptional position: she becomes a marginalised white person in a non-white society. Like the chimpanzees in *Planet of the Apes*, the Iranians she meets do not understand that they are her cultural inferiors and, absurdly, they keep treating her as if she was their inferior! She refuses to assimilate their values, but she is terrified that her daughter might, and she watches anxiously when her daughter starts to use Farsi, or begins to forget that Iranian schools are filthy. Thankfully, Mahmoody herself never forgets that she is American, and she is able to rescue her daughter from the Alice-in-Wonderland farce of contemporary Iran, and return to the sane, Christian normality of America's racialised hierarchy. Goo goo ga joob, as John Lennon might have remarked at this point.

Celebrity and its discontents

There is another, more subtle form of alienation that the modern Muslim writers sometimes experience: the sudden intensity of publicity being focused on them. Rather than individuals telling their story on behalf of a larger group and so educating the wider community formed by their readers, the opposite is often true: they become empty pages on which someone else's story is written. Just as Basrawi was disappointed by the 'patronizing pity' that surrounded her, so the Iraqi exile Zainab Salbi slowly grew more sceptical about the sympathy which Americans showed her during the first Gulf War, following a story concerning her on CBS News.

> I wound up as a kind of national poster girl for the 'Iraqi side' of the story, innocent victims caught up in war. People would recognize me in the Hallmark store and say, 'Oh, you're that poor girl from Iraq, aren't you. Have you heard from your mother yet?' I was the lucky one, the innocent, nonthreatening Iraqi who got to see only nice kind people while other Iraqis I knew were being called 'sand niggers' and having their cars smashed and houses attacked, even though some of them had been born in the United States.[85]

Rania al-Baz also had to face similar issues. While still in hospital, recovering from the horrific attack she had suffered and having to confront her newly disfigured face, she also had to face processions of photographers and journalists. She heard that her name had even been cited in the US Congress. 'I asked myself whether I was a martyr or, despite my intentions, a militant.'[86] Instead of being Rania al-Baz, she became the Rania al-Baz case. Like Salbi, she began to feel sceptical about this process, for the Western media was citing her experience in order to sustain arguments that she did not accept.

> The status of women in Saudi Arabia is often presented in a simplistic manner. She is portrayed as a slave, with no nuances. No one says that [Saudi Arabian women] are devoted to their religion, their culture, their traditions, and when these impose duties on her, she accepts them without great suffering. It is only the excesses, the deviations which should be denounced . . .
> I respect both Saudi Arabia and Islam, and I do not want people to believe that I oppose either one or the other . . . I do not criticize our traditions, our culture or our rules; I only protest against those who have perverted them, and created a new law code in the name of Allah.[87]

Al-Baz's case is interesting for another reason: this was a woman who had worked in Saudi Arabia as a television presenter. She has some familiarity with the manner in which modern mass media works, and she realised quickly how her experience could be misunderstood or manipulated.

Talking cure

One final point needs to be made on the theme of 'dangerous words'. These books can clearly have one further function for their authors: they can be part of a healing process. An essential part of coming to terms with a traumatic event is learning how to turn the event into a coherent narrative: not necessarily 'the truth', for often a traumatic event provokes emotions of such depth that it is quite impossible to find the words that capture the complexity of feelings aroused. But the simple, lesser task of being able to register the events as coherent prose can aid the victim's recovery, for it is a sign of mastery over trauma.

This point suggests a different way of looking at the search for dialogue. Maybe the important point here is not necessarily the rational construction of a mutually acceptable programme, but rather the creation of a space within which experiences can be voiced and – above all – listened to without preconceptions or manipulation by the audience.

Self and other

The material reviewed so far in this chapter suggests how challenging the construction of a functioning 'self' is for many of these writers. This is an issue for every writer, but it is made more difficult for these writers because here the self is created with reference to an 'other'. At first sight, this looks like a simple pattern of opposition. For the orientalist, that other is Muslim; for the Muslims, the other is Western. One simple solution to any difficulties encountered in such presentations is that preferred by many of the older orientalists. They were confident in their status, and so they could easily slide into a self-deprecating, mock-heroic voice, and thus side-step the need for any definitive statement of their true thoughts.

In practice, some of the paths these authors travel are more complex: for example, what of the Iran-American writers who 'return' to an Iran from which they have been absent for decades? What of Western Muslims who travel to Muslim-majority countries? What of the Lebanese Christian Arabs who are constantly being mistaken for Muslims? What of Westerners who are undergoing a conversion experience? For such people, the creation of a public 'self' for the purposes of writing a book can be an extremely difficult challenge.

How do these writers portray the 'Other'? Let us begin with the clearest examples: the orientalists on their journeys to the East. In most cases, these are relatively wealthy women, with relatively secure positions in Western societies, who choose to travel. Usually, they are open-minded in the sense that they also wish to study and to learn from what they see. Of course, this is not always the case, and here it may help to cite an example of negative orientalism. Pamela Bright visited a number of Palestinian refugee camps in the mid-1960s. She quickly changed from feeling initial sympathy for the refugees to feeling intense, irritated frustration:

> As I went from UNRWA village to UNRWA village, and saw how well housed, well clothed and healthy they were, I got infuriated by repetitive complaints, and I wondered how the Agency had stood it these seventeen years, and why they should stand it any longer [88]

Perhaps more seriously, as she considers the situation in the different camps, another tone emerges in her writing. She sees one enterprising refugee woman, and wonders why more do not follow her example. 'Their religion was still too inexorably woven into their habits and thoughts to follow her ways.' When rumours circulate around one camp, Bright comments 'the herd stuck together to resent it'. In another camp she finds 'a pavement café with Orientals, who had, it seemed, hours to sit and a life-time with which to analyse emotions'. There was 'no recreation but dispute, no assuagement but lethargy'. They showed 'this natural sloth, born of ignorance . . . the familiar indolent pose of the underbred Arab'; they were 'whining men and greedy women'. [89]

These are provocative words. First, we must acknowledge that they have some documentary value. When a people has gone through some form of intense collective suffering, they do not necessarily come out of it as heroic, assertive fighters, nor even as virtuous victims, grateful for whatever assistance is given them, seizing opportunities to improve themselves. Bright shows a third option: a collective demoralisation, which is unattractive and disturbing to encounter. But Bright does not explore the reasons for this social and collective experience. Instead, she explains their situation with reference to some long-established Orientalist concepts: their religion (Islam), their culture (Oriental), their ethnicity (Arab). In the last chapter it was shown that the orientalists could enjoy their travel and the sights that they saw, and how often they would praise these with a familiar and rather limited vocabulary, whether with reference to the *Arabian Nights*, the attractive simplicity of their lives or the wonders of their religion. Yet, where Murphy, Wharton and Sackville-West found beauty, Bright finds sloth, indolence and whining. The two visions, however, are not as radically different as might seem. What these writers share is a similar conceptual vocabulary, which explains why Bright should still be categorised as an 'orientalist'. They all consider that they 'know' the Orient. The key concepts of 'Orient', 'Islam' and 'Arab' are the shared basis of this knowledge, and explain the confidence which the orientalists felt in their knowledge. They find no real surprises, merely confirmations of their preconceived ideas. The Orient may be beautiful, or it may be indolent, but it is definitely Oriental and therefore different from the West.[90] The sights that Bright sees do not lead her to question herself or the basis of her knowledge.

A consequence of their absolute certainty in their 'selves' as writers and in their knowledge is their inability to enter into dialogue. As they begin their journeys considering that they 'know' the Orient, there is nothing substantial that can be learnt from it: while they can gather more knowledge, they do not question its substance. At its limits, the Orient can serve as a type of sighting mechanism, allowing one to judge the nature of Western superiority. Certainly, the East was backward: but did this necessarily mean that it was worse than the advanced West? As we have seen, many orientalists enjoyed being cheerfully provocative, and would even claim that they preferred the simplicity of the primitive East to the amenities of the modern West. Marguerite van Geldermalsen considered such arguments. One evening, she and her Bedouin husband were visited by Jordanian girls who were fascinated by Geldermalsen. Afterwards, the couple bickered about the visit. Mohammad says: 'They are just young girls. They find it interesting that you can leave the world of paved streets, cars and houses to live in a cave in the middle of the desert.' She replies: 'I don't care what they find interesting . . . I live in a cave in the desert to enjoy quiet afternoons with you, not to show a generation of Arab girls that there is more to life than a tile floor.'[91]

The point where any questioning ends, however, is when it comes to questions about oneself. Here, Geldermalsen really is different from the older orientalists: she does wonder how she appears to the Bedouin among whom she is living and, after considering this point, she is willing to modify her behaviour, without complaint. For the older orientalists, and for Mahmoody in Iran, the possibility that they might be wrong is simply not considered. Indeed, *Not Without My Daughter* could be summarised as an extended 'no' to all things Iranian. This point leads us to note a significant difference between the writers. In general, the Muslim female authors are extremely sensitive about how they might appear to others, and modify their behaviour in light of this. 'Sabrina' is a 25-year-old French woman, a law student and a Muslim. At one point in her life, she decided that she wanted to wear a veil, but she was concerned how the French people around her would react to this. In particular, 'I felt that for many people, black veils make them scared, and make them think about what's happening abroad.'[92] Sabrina therefore chose to wear light, brightly coloured veils. The majority of Western women writers, from the older orientalists to the new polemicists, would not dream of willingly modifying their behaviour after considering what local people might be thinking of them.

Writing as a woman

Surprisingly, the one point at which the older orientalists considered questions about their own identity was in relation to their gender. The 'Orient' of the French and British empires was often assumed to be a quintessentially male territory.[93] Yet, by travelling to its more far-flung countries, the women orientalists could discover something else: a certain relaxing of the codes which governed women's behaviour, and therefore a strange blurring of gender roles. Maillart was amused rather than horrified to see Turkish and Afghan officials assume that the trouser-wearing 'Christina' was a boy.[94] In the early 1970s, Sarah Hobson was keen to study Iranian carpets. For no obvious reason, she decided that in order to do this, it would be better if she travelled to Iran 'as a boy', and her *Through Persia in Disguise* includes protracted, semi-comic passages concerning her often unsuccessful attempts to pass as male.[95] Hobson's attitudes seem anachronistic: in her fictional *The Map of Love*, Ahdaf Soueif invents an Edwardian aristocratic woman who decides to dress as a man in order to go riding in the Sinai desert: this seems just about believable.[96] Curiously, Hobson's work sounds more like fiction.

This small zone of relative freedom did not necessarily lead the writer to accept any form of collective female solidarity. Stark recalls a telling incident concerning her journey in the Saudi Arabian desert. She was taking some photos. A local woman protested loudly and repeatedly, to the point that Stark grew worried that the local tribal authorities would also object to her camera:

> 'One thing,' I remarked, 'is ever the same in your land and in mine.'
> 'And what is that?' said they.
> 'The excessive talk of women.'[97]

The men were delighted by her remark; they laughed, and the tension was over. Murphy also made the following, more thoughtful, observation of her gendered identity while travelling in Afghanistan: 'I have all the advantages and none of the disadvantages of their own womenfolk.'[98] Åsne Seierstad draws similar observations from her stay in a Kabul household:

> I imagine they regarded me as some sort of 'bi-gendered' creature. As a westerner I could mingle with both men and women. Had I been a man I would never have been able to live so close to the women of the household, without gossip circulating. At the same time there was no obstacle to my being a woman, in a man's world. When the feasts were split, men and women in separate rooms, I was the only one able to circulate freely between the groups.[99]

Seierstad does make a brief reference concerning how she must have looked to others, but this provokes no further reflections from her. These opportunities to act as if they were men can actually lead female writers to feel more distant from local women, but to enjoy this privilege nonetheless.

Modern female war reporters often experience similar pressures in a far more intense form. Lamb provides the following description of the international reporters in Afghanistan:

> There was an American Club where one could drink Budweisers, eat Oreo Cookies ice-cream and listen to middle-aged male correspondents in US Army jackets with bloodstains and charred bullet holes on the back hold court with stories of conflicts and 'skirt' from Vietnam to El Salvador. Their eyes had seen so much that they saw nothing, they knew the name and sound of every weapon ever invented, their faces were on the leathery side of rugged and even at breakfast there was Jim Beam on their breath . . . most had children in various places

but they never carried their photographs, and all of them went to the Philippines for R and R.

It was different for me. I was a young girl in a place where women were regarded as property.[100]

Her *Sewing Circles of Herat* documents her attempt to find a way out of this hyper-masculine world.

Hadani Ditmars recalls working in similar conditions in Iraq. All the people around her, whether American, Iraqi or from other nations, were men. 'This absence of the X chromosome factor threw me into a kind of gender amnesia; I travelled in psychic drag.' She found she could adapt: 'My status as a foreigner outweighed the baggage of my sex.' And so, 'I was one of the boys.'[101] Hala Jaber, facing the same issues, concluded 'I would have to work like a man to stop thinking like a woman.'[102] This ultimately proved to be impossible. 'However hard I tried to bury myself in the new role of action-girl foreign correspondent, something within me would resurface in Baghdad, my maternal instincts disarmingly intact.'

There are some interesting continuities here. Both the older generation of orientalists and the newer female war reporters find that their journeys raise questions about their gender. Occasionally, both will sometimes rehearse arguments concerning the advantages of being exceptional women in extraordinary places: for example, Jaber makes some claims regarding her affinity with Iraqi mothers. But usually they experience their gender as an anomaly: to be laughed off by the orientalists (imagine being taken for a man because I was wearing trousers!), to be overcome by the war reporters. The war reporters' texts also work as 'talking cures': they tell of their journey back to a feminine sanity. The orientalists do not experience anything resembling an identity crisis; issues about their gender role and status do not lead them to question themselves.

Western writing, Muslim writing

Being concerned about how one appears in the eyes of others is clearly an important component of any form of self-consciousness. In the difficult meeting of self and other in these works, there are clear differences in the reactions of the Western and the Muslim women.

In general, comments concerning how the West appears in the eyes of the East are reduced to brief expressions of exasperation. Anthropologist Veronica Doubleday at first felt some frustration when she met Afghan women. 'Often I came away from the women weary and confused, hurt by their ridicule and tired by their questions. I disliked being an object of curiosity, little understood as a person in my own right.'[103] Something rather more worrying happens to Lamb. Travelling in Pakistan towards the Afghan-Pakistan border, she stops at the town of Akora Khattak. She walks through with her translator, and they meet two schoolboys from the local *madrassa* in the street. The two signal their admiration for Osama Bin Laden aggressively. Her translator begins to look worried, and Lamb fears that the two may attack them.

> I had become an enemy just for being white and western, and hated above all for being female. It was an uneasy feeling to be hated by strangers so nakedly, particularly in a country I had once felt at home in. I was finding the front-line of this war in more and more places.[104]

She makes no further attempt to consider why these feelings might exist. Beyond these semi-humorous, semi-worried, irritated asides, the Western writers are confident in their identity, and never question themselves as a result of their experience travelling. Above all, even where they note how their identity is misunderstood by the other, with the exception of very rare writers like Geldermalsen, they never consider that they have something to learn from the other.

The Muslim migrants have far greater problems in establishing their identity in the eyes of the other. Indeed, one could even suggest that one reason they write is to try to trace a coherent route of identity-development. Malik recalls: 'I was trying to straddle, balance, juggle, whatever, my life at home with my life at school.'[105] Basrawi, growing up in the Aramcom enclave, finally reached a decision: 'My reaction to this untenable situation was that I, as a Saudi daughter, and I as an Americanized Saudi teenager, became two different people. I was one person at home and someone else the moment I stepped outside the door.'[106] Ghada Karmi's parents refused to take issues of assimilation or identity seriously: her father retained the myth that their stay in London in the 1950s was only temporary, and so all would be resolved soon. Her mother simply tried to ignore everything English. Ghada and her sister were left to their own devices:

> As a result, we were left to find our own accommodation to the schism in our lives between our Palestinian Arab origins, so zealously maintained by our mother, and the new society we had joined; between our identity as Arabs and Muslims and that of the European, Christian country around us; and above all, between the awareness of our bruised and dislocated history and the British indifference and hostility towards it. I resented my parents deeply for throwing us so unthinkingly into this cultural and political morass. In the years that followed, we were forced to feel our way forward uncertainly, trying

to make sense of these contradictions and resolving them in our own different ways.[107]

Latifi records that she and her sister were dorks, nerds, weird and freaks in the United States.[108] Salbi was interviewed by a reporter from the *Los Angeles Times*:

> She asked how I had come to be in the United States. It was a simple question with such a complicated answer I didn't know what to tell her. I didn't even know how to describe myself. I wasn't a refugee. I wasn't a tourist. I had come here as a bride, but I wasn't a wife . . . So I told her half of the truth.[109]

For these travellers, this issue of identity is not raised through a brief moment of exasperation or fright, nor something that could be easily laughed off. Malik speaks eloquently of this point: while growing up, she faced 'constant T-junction dilemmas . . . should I turn left towards White England or turn right towards Muslim Pakistan?'[110]

This reveals a highly significant difference between the Muslim writers and the Western writers. The Western writers have the confidence and security to be able to laugh. There's a nice example of this in Geldermalsen's book. As part of the process of registering her marriage to Mohamed, she has to obtain a certificate. She produces her passport: while her name is long and strange, the clerk is able to copy it down. Then come further questions: what about her father? Her grandfather? Her tribe? She grows exasperated, but then decides to say nothing. The clerk stares at her passport, and eventually decides: 'Marguerite, me; Jane, my father; van, my grandfather; Geldermalsen, my tribe.' When finally read out in Arabic, the result is 'Marghreet Jeen Faan Jeldrrmalsn.'[111] For her, this is funny. She has the confidence of holding a New Zealand passport, and the promise of her parents to support her whenever she needs it. The Muslim migrants feel more vulnerable. They lack these resources, and when they see challenges to their names or their identities, they feel a need to defend themselves from what appears to be an attack. Their writing 'self' needs to be constructed in the face of a public that is sometimes openly hostile, sometimes demanding and usually misinformed. Sackville-West could optimistically face her reader 'as a familiar friend'; the Muslim writers are usually more defensive, more cautious about their readers.

The Muslim writer as individual

There is a strange difference between the most typical reading of the more modern works, which understands them as case studies that demonstrate a collective Muslim misery and the stance taken by the writers. This is revealed in a scene that is repeated in these works like a recurring dream.

Nahal Tajadod's semi-comic sketch about Iran tells of the difficulties she experiences in trying to renew her passport. In one passage, when approaching one of the many offices she visits, she is stopped by a crowd of women in the street.

> A great black roll of cloth seemed to cover the entire street – a cloth pierced here and there by holes through which one saw arms and faces. There were hundreds of women, all wearing black chadors, sitting in silence on the ground, in the street. I immediately thought that it must be a demonstration organized against Bush or Israel.[112]

Her first impressions are wrong: these women form the queue for passport applications, the one she is seeking to avoid. Later some of these women realise what Tajadod is trying to do: one grows furious, and threatens her: 'We didn't make the Revolution so that women like you could pass before us!'[113]

Tehmina Durrani goes in a car to visit her husband in Adyala Jail in Rawalpindi in Pakistan. She is recognised by the thousands of people outside, who have walked there to demonstrate their support: 'Clouds of dust rose. I felt the downtrodden, lowly dust, tramped for centuries, had finally begun to rise. I was recognised. I did not dare roll my window down as the adulation of the mob can prove dangerous.'[114] Haddad, always provocative, states 'I grew up in a country that hates me'.[115] Carmen Bin Ladin has her own 'not without my daughter(s)' moment while living in Saudi Arabia: 'I could not face the prospect that my daughters might grow up to become like the faceless, voiceless women I lived among.'[116] Farmaian states 'My interest has been to record what happened to me – and only to me.'[117] Salbi seems to reach a similar position: 'The last thing I would claim is to represent all Iraqi women, let alone all Arab women or all Iraqis.'[118] Most of these writers watch the crowds, rather than march with them. This repeated theme draws attention to the isolated individuality of the writers.

Rather than presenting themselves as typical Muslims, many of these Muslim women are trying to do the opposite: assert their individuality, distinguish themselves from the crowd. Sometimes this is done explicitly as a means to prevent their works from contributing to the 'image of

uniformity' by which 'other' societies are first identified and then deni-
grated.[119] Their pronouncements fly in the face of the logic of the
marketplace: their works are only valued by publishers because they seem
to be useful contributions to the 'Condition of Muslim Society Question'.
Readers are not really concerned with the individual experience of a
Sattareh or a Zainab: they want case studies or precedents which sustain
the nightmare visions of *Not Without My Daughter*.

Conclusion

This chapter has discussed some unusual forms of autobiography. The
original model, that popularised by the orientalists, could function almost
as a type of anti-autobiography, allowing the author to play games with
their self and their identity. The market currently demands Muslim misery
memoirs: some of our authors, such as Hirsi Ali, Ali and Djavann, respond
almost directly to this call. But the 'selves' which are created in most of
these Muslim-authored works do not correspond exactly to the model of
the misery memoir. Just as female war reporters find themselves occupying
a curious position, living a hyper-masculine lifestyle but considering
themselves neither traditionally feminine nor pseudo-males, so the
migrant Muslims have an awkward relationship with their old home
communities, somewhere in between rejection and attraction. This
problem is compounded by a similar problem with their new host communities. Some have a sense of 'Never feeling you belong anywhere.'[120] Even
as zealous a defender of French values as Djavann draws back from
declaring herself to be French. In a semi-fictional work, she talks of a character as knowing 'she would never be French by her biology or by her
birth; she wanted to be [French] by her language'.[121] While these works are
frequently read as case studies by typical Muslims who represent established communities, in fact a different quality comes from them: their
authors appear as hyper-individual, neither typically Muslim nor assimilated Westerners, and they point towards a different type of global culture,
for the obstacles that they have confronted and the dilemmas that they face
are not specific to Muslims, but are shared by the great mass of humanity
encountering the newly interconnected cultures of a globalised world.
This suggests a significant difference in the manner in which we can classify these works: at first, simple binary divisions between Muslims and
non-Muslims, or Easterners and Westerners seem the most obvious. In
reality, the most important distinction may well be between those with an
(apparently?) clear sense of their identity, whether Muslim or not, and
those for whom identity is obviously a serious problem.

CHAPTER THREE

The Politics of Time and Space: a Fractured Modernity

'We found ourselves at the collision point of two dissimilar civilizations.'

Raymonda Tawil[1]

Edith Wharton's *In Morocco* was first published in 1919. By the time the second edition came out in 1927, she was irritated. *In Morocco* was originally written as a type of elegy for an ancient Morocco which was passing, and which in 1919 she assumed the reader would never see. 'With a few years far more will be known of the past of Morocco,' she noted in the first edition, 'but that past will be far less visible to the traveller than it is today.' The problem for Wharton was that in 1927 this clearly was not the case. Five thousand miles of new railways and roads had opened up the country in a manner she had not anticipated. Hubert Lyautey, the French resident-general of the country from 1912–25, had acted with energy and foresight to conserve elements of Moroccan culture and traditions. Old palaces had been converted into 'luxurious modern hotels' so that 'from the vantage-ground of the new Morocco, the tourist may still peep down at ease into the old'.[2]

Wharton's comments are more complex than they might seem. We can note the moral superiority that she assumes: whatever her one-month dash through Morocco in a military car in 1917 might have been, she considered that it did not qualify her as 'a tourist'. Why not? First, because she had not been 'at ease'. But, more importantly, because she was claiming to do more than 'peep' at the old Morocco. Like the other orientalists, she voiced some sense of wonder at what she saw, and she assumed that a mere tourist, marshalled into a Cooks tour, would not be able to do this. A more curious aspect of her comments, however, is that she seems to be describing a form of time travel. How could 'the new' and 'the old' co-exist in the form that she suggests? Does she simply mean that the tourists lived in the most modern buildings, and they looked out at those who lived in a more old-fashioned manner? At first, this seems the most logical explanation of her statement; in fact, it probably is not what she meant. Like other orientalists, and like so many other travellers to the East, she considered that

Muslim societies existed in a completely different time zone. Travel to the East was also travel through time – into the past.

In this chapter, we will discuss how a sense of time affects our travellers' understanding of each other and the societies that they visit.

A note on definition: modernity and the modern

As will be seen, many of our writers are confused about the implications of terms such as 'the modern'. The two most common mistakes are, first, to assume that a comparison between the new and the old necessarily leads to an outline of a line of development, through which the old must inevitably become like the new. The second error is to attach some sort of moral value to the modern. Here, one should remember that Hitler and Stalin were both very 'modern' leaders, who tried to make their societies more techno-logically sophisticated and more efficiently organised, and that the concentration camp and the nuclear bomb are both 'modern' devices. There is nothing inherently morally good about something that can be classified as 'modern'.

This second mistake probably stems from confusion between 'the modern' and 'modernity'. The latter term refers to something quite distinct: a philosophical and political project that inspired some of the best Western political thinkers from the eighteenth century to the present. Here, we are examining an idea that has taken many different forms, and therefore is difficult to tie down to a precise definition or programme. It might be best to think of modernity as a question, rather than a solution. The question could be put this way: despite the enormous variety of cultures, civilisations and religions in the world, some concepts appear to be constant. A mathematical formula such as 'two plus two equals four' is accepted by an American, a French person, an Indian and a Korean; by a Jew, a Christian, a Buddhist, an atheist and a Muslim; by a city-dweller, a villager and a nomad. If this is so, is it then possible to create a form of global culture, based on similarly mutually acceptable precepts? Throughout the history of modernity, different disciplines have been put forward as instruments of modernity: initially mathematics was the preferred route, but then biology and linguistics were each considered as providing the key. Voltaire thought he could see a form of modernity when he visited eighteenth-century London:

> Go to the London Stock exchange, a place which is far better behaved than most stock markets, and there you will find representatives of all the nations, gathered to help mankind. There, the Jew, the Mohammadan and the Christian treat each other as if they shared the

same religion: the only people that they call 'faithless' are the bank-
rupts; there, the Presbyterian trusts the Anabaptist, and the Anglican
accepts the Quaker's word. When they leave these free, peaceful
assemblies, some go to the synagogue, others to the pub.[3]

In part, Voltaire's admiration for the stock exchange is stimulated by its use
of numbers: once again, these seemed neutral, apolitical and therefore
potentially universal. Other interpretations of modernity are possible, and
recent debates about globalisation have stimulated some further original
thinking.[4] Doris Lessing seems to be considering Marxism as a vehicle for
modernity when she writes that, 'I think it is possible that Marxism was
the first attempt, for our time, outside the formal religions, at a world-
mind, a world ethic.'[5] The project outlined in such ideas is certainly
optimistic and future-orientated, but the hope is that progress will bring
not just iPods to replace Walkmans and DVDs to replace VHS, not just
almost-immediate worldwide knowledge of Janet Jackson's 'wardrobe
malfunction', but also a different, wider consciousness, a global consciousness, through which the basic proposition that there is 'one world' becomes
a mental reality for the whole of humanity.

This idea is of particular relevance to our study. If it is possible to
construct mutually intelligible concepts, acceptable to people from
different cultures, then it is also possible that our hundred female authors
could agree about – for example – the nature of the veil. If this is not
possible, then perhaps some of the older orientalists were wiser than we
might think: some were willing to state, quite bluntly, that the East is East
and West is West.

Exploring the past

Like Wharton, many of our authors describe their journey to the East as a
journey in time, back into the past. The landmark figures that they cite –
T. E. Lawrence, Alexander the Great – all lead them to past glories.
Probably the most common time-related term that they use to describe
Muslim societies is 'medieval'. Arriving in Dilijan in Persia, Vita Sackville-
West thought that 'the village was like a walled city of the Middle Ages, as
labyrinthine, and as secret'.[6] Driving down an Afghan hill to Bala
Murghau, Ella Maillart 'felt as if plunged into the Middle Ages. Smoothly
flowing, life seemed changeless. The bazaar was peaceful, even somno-
lent.'[7] Carmen Bin Ladin explains that her distant relative Osama Bin
Laden was 'fashioned by the workings of an opaque and intolerant medieval society'.[8] Other comparisons suggest still longer journeys across
millennia. When travelling across the plains of Persia, Annemarie

Schwarzenbach observed that the landscape had not changed with the days of Alexander the Great, and probably would never change.[9] Arriving in the Ghorband valley, Dervla Murphy excitedly commented 'surely this must have been the Garden of Eden – it's so beautiful that I was too excited to eat the lunch my hostess had packed for me'.[10] Juliette de Baïracli Levy met shepherds by Lake Tiberias: they were 'aged men of the typical Old Testament type'.[11] Arriving in the Sinai desert for the first time, Laura Blumenfeld's mother commented 'wow, this is Sunday-school land . . . All those years learning about Moses in the wilderness and here I am.'[12] Pamela Bright meets a Palestinian peasant who 'had the dignity of an ancient Egyptian bas-relief'.[13] Visiting a bazaar in Herat, Veronica Doubleday felt that she had 'stepped back centuries in time'.[14]

At first sight, these comments make sense: what else do you call a village without cars or phones, if not 'medieval'? But the more these metaphors are used, the more problems they cause. They imply some sense of historical transition: in Europe, the medieval period, or the Middle Ages, signifies the period between the ancient Greco-Roman world and the revival of European civilisation after the Renaissance.[15] Initially, the term was almost pejorative: the medieval period was merely a 'middle' period of barbarity and decline, in between two glorious periods of civilisation. If Muslim societies are 'medieval', how then should they be situated historically? What form will their revival take? Such points illustrate how difficult it is to apply a term drawn from European history to another region of the world: is it really true that twentieth-century 'medieval' Dilijan resembled – for example – the thirteenth-century French medieval village of Montaillou? Did it possess the same shambolic economic forms? The same decentralised, overlapping power structures? The same demographic balance, teetering on the brink of over-population? The same tension between religious orthodoxy and widespread heterodoxy? If these qualities are not the same, then what is the point of applying the term?

There is also a second problem with the medieval metaphor. European medieval societies did not term themselves 'medieval', and had no clear idea of the societies that would develop in the future. Muslim societies are in a different situation: they live with a clear knowledge of several possible futures. Since at least the eighteenth century they have been highly concerned about the West, and have had to define themselves in comparison with the West. There have been permanent structures of communication and exchange between the two, whether these are acknowledged or not. Freya Stark provides a nice example of this point: she rode a camel in an isolated sector of the Saudi Arabian desert into which very few Europeans had ever travelled. 'We came to an edge and saw Romance in the varied light of evening – a little castle, walled and towered.' They approached, and met the family who lived nearby. Then they spotted the son of one of Stark's Arab servants playing with something he had found near the castle. It was 'a tin bucket with Charlie Chaplin stamped in gaudy colours'.[16] Even in this apparently most isolated of places, there was clear evidence of the presence of Western society. Writing in a different context, Carmen Bin Ladin also notes that constant exchanges between the apparently 'modern' West and 'medieval' Saudi Arabia:

> In a physical sense, Saudi Arabia had changed immensely. No country anywhere developed as quickly as Saudi Arabia did in the first five or six years I lived there. Half a century before, people wrapped themselves in wet sheets at night to get cool enough to sleep; now, everyone seemed to have air-conditioning. There were car dealerships everywhere: at some, you could even part-trade camels for a new Toyota.[17]

Qanta Ahmed spots the same quirk during her pilgrimage to Mecca. As she packs to leave, she runs into Qudsia, a colleague, munching delicacies from an eight-piece bucket of Kentucky fried chicken and washing this down with a giant cup of soda from Dunkin' Donuts.[18] If we return to the medieval metaphor, these examples would be like Emmanuel Le Roy Ladurie researching the thirteenth-century French medieval village of Montaillou and suddenly coming across evidence of a laptop. They suggest more shortcomings inherent in the medieval metaphor: unlike European medieval societies, contemporary Muslim societies have constant connections with other civilisations in different stages of development. In practice, Muslim societies present a picture of great diversity: elements are as technologically sophisticated as anywhere in the West; other elements seem less sophisticated, but are certainly not medieval in any meaningful sense of the word; elements that are genuinely and profoundly different. But no matter how primitive conditions in some Muslim societies may appear, this clear consciousness that they all possess of other societies makes them very different from European medieval societies.

The medieval metaphor also locks the writer into a very simple concept of development, according to which the East is the past, and the West is the future. Some intractable conceptual problems then arise. If the West represents the future, is it then inevitable and/or desirable that the East must evolve into the West? At first sight, the logic of the medieval metaphor would seem to suggest precisely this, yet so many of our writers seem to deny this interpretation emphatically. To return to Wharton, she explicitly congratulated Lyautey, 'the great Administrator', for preserving 'the old monuments of Morocco from injury, and her native arts and industries from the corruption of European bad taste'.[19] Her comments clearly suggest a wish to preserve the old Morocco, rather than a desire to see it develop into something resembling the modern West. Lesley Hamilton explains her fascination with the Sinai desert in similar terms:

> I *wanted* to turn back the clock and see this desert when it was still wild and unknown, when there were no roads and air routes, when the Beduin were still nomadic raiders, and when a handful of iconoclastic explorers were the only Westerners to venture there.[20]

Rather than welcoming the modernisation of the East, the old orientalists often seemed instead to value the East precisely because of its archaic nature.

Ideas concerning the social evolution of the East raise other issues for the orientalists. Was it possible for Muslims to become Western? Were they not fated, by biology or destiny, to remain as they were born? Some orientalists argued that attempts to introduce Western education and science into Eastern societies did not result in their improvement, but rather in decadence and de-culturalisation. When Murphy visited young Afghans who had received a modern education, she found 'a general restlessness, rootlessness and discontent. They repudiate their native culture yet cannot succeed in adopting an alien civilisation which they imagine is superior, though they don't understand the first thing about it. Give me the nomads' outlook every time.'[21] Sarah Hobson seemed to feel something similar when she visited Shiraz in Iran in the early 1970s:

> As I explored the town, I felt . . . that the reputation and image far exceeded the reality. Where were the roses and nightingales? True, there were cypress trees, but where was the wine, and the poetry of the place? Perhaps the wide tarmac roads, the hotel blocks, the huge new hospital, were now poetry to the Shirazis, but it was not my idea of Persian poetry.[22]

This anti-development position leads to Wharton's wildly contradictory observations, in which she celebrates the apparent ability of a modernising French imperialism to save the ancient treasures of Morocco's past. It also explains the orientalists' cult of the Bedouin, praised as being 'true' Arabs because they appear uncivilised, while Arabs who lived in cities or who developed modern agricultural practices in villages were seen as mongrels, belonging neither to one culture or the other. For such writers, the 'medieval' East is not in the 'middle' of any stage of development, it is (or should be) simply stuck in the past.

Others have adopted almost exactly the contrary argument. Recent writers such as Chahdortt Djavann, Leïla Sebbar, Wassyla Tamzali and

Hélé Béji certainly speak in different registers, but they all celebrate the civilising values of the French schooling system, and even praise the 'universal values' that it promotes.[23] Hirsi Ali argues that just as Muslims have been able to learn from the Wright brothers and adopt air travel, so they must also learn other values and techniques from the West.[24] For these writers, the evolution of East into the West is both necessary and inevitable.

Perhaps in order to avoid some of the conceptual problems with the medieval metaphor, other writers have preferred to use terms such as 'timeless'. Looking at Lebanon from her plane, Pauline Cutting thought that the country had 'a timeless, striking beauty'.[25] Rona Randall found that the Middle East is marked by 'a feeling of eternal continuity, a timelessness that lays its spell on you . . . All the time I was in Petra I felt her timelessness reaching out to me.'[26] She elaborates on this theme when visiting the then-Jordanian controlled East Jerusalem.

> It is difficult to describe a place like Jerusalem, for it is so much more than a place. It is an experience, an encounter that leaves its imprint for ever. From the moment of arrival you are aware not only of a sense of history, but of a feeling of eternity, as if the city has always lived and breathed and always will . . . There is no place like it in the world.[27]

As historical observations, these are simply nonsense. All societies change: even the most primitive, non-technological cultures still adapt to changing ecologies and produce innovations in their apparently fixed traditions. But as a means of expressing some of the differences between Muslim and Western societies, the term 'timelessness' may be less inaccurate than 'medieval', for Muslim societies often seem to stand outside Western concepts of time.

Several of the Muslim authors note particularities in Muslim concepts of time. One important point is that the cult of the birthday is a Western tradition.[28] Prior to the entry of Western colonial powers, many Muslim societies had no equivalent of the birth certificate, thus making it difficult to estimate an individual's age with any accuracy.[29] When Waris Dirie arrived in London, just before passing through customs, a friend told her that her passport declared that she was eighteen. Dirie was surprised and replied:

> 'I am NOT eighteen . . . That's old.'
>   'Well, how old are you?'
>   'I don't know – maybe fourteen – but I'm not *that* old!'[30]

Some Muslim societies have grown outside Western concepts of time. Days, years and centuries are measured differently: not necessarily in a better or worse manner, simply in a different manner. They could therefore be described as 'timeless' in the sense that their understanding of time is not that of the Western traveller.

Growing contacts with the Western world stimulated the widespread but often incomplete adoptions of new techniques in the East, some of them consciously copied from the Western world, some of them adapted in a more autonomous manner by Muslim-majority societies. (Here, a note of caution needs to be sounded: when, for example, Azar Nafisi reports that her Iranian students enjoy Michael Jackson's music, we should not immediately think 'Westernization'.[31] The Michael Jackson that is seen and heard in Tehran is not the same as the one who appears in Los Angeles: his movements, his singing and his lyrics can acquire different meanings in different contexts.[32])

Frequently, this process of modernisation has been confused with moral improvement or social reform. For example, consider how Raymonda Tawil describes the journeys undertaken by Palestinian exiles to Saudi Arabia in the 1960s: 'These sophisticated people from the modern towns of Haifa, Acre, Nablus, and Jerusalem were forced to conform to the lifestyle of backward Bedouin tribes.'[33] Here, it is clear that Tawil is not merely offering some form of chronological annotation: for her, the words 'modern' and 'backward' have obvious moral and political implications. Carmen Bin Ladin made the same error. She was concerned about the status of women in Saudi Arabia, and anxiously searched for signs that it was 'entering the modern world': she cited veils being lifted, the opening of a bank that accepted women's accounts, an English-language TV channel and a new bookshop.[34] While Bin Ladin may well be right in welcoming all these developments as offering some greater autonomy for women, it is conceptually confusing to conflate such innovations with being 'modern'. As Bin Ladin herself notes elsewhere, Toyotas and air conditioning are also modern, but they do not necessarily lead to greater freedom for women.

We will end this section by noting that modernisation can take some dreadful, tragic forms in the Middle East. Driving from the airport to the centre of Baghdad after the second Gulf War, Hala Jaber describes some of the changes that she saw:

> The thousands of palm trees that had always lined this route in two neat rows, greeting visitors with a vision of orderliness and verdant vitality, had disappeared . . . The Americans had decided the safest course of action would be to take their bulldozers to every one of the

majestic trees. Generations of resilient beauty had been flattened in less than two years . . .

This once unified city of 6 million souls had become a labyrinth of concrete blocks and barriers, bricked-up windows and walls up to 20ft high, dividing Sunnis from Shi'ites. The Americans had turned it into a maze complex enough to confound the most sophisticated sectarian killer . . .

'Dear God, what have they done?' I said out loud.[35]

Emma Williams could be described as a traveller who was tricked by history. She planned her move to Israel/Palestine in the late 1990s, during the optimistic period following the Oslo Accords of 1993. But she arrived weeks before the second intifada of September 2000, which marked the definitive end of that optimism. Unaware that she was enjoying the last few weeks of (relative) peace, she learnt how difficult it is to travel in Israel when, in her own car, she tried to follow her husband, Andrew, but lost him just as she approached an Israeli checkpoint:

My first checkpoint and I was clueless. All the vehicles were funnelled into one lane that chicaned through a row of concrete cubes a metre high. Pedestrians were channelled through another chicane. I would soon learn that the crux of the checkpoint is the Israeli soldier, armed, bored and powerful. He decides if you pass or not. Only the speed varies: permission can be instantaneous – the soldier's nod – not for hours, or not at all. Faces in the queue show resignation, irritation, humiliation. There were few discernible security measures, no searches, little screening of ID. Hang on, did I have the right ID? I swallowed panic. The soldier glanced at my car and waved me through. Andrew was waiting for me on the other side, patient as I threw my angry fear at him.[36]

The point to be stressed here is that the sights and obstacles which confront Jaber and Williams in Baghdad and Jerusalem are also modern. Alongside banking facilities for women, TV channels, air conditioning and bookstores, modernisation in the Middle East has also meant destruction by bulldozers, obstruction by checkpoints, surveillance of ID cards, concrete blocks, barriers and surly soldiers. If nothing else, this point explains why many Muslims are ambivalent about 'the modern'.

Old futures, new pasts

A theme runs through many of these texts, like a thread weaving in and out of a carpet. This is the ideal of a type of historical alignment: a position at which a society can feel at peace with itself, for its sense of its past is compatible with its identity in the present, and this sense of assurance is the foundation for a confident optimism about the future. While not using precisely these terms, it is clear that many of these writers consider that their societies do not possess these ideal qualities, and they are acutely aware of being 'out of time'. This type of chronological dissonance is probably felt most acutely among the most modern Muslim writers of our sample, but one can find echoes of it in almost all of them. In a sense, when the orientalists gazed in wonderment at the glories of the Islamic past, they had already faced a similar question: how was that past to be fitted into the world's future? They never found a satisfactory answer, but their confidence in their status and their position in historical evolution allowed them to laugh off easily anything that appeared as a challenge. This type of question seems to have grown more difficult and more troubling in recent years.

The significant shift away from the orientalist structures of historical interpretation did not occur until quite late in the twentieth century. The Iranian revolution of 1978–9 may well have been a turning point: it certainly challenged the idea that the East could only follow the West. The widely publicised image of the woman in the face-masking burqa, often presented as *the* image of Islam, works in a similar manner: it suggests an obstinate refusal by the East to accept the necessary modernisation along Western lines.[37] The interventions by Saadawi and Mahmoody both, in quite different ways, suggest challenges to the cultures and structures of orientalism: Saadawi by explicitly criticising Western models of development, Mahmoody by so vividly dramatising a new sense of a threat from the East, and suggesting that – in the form of Muslim migrants – this threat was now even present within the West itself.[38]

Let us briefly consider how three of our authors respond to issues of historical identity.

Making a past: In Search of Fatima

Of the hundred works under consideration, Ghada Karmi's *In Search of Fatima* is one of the fullest, most informative and most genuinely autobiographical. Born in 1940 in Palestine, Karmi lived through the political violence that marked the last years of the British Mandate, was briefly exiled in Jordan, and then travelled with her family to London in 1949. Within the work, Karmi makes a number of telling points about both her individual relationship with her past and the more general issue of Palestinians' relationship with their past. Like some of the other Muslim migrants, Karmi does not know the exact date of her birth: her registration documents were left behind in their house in Jerusalem in 1948. Her exile really does make her 'out of time'.

The 'Fatima' in the title of her autobiography is an Arab peasant woman who was employed to help her mother in their house, and who often came to act as a substitute mother for Karmi. *In Search of Fatima* uses this memory to initiate a wider discussion concerning the status of the peasant in early twentieth-century Palestine: they were seen as uneducated and backward; peasant origins were a source of shame among Palestinian townsfolk.[39] On the other hand, peasant villages were the source of many artefacts and customs which were seen as distinctively Palestinian: Hebron glass-making, Majdal weaving, village pottery, the *dabka* dance. With the experience of mass exile after 1948, peasant life was suddenly revalued: their 'tenacity, simplicity and steadfastness' now seemed useful attributes.[40] Even the unfashionable peasant caftan, sown in different shades of red to indicate specific villages, was seized on as a key symbol of Palestinian identity.

> No one then could have known that after the loss of Palestine in 1948 this despised peasant costume would become a symbol of the home-land, worn with pride by the very same women who had previously spurned it . . . What had started out as a solely peasant custom was now transformed into a precious national heritage.[41]

While this establishment of a usable past suggests the possibility of a future Palestinian identity, it is obvious that sixty years of struggle still has not created a viable Palestinian nation. The 'past' here is therefore still an unanswered question, for what is the point of a past that does not lead to a future? Karmi's attempts to re-establish her identity following her decades of residence in Britain prove difficult. Her book ends on a pessimistic note: she is unable to feel truly at home in either the East or the West.

An old future: Islam Pride

Hélé Béji's *Islam Pride: Derrière le voile* (Behind the Veil) is somewhat different from the flood of French-language books criticising the practice of Islamic veiling. The title itself demands some explanation: at first, Béji seems to be suggesting a similarity between Islamic identity and the concept of 'Gay pride'. French gay activists have used the English-language term 'pride' to signal that they share concerns with similar activists in other countries and cultures. Béji's use of the word does not follow this pattern: she intends her title to be critical and ironic: like other French neo-Republicans she uses English-language words to suggest something insubstantial, artificial and superficial.[42] For her, the term 'Islam pride' suggests how ridiculous it would be to see current Islamic revivals as being 'modern', like Gay pride, because they are inherently archaic.

Béji, a French-Tunisian, is proud of the independence of Tunisia in 1957, but she belongs to the generation of North African militants who, while they fought French political power, still accepted France as a social and cultural model to imitate. She provides the following description of the post 1957 culture of her home.

I grew up in an environment of feminism inspired by Bourguiba [the Tunisian president after 1957], in a liberal Muslim family, struggling against colonialism, fighting for the republican ideal. At home, it was not unusual to hear free-thinkers joking about bigotry, lively women criticizing the faithful, and brave young women willing to defy established customs. In my family, the majority of women, whether young or old, did not wear a veil when they went out.[43]

Béji sums up the joyful mood in Tunisia immediately after its liberation in 1957 with the phrase 'we had become modern'.

Her essay attempts to understand why a new generation of Tunisian women choose to wear the veil. Her first thought on seeing such women is that 'they are backward'.[44] The work turns on her encounter with a female relative who has suddenly adopted the veil. Half-jokingly, Béji makes an attempt to pull the veil from her relative's head. She replies 'Don't! That's rude! [honteux]'. Béji retorts that the relative is being rude to the legacy of Bourguiba and the rights established by independence.[45] (One weakness of the essay is that these are the only words by a veil-wearing woman that Béji cites throughout the whole book.) Béji notes that her relative's new veil is not, strictly speaking, traditional: when she was young, before 1957, Tunisian women wore large, loose veils of white silk, while the new generation wear black veils tightly wrapped around their heads. Béji speculates that the veil has changed its meaning:

In a post-liberal society, [the veil] is a form of dissidence by the children of liberty, by the least well-off, [a protest] against a life without a future, in which they held in place [clouée] by their origins or their religion, viewed by society with a pitiless scorn.[46]

In this sense, the new veil suggests a complex relationship between past and future: it re-reads Islamic tradition in a form which Béji does not recognise, and suggests a future which she finds unfamiliar. Béji's own uncertainty is clear. In 1957, while Tunisia certainly faced problems, there was a sense of optimism and hope. Today, Béji feels disturbed by the sight of this new generation, and cannot easily place them in relation to the images of the past and future with which she is familiar.

An American future: The Kabul Beauty School

Deborah Rodriguez's *The Kabul Beauty School* is a fascinating and original work, written by someone who clearly relishes her 'non-expert' status. In 2002, Rodriguez volunteered for aid work in Afghanistan as part of an American Christian charity. In the processes of preparation and arrival, she grew acutely aware of the difference between her specialism and those of her co-workers: 'All around me, I heard people introducing themselves as teachers, engineers, nutritionists, agricultural specialists, and experts of all sort. Not once did anyone else introduce herself as a hairdresser.'[47] However, when she arrives in Afghanistan, she suddenly finds that her chosen profession is highly valued: first, because none of the hundreds of aid workers has had a proper haircut for months. But then, secondly, she realises that she can do something even more valuable than cut her colleagues' hair: she can also help their aid programme in a unique way.

> I was excited. It seemed that I had discovered the one thing I could help to do to help the Afghans – and only I, out of all the talented and dedicated Westerners I'd met here, could do it. I knew that I could help the Afghan women run better salons and make more money.[48]

Her book tells of her work to establish a beauty school in Kabul.

The Kabul Beauty School would be easy to caricature: 'Hi, I'm Debby, and I'll be doing your hair today. Did you hear about that Taliban attack? Heck, those are some bad dudes . . .' But Rodriguez always has one trump card, which she plays well: if one key purpose of the international campaign is to stimulate women's economic activities, then she has devised a viable strategy to achieve this goal and, arguably, a better strategy than those previously attempted by better-qualified aid workers.

It is interesting to compare this text with previous orientalist works. Curiously, the badly chosen image on the cover suggests a clear continuity: it is a delicately coloured photo, focusing on the face and shoulders of a beautiful, slightly melancholy, Asian-looking woman, with an elaborately embroidered veil loosely draped over her head, whose heavily made-up eyes look downwards, away from the reader. The model resembles an Indian woman: she certainly shows none of the features of any of the main

ethnic groups in Afghanistan. Furthermore, this delicate, shy image is
completely at odds with Rodriguez's writing, which is a fine example of a
no-nonsense American can-do spirit, occasionally relieved by some self-
deprecating humour. There are some other continuities with the older
works: it is interesting that Rodriguez refers to Afghans almost as if they
were natural aristocrats: 'I must say that, in all my time in their country,
I've never met a rude Afghan. Even when they're pointing a gun at you,
they're polite.'[49] There is also a strange echo of another older theme.
Rodriguez is looking for a cure whilst in the East: an escape route from a
mean husband and a failed marriage. But it is the differences with the
older works that are striking. While the previous orientalists were 'free',
leisured travellers, who understood their journeys as an emancipatory
experience, Rodriguez travels as an aid worker in an organised group. She
feels no sense of wonder and certainly does not expect any spiritual experience, but she does feel something like a sense of destiny fulfilled: 'I knew
that, for the first time in my life, I was going to the right place at the right
time.'[50] In general her remarks about Afghan culture are pejorative and
dismissive. Comparing Afghan and American cultures, she does not for a
single second consider that any aspect of Afghan culture might be superior
in any form to American culture.

The manner in which she makes contact with Afghan women is interesting: not through any shared spiritual values but through an – assumed
– shared feminine culture. Rodriguez is explicit and eloquent on this
point. Entering a semi-clandestine Afghan women's hairdresser she notes:

> Aside from those differences, I felt the same warm, welcoming
> atmosphere that I'd spent most of my life in. There were women's
> voices, women's laughter – and that feeling of women relaxing with
> one another, laying hands on one another, telling one another the
> details of their lives and news of the lives around them.[51]

After establishing her own school, she makes the same point:

> There was the music of women's voices, women's laughter – the
> sounds of women taking care of one another – that is just part of a
> salon and beauty school. To me, these sounds are a sensory feast – like
> stepping into a hot bath or opening the door of an oven where cookies
> are baking – that always makes me feel good.[52]

There is, however, an important qualification to this channel of communication: it only works one way. Not surprisingly, Rodriguez is dismissive of
the burqa, but actually says little about it. More thought-provoking is the

manner in which she is really quite rude about the manner in which Afghan women dress, even when they are making efforts to present themselves in a glamorous and memorable fashion. One bride is described as 'wearing her own body weight in eye shadow, false eyelashes the size of sparrows, monumentally big hair and clothes with more bling than a Ferris wheel'.[53] Twice she compares Afghan women who have dressed for public occasions to drag queens: in this context, it would be hard to imagine a worse insult.[54] There is no cross-cultural dialogue here: Rodriguez offers Afghan women liberation through *Vogue* and Clairol products, and does not feel a flicker of doubt about her proposal.[55] While frequently expressing her love for Afghan women, Rodriguez does not once include a positive assessment of any aspect of their lives: she has nothing to learn from Afghanistan or its women. Without any doubt, here the modern is Western: the originality that Rodriguez brings is that she suggests a feminine-modern, which can be presented as apolitical and non-controversial, *because* it is feminine.

These three works suggest how difficult it is to align past, present and future within contemporary Muslim societies. Rodriguez certainly accomplishes this task, but only by ignoring or dismissing almost all aspects of Afghan culture, and blithely assuming that *Vogue* and Clairol products will be readily and unquestioningly accepted by all Afghan women. Béji and Karmi suggest more troubling pictures: neither future nor past are clear, and therefore the present seems threatening. Arguably, they are more typical of the modern Muslim writers, and even Rodriguez's easy confidence is unusual among modern Western writers.

Past, present and future

The country in the Middle East which has struggled hardest to align past, present and future is probably Israel.[56] Here, claims about biblical legacies are joined with contemporary geo-political confrontations and diplomatic ambitions to create the cultural-historical synthesis which defines Zionism. Frequently, Western observers are struck by the differences between Israel and the surrounding Muslim societies: to them, it seems clear that Israel is a distinctively welcome, modernising force. Thus Colette Modiano was surprised by the sight of the 'rectangular concrete of the kibbutzim' on the hills of Galilee.[57] Lesley Hamilton differentiated between the Israeli initiatives and the previous colonial presence:

> In 1948, [the Israelis] became the first to venture into this desert not
> as an extension of empire, but as part of a deep historical sense of

homecoming, a return to the place where their ancestors had roamed long before the empires of the world had come and gone.[58]

In other words, Israel was a legitimate presence in the region because it supplied an appropriate past. Western journalists such as Martha Gellhorn were forthright in their admiration for Israel, and swift to condemn Palestinian nationalism: after she visited Palestinian refugee camps, Gellhorn commented that 'The echo of Hitler's voice is heard again in the land, now speaking Arabic.'[59] The Israeli presence seemed to represent a new historical framework for the region; its claim 'to make the desert bloom' promised the transformation of the Muslim past through a dynamic, forceful, technocratic implementation of Western science. Here, at last, there appeared to be a practical answer to the old orientalist dilemma of how to align Muslim past and Western future. Such points explain much of the sympathy voiced by Western commentators for the Israeli presence in the 1950s and 1960s.

The Israeli programme to transform the region's past can be compared with other attempts to create 'new pasts'. In France today, schoolchildren are still reared in an Asterix-like cult of veneration for 'our ancestors, the Gauls'. The lesson they are taught can be dated back to political-historical initiatives by Napoleon III, who ruled France from 1851–70. Napoleon III encouraged academic and archaeological research into the pre-Roman presence of the Celts (or Gauls) in France, not in order to celebrate their culture and civilisation, but in order to demonstrate a historical continuity: France's ability to conquer and absorb 'other' peoples.[60] The cult of 'our ancestors, the Gauls' therefore commemorates not the greatness of the older Celtic civilisation, but the process of historical absorption and synthesis carried out by what is claimed as a continuous French polity, stretching from Charlemagne to Sarkozy. Something similar happened in the growth of the USA: European observers in the sixteenth century were perplexed by Native American cultures. Were they undeveloped versions of humanity who could be redeemed by education and evangelisation? Or were they just vicious savages, standing in the way of imperial progress?[61] Such questions were never resolved but, once the West was won, the Native American presence was then commemorated in the strangest fashion: by the Apache helicopter that has seen action in Iraq, by Tomahawk missiles and the popular Redskins football team. In these examples, rather than rejecting and denying the presence of the 'other' past, the dominant, conquering power appropriates and absorbs the other's presence into its sense of the past.

As a generalisation, this process of absorption and appropriation through commemoration has not been applied by Western powers to

Muslim cultures. Occasionally, one can find initiatives that suggest this type of strategy. Some confident nineteenth-century orientalists spoke as if Muslim civilisations had died, and therefore Western domination in some form was the only possible future for the East.[62] Lyautey took pride in his administration's ability to preserve the old Morocco more effectively than the Arabs had. Religious scholars and Christians sometimes speak of Jerusalem and the Holy Land as representing 'our' past. Lastly, the interest and even affection that some Israelis show for Bedouin cultures is perhaps also a type of echo of the processes of appropriation which have been carried out elsewhere. But these examples are all exceptions to the rule: the historical relationship of the East with the West is still, for the most part, an unanswered question.

A new concern has been brought into this complex, awkward relationship by the more recent polemical essays. While Rodriguez may still feel certain that the future is American, the new writers treat the new, long-term Muslim presence in Europe as a dangerous attack on European identities. In *Londonistan*, Melanie Phillips rehearses such arguments: even the title of her work suggests invasion and conquest.[63] Phillips invites her readers to celebrate the British character, with 'its belief in the rational, the everyday and what is demonstrably evident, and its corresponding suspicion of the abstract, the theoretical and obscurantist'. Indeed, reason is 'the supreme national virtue' of the British. However, in the current climate, even this virtue can become a weakness. 'Presented with a ranting ideologue, the British are less likely to succumb than to scoff.'[64] They therefore underestimate the dangers represented by the Islamists on their own soil. Phillips's preferred solution is a revival of the national spirit. 'This was . . . the country that was a byword for bloody-minded independence and a refusal ever to knuckle under to tyranny. This was the bulldog breed that in the 1940s had endured the horrors of the Blitz and vowed never to surrender.'[65] Alongside her references to the bulldog values of 1940, readers are also invited to accept 'the litmus test', the defence of Israel, which is in the front line of the international war against terrorism.[66] Plucky little Israel and bulldog Britain are joined in a single image of the bulwark, defending the Western world and its past against the destructive Muslim hordes. Similar arguments have been produced by French neo-Republican thinkers, who also construct a model of Muslim culture as uniquely incompatible with French secular values.[67]

These examples show how difficult the project of modernity has become. In place of a confidence in the development of a universal language that will enable thinking on a global scale, we find signs of ever deeper and more serious splits, and an increasing sense of uncertainty. Many Muslim writers are often less willing to accept the West as the model of their future; the Muslims who continue to do so find that their future now appears curiously antiquated; Western writers see the Muslim world as no longer simply an irritating exception to an assured vision of a welcome future: for some, it is now even a threat to a secure sense of the past.

The project of modernity, however, has not ended. It remains the best option, even the only option, available. Concepts of postmodernity, while presenting some accurate and perceptive criticisms of the political implications of past visions of modernity, cannot construct anything to replace it.[68] More conflict-orientated scenarios, such as Samuel Huntington's 'Clash of civilizations', threaten humanity with a terrifying, unending cycle of battles and discord. Rather than demonstrating that modernity is impossible, our hundred authors show some of the challenges it presents, but also suggest a different kind of scenario: a fractured modernity, in which advances are made in partial, piecemeal, uncoordinated form.

A fractured modernity

The modernity which the modern Muslim writers encounter is not a seamless evolution of historical logic, drawing in the diverse strands of humanity into one glorious, multicoloured, harmonious tapestry, but rather an improvised, rather grubby, patchwork. If we put to one side the self-conscious radiance of converts to Islam such as Evelyn Cobbold and Na'ima Roberts, one striking point is how little ideas and thinkers guide our writers on their journeys.[69] Even the joyous rebels of the Arab Spring of 2011 based their protests more on a simple, apolitical, ethical stance, rather than a political programme.[70] The social identities of our Muslim migrants are built around mean little confrontations and banal incidents in anonymous institutions: airports and schools, prisons and border checkpoints, sometimes also libraries, hospitals, shops, cinemas and even (according to Rodriguez) hairdressing salons.

Occasionally, the Western travellers express a certain delight in the world-shrinking capacity of these technologies.

> It is fantastic but true that today you can shed the Western world in little over five hours, flying non-stop from London airport far more speedily and comfortably than by any magic Arabian carpet and stepping down not merely into the heart of the Middle East but into a place steepened in Biblical and pre-Biblical history.[71]

But for the majority of Muslim passengers, there is little sense of celebration of the wonders of modern technology. Airports are uncomfortable, liminal places, in which autonomy is challenged, authority confronted and identities forced. 'No, YOU shut up!', shouts Fadia Basrawi on the third page of her *Brownies and Kalashnikovs*: she is trying to return to Saudi Arabia from Lebanon and, as ever, the airport officials seem to delight in asking the 'most inane questions'. Basrawi's long-suffering, well-mannered father sighs: 'Do we have to go through this every time?'[72] Susan Nathan listens to the stories that her Palestinian neighbours tell her, and then concludes: 'There cannot be an Arab citizen of Israel who has travelled abroad who does not have his or her own personal horror story of dealing with the security procedures at Ben-Gurion Airport, just outside Tel Aviv.'[73] Karmi's work also begins in London airport, before it turned into Heathrow. She was amazed at the 'crush of people, strangers pushing, rushing, jostling'.[74] It bewildered her: this was the first time that she had encountered a crowd of strangers. The travellers flow past each other, but sometimes stop and stare. Qanta Ahmed watches the Saudi voyagers forming symmetrical lines, and then praying for twenty minutes at John F. Kennedy airport: while the elegantly dressed men remain distinct individuals even as they follow the rituals, the women soon become just 'a mass of black bundles'.[75] The flights themselves work like time-machines, throwing women out of one civilisation and into another. Chahdortt Djavann sets her celebrated sketch concerning the humiliation of having to wear a veil on an Iran Air plane coming into Tehran.[76] Dirie felt a mounting astonishment and anxiety as she took in the sight of her pale-skinned fellow passengers on her flight from Mogadishu to London: so many of them looked cold and sickly. They must have been out of the sun for too long: whatever it was, it had to be 'a temporary condition'. Perhaps, she thought, if she rubbed their skin, they might be black underneath.[77]

Schools perform similar functions. Rather than ordered, clear pathways to knowledge and reason, they initiate our travellers into the irrational rituals of prejudice and conformity. The experience leaves the Muslim migrants with some varied impressions, by no means entirely negative. The 12-year-old Raymonda Tawil was pleasantly surprised by the Catholic convent school at Haifa: it was attended by girls from European Jewish families who had converted to Christianity during the war years. Their presence, and the actions of some open-minded nuns, made for a 'creative, intellectual atmosphere'. They were even taken to the beach once a week, where they were allowed to wear bathing costumes.[78] Farmaian remembers the extraordinary freedom and the 'encouraging and liberal atmosphere' at the American school in Tehran to which she was sent in the 1930s.[79] Sometimes there were surprising congruities between different cultures. Nahid Rachlin travelled from Persia to the USA in the 1960s. When she arrived at Lindengrove College, she registered for a home economics course on the grounds that it would not require advanced English. Part of the course was on 'charm' and she was delighted to realise that this concept was not so different from *taarof*, the elaborate Persian code of politeness.[80] Karmi found good and bad in the Catholic convent school she was sent to in London: while from the start 'the nuns were the epitome of kindness', she still felt isolated and confused: 'I cannot remember so much misery as I felt in those early months.'[81]

On some occasions, schools could be the arena for outright xenophobia and racism, as was seen in the last chapter. Another complaint that comes through so many of these books is that these authors, as young girls, were left unassisted to confront major cultural issues. One line from Latifi's *Even After All This Time* seems to sum up their experience: 'If the classes were generally confusing, the breaks between classes were downright terrifying.'[82] Basrawi is frightened when she realises that the teacher really cannot speak Arabic, and then bursts into tears at the sight of a thin ginger girl with freckles.[83] Our writers find a fair amount of outright nonsense exists in schools. Rachlin came from a liberal, even moderately sceptical, Persian Muslim family, in which no one wore a veil, observed the Ramadan fasts or prayed. At Lindengrove College, the dean requested a special interview with the school's four foreign students prior to parents' day. She told them that in order to welcome the parents, they must dress in their 'native costumes'. For Rachlin, this meant a veil. Rachlin protested that she had never worn a veil in her life; the dean insisted: 'I still want you to wear it for this occasion, to show a little of your culture to us.' Rachlin then had to make her first veil. She meditated on this contradictory experience: 'Here I was in this land of freedom and more or less forced to wear it.'[84]

Azar Nafisi's *Reading Lolita in Tehran* is set in a different context (a university) and written from a different perspective, that of a lecturer, not a student. But the final impression is remarkably similar: the distinctive crashing together of diverse, incompatible demands, with the students or pupils left to reconcile the irreconcilable as best they can. The strange feature to note is that these important confrontations and exchanges take place in an educational context, not a political one: the school (or university) almost seems like a substitute parliament for many of these authors.

Reading Lolita also suggests a different perspective on modernity and culture, in which culture does not play a simply educational or propagandistic role, but rather exists as a separate space, perhaps like the Orient for the orientalists, in which participants can experiment with identities and histories. In Nafisi's work this perspective is given a particular political edge: at times, she suggests (or seems to suggest?) that a specifically Western literature can play the role of a counter-culture to the Islamic republic. But other perspectives are also present in her work. Musing on the legacy of the thirteenth-century Sufi mystic Rumi and the ninth-century Persian poet Ferdowsi, she remembers that her father had commented that:

> our true home, our true history, was in our poetry. The story came back to me then because, in a sense, we had done it again. This time we had opened the gates not to foreign invaders but to domestic ones, to those who had come to us in the name of our own past but who had now distorted every inch of it and robbed us of Ferdowsi and Hafez.[85]

Certainly, many of the Muslim writers in my sample explicitly praise the value of literature in their personal development which – significantly – they usually present as something that they discover for themselves, rather than in a classroom. Latifi tells a genuinely touching story: she suddenly realises that even an Iranian refugee living in the USA is allowed access to a public library, without having to pay. There, she discovers Jane Austen: 'Reading her books filled me with hope.'[86] Disappointment then follows: she is 'crushed' to learn that Austen is dead, and that having read the last volume by her on the library shelves, there will be no more. Karmi finds similar joys in her local library in north London, 'a place of hidden treasures and delights . . . [Books are] better than people, I used to think, they never talk back and never let you down'.[87] Left to her own devices, she works through the shelves from A to Z, choosing books by their covers. Growing up in the Shah's Iran, Rachlin finds a translated copy of Victor Hugo's *Les Misérables*, which she read 'like a child starved for food'.[88] Tawil goes through a similar experience in Israel/Palestine in the 1950s:

> Shifting from school to school, I came under many different influences. My mother tongue was Arabic, and I was largely formed by my Arabic heritage. But my home also imbued me with a deep affection for Western culture, particularly that of France. Father used to say that everyone had two homelands: his own and France. French was my second language, reinforced by the French nuns at the convent.
>
>   I soon discovered the world of books. My romantic soul found its reflection there, mirrored in the works of Victor Hugo, Dickens, the Brontë sisters, and Guy de Maupassant.[89]

Haddad, deliberately and provocatively adopting a bad girl image, makes a similar comment: 'I used to think that only two things were worth doing whenever I had the chance of being alone: reading and masturbating.' A few pages on, she reflects more seriously: 'I am convinced that reading is one of the most important tools of liberation that any human being, and a contemporary Arab woman in particular, can exploit.'[90]

One cannot help noting the prominence of classical Western authors in these lists of discoveries. Is this Westernisation in practice? Mai Ghoussoub makes some interesting points concerning this issue:

> The novel is a European invention. But I would add that this fantastic European invention has pervaded the world; it has become global before the word 'globalisation' became fashionable. Moreover, the Arab novel has benefitted from the influence of the West as well as from its local tradition of storytelling or the infinite love of the word in Arabic culture and poetry.[91]

Furthermore, in reading the great classic novels of Western literature, these Arab and Muslim women are not therefore subscribing to any specific political programme. Nafisi herself nicely illustrates this point, perhaps unintentionally. Having read *Lolita*, she then proposes a genuinely daft reading of the text, suggesting that Nabokov's work was an anti-totalitarian parable. Somehow, these novels provide a space for thought and reflection, rather than acting simply to propagate pro-Western political values.

Alongside the examples of high culture, Western pop culture also permeates the Muslim memoirs. Following a series of tense negotiations, Basrawi's father finally allowed her to see the Beatles' *A Hard Day's Night*, on condition that he accompanied her to the film. He then insisted on watching her, rather than the screen, throughout the whole film. He was terrified that she was going to become a 'wild woman' during the performance; she was mortified by his presence: their confrontation is a telling illustration of conservative Arab fears.[92] Hadani Ditmars flew from Canada to Baghdad in late 2003. She was met at the airport by an SUV and Omar, a trained orthopaedic surgeon who had realised that he could earn more money as a hotel driver. As they reach the centre of the city, he puts Britney Spears's 'Oops, I Did It Again' on the car's sound system. Prior to the Taliban's takeover of Kabul, Latifa's bedroom was decorated with posters of Brooke Shields, Elvis and stars of Bollywood films. Even at the worst moments of Taliban repression, pirated copies of *Titanic* still circulated in Kabul: Latifa enjoyed its passionate story.[93]

Like Stark's example of the Charlie Chaplin bucket in the isolated Saudi Arabian desert, these items are now ubiquitous. The key difference between the examples of high culture and pop culture is that these young women tell of their discovery of Jane Austen or Victor Hugo as important, even life-changing, moments. They speak of pop culture with some affection, but with no great respect: it is simply part of the soundtrack of their lives, something that they assume will be there, whatever their conservative parents or peers might wish.

The evidence in this section shows that the technology of modernity is omnipresent: frequent, relatively cheap air flights abolish the sense of distance that made Wharton's trip to Morocco an adventure; the culture industry (and associated freelance pirates) market the products of Western pop to all corners of the Muslim world; the internet can allow almost immediate access to a vast range of artefacts and experiences. But none of these media, in themselves, produce a change in consciousness. Paradoxically, rather than a rational, egalitarian form of dialogue, suspicion and xenophobia seem to be on the rise in this technologically sophisticated context. Above all, these women find political discourse difficult.

The public, the private and the global

It's an old rule that tragedies come in threes. Tawil's autobiography illustrates this point. In 1948, her Palestinian mother suffered successive blows: 'Coming on top of the divorce, the 1948 war and the partition of Palestine divided her irrevocably from her sons, my brothers.'[94] What is striking here is the different nature of the threats that challenge her life: her arguments with her husband, the distance from her sons, the political violence of war and the trauma of exile. Such lives are difficult to document, difficult to contain within a single narrative. Many of the works by Muslim writers are endlessly caught between two stories: the small narrative of their private lives, their families and marriages, and the big narrative of public, political events which crash into their private lives. Deborah Kanafini seems to note this point in her introduction: 'This book is about people who try to find new endings, from the large-scale arena of global politics to a woman's freedom in her own household.'[95]

Our hundred writers have confronted a difficult challenge: how to tell these diverse stories within a single life. For some, the answer is a pattern of alternating chapters, swinging between the intensity of their private lives, to rather more general, textbook-like surveys of the public life around them. In general, they sound more confident, more convincing when discussing their private lives; less assured when discussing more general issues. Tawil, Kanafini and Karmi certainly have something interesting to say about the nature of Palestinian political culture. More often, other authors seem to consciously turn away from politics, to present women's lives as safe, intimate and apolitical. This also means that these reasonably successful works are poor vehicles for the construction of dialogue between different cultures, for so often they sidestep the largest issues.

One difference between the Western writers and the Muslim writers is significant: their approach to the concept of fusing cultures. None of the Western writers claim to 'belong' to the West and the East; some of the Muslim writers make precisely this claim about the West, but often in very guarded or combative terms; some state that they belong nowhere. Salbi is one of the rare optimists: 'I am a mix of the cultures and times in which I have had the privilege to live.'[96] Hala Jaber makes a similar claim: 'As a Lebanese and a Muslim, I knew the Arab perspective. As the wife of an Englishman and the employee of a London paper, I understood the Western way of thinking. I was in the privileged position of being able to straddle two worlds and explain one to the other.'[97] Ghoussoub, from a Lebanese Christian background, founds her publishing firm on such a claim: 'We wanted to be . . . a roundabout, where languages met, where one could no longer tell where the East starts and where the West ends.'[98] But such writers represent minority opinions. Latifa's downbeat ending to her story is more typical:

> I am for the moment a privileged exile who eats her fill, has no fears about the winter cold, and can hold her own with Westerners. So I can now express, without fear, my instinctive anxieties about the future – for that too is a privilege.[99]

Latifi's brief 'return' to Tehran provokes her to write a similarly subdued conclusion:

> Tehran was still a beautiful place – the bazaars teeming with life; the mosques with their cool, blue tiles; the towering, snowcapped mountains in the near-distance – but I didn't know where I fit in. It was very confusing. Back in America, I would tell people I was from Iran. But now I was home, as it were, I didn't really know what that meant.[100]

Karmi is openly pessimistic: 'I was truly displaced, dislocated in both mind and body, straddling two cultures and unable to belong in either.'[101] As we will see in the next chapter, the people who face this dilemma in its most pressing form are those who enter into cross-cultural marriages.

The simple truth seems to be that these women face too many barriers. Almost from the first page, they are forced to choose their camp: are they Muslim or secular? Arab or European? Or American? Conservative or

modern? Palestinian or Israeli? The struggle to find their way through this
maze of walls exhausts them: the idea of transcending them seems impossible. One way out is to consider Islam itself as a vehicle for modernity: an
argument which will be discussed in chapter 5.

Conclusion: on Jane Austen and the Goon Show

Latifi did meet modernity, of a sort. She even shook hands with it (or
him?). After nine years as a semi-orphaned Iranian refugee in Austria and
the USA, her family was reunited, and at last she went to Disneyland. This
incident refers back to a standing joke within her story: whenever she
began to protest about leaving home, she was calmed by the promise of a
trip to Disneyland – a treat that had been offered to her countless times,
but had never materialised.

> At long last, I met Mickey Mouse. I even went up to him and shook
> his hand. I, Afschineh, age nineteen, grinning from ear to ear and
> shaking the hand of the elusive Mr Mouse. It wasn't the earth-
> shattering experience I'd been expecting, but then again, I wasn't the
> same girl.[102]

The modernity that the Muslim writers meet is not the glorious global
ideal that inspired Voltaire. Instead, it resembles the vision of globalisation
evoked by Zygmunt Bauman: 'The deepest meaning conveyed by the idea
of globalization is that of the indeterminate, unruly and self-propelled
character of world affairs; the absence of a centre, of a controlling desk, of
a board of directors, of a managerial office.'[103] But this is, nonetheless,
modernity. These migrant women have learnt a global vocabulary: when
we laugh at Dunkin' Donuts and KFC thriving in Mecca, the next question should be to ask why we find this funny, incongruous or inexplicable.
Spirituality and vulgar commerce can co-exist in both the East and the
West: these women are familiar with *Vogue* and Mickey Mouse, with the
Brontës and Michael Jackson, with Victor Hugo and *Titanic*.

Karmi provides one last image of this strange, fractured modernity.
While her parents, in different ways, resolutely refused to adapt or to
assimilate to British culture, she and her sister were intrigued by the new
sounds flowing out of the radio. In particular, they were entranced by the
Goon Show.

> The three of us were soon hooked on this strange programme . . . It
> was zany, crazy and to us extremely funny, though how on earth any of
> it related to our culture or experiences no one understood. 'Look at

them. What on earth can be so funny?' our mother would remark to our father as they watched us in bafflement reeling about with laughter, imitating the voices and repeating the jokes to each other. No Arab could have understood the English innuendos and allusions in the programme, certainly not our parents, and it was like a bond between us children.[104]

Karmi presents this as idiosyncratic: the *Goon Show* exhibited the sort of humour that is promptly labelled quintessentially British – how could she, the young daughter of a Palestinian exile, have understood it? But there were some deeper connections. Sometimes explicitly, more often implicitly, Spike Milligan's comedy assumed a colonial setting. His parade of stupid, pig-headed authority figures, with their incomprehensible orders and absurd rituals, set in surreal landscapes, could easily make sense to any Muslim immigrant once they had made the link to colonial practices.[105] There were even connections with the lively semi-legal Egyptian satire scene: what better use of the celebrated Western value of freedom of speech than to mock one's rulers? All the migrant's dilemmas – the hypocrisy of the standards by which they meant to live, the strange conventions that they were supposed to understand, the incomprehensible language that they had to learn – were there, and they were funny.

CHAPTER FOUR

Voyages in Manistan: the Female Traveller and the Secret Woman

'To be a woman writer in an Arab country means to need to be rather cunning and slippery, to show a bit here and to mask a bit there.'

Joumana Haddad[1]

'Civilisations do not clash over whether love exists or not.'

Shelina Zahra Janmohamed[2]

When Deborah Rodriguez opened her beauty salon in Kabul in 2003, she often stayed late after the other workers had left in order to clear up. She would leave as the sun was setting, and then realise that she was the only woman on the street. Men would stare at her as she passed by, making her feel uncomfortable. 'I'm starting to think of this place as Manistan', she grumbled to one of her colleagues.[3] Her comments applied to Afghanistan but – in a sense – all our writers travelled to Manistan. Nearly all of them describe similar moments of isolation, when they appear as single women confronting male power structures. These moments are relieved by some descriptions of female groups, but one's lasting impression is of single women working in difficult circumstances, whether adjusting their veils so as not to attract the attention of the Iran security police, trying to make themselves acceptable to male journalists by acting as 'one of the boys', negotiating with male chauffeurs and mechanics in order to be able to continue their journeys or confronting male officials at checkpoints and border posts.

As we have seen, our hundred authors travel for different reasons: to see the countryside, to find enlightenment, to escape persecution, to seek a better life, to confirm statistical data, to uncover archaeological evidence, to satisfy curiosity or to conduct interviews. Given the frequency with which they confront or challenge male authority, it is striking how rarely they reflect on the issues that these incidents raise and – above all – how little they say about their status as women in a cross-cultural context. No general theory about women's writing emerges from their works: a situation that seems quite different from that of earlier generations, as Billie Melman shows. In the nineteenth century a certain type of philanthropic activism and a linked form of writing were seen as suitable for women: it allowed them to demonstrate 'their unlimited capacity for "empathy" and identification with the "other" . . . their sensitivity to detail, rather than the whole; their genius as collectors of evidence, rather than analysts'.[4] From these points, one could construct a justification for women's writing on the Orient.

The modern writers do not explicitly consider such issues. One surmises that this issue is at once too awkward and too obvious to be discussed. For example, Melanie Phillips is a writer claiming to represent the moral majority of conservative Britons: she may well consider that, in this context, it makes little sense to draw attention to the exceptional nature of her intervention. For others, discussing the gendered nature of their writing may seem a bridge too far: having confronted religious, national and international barriers, the idea of also surmounting gendered frontiers may appear excessive. Occasionally, a self-consciously flamboyant and provocative writer such as Joumana Haddad will parade (or strut?) her femininity in front of her audience; more typically these writers will work by assumption, and present their female-centred books to an apparently female audience with little fuss.

At some points, however, most of these writers do discuss women's lives. This is usually presented as a type of secret within Muslim societies, and the great panoply of stereotypical veil-related phrases are then mobilised: 'behind the veil', 'unveiling Afghanistan' and so on. Many hit upon the theme of the 'secret woman': this issue leads us to consider a range of gender-related issues, concerning romance, sexual morality and marriage.

The orientalists' secret

Melman suggests that research into women's lives was a prominent theme for nineteenth-century female orientalists. Among the orientalist works I have consulted from the early and mid-twentieth century, there is little evidence of a similar concern. Vita Sackville-West concentrates on describing men;[5] Edith Wharton does include a couple of descriptions of harems in her *In Morocco*: while claiming to depart from the clichés of 'sensual seduction', she describes 'beings imprisoned in a conception of sexual and domestic life based on slave-service and incessant espionage. These languid women on their muslin cushions toil not, neither do they spin.' In another passage, she even claims that Jews were prominent in supplying young girls from Georgia to Moroccan aristocrats.[6] These sections occupy less than ten pages in her 200-page book: they can hardly be described as prominent, and they do not appear particularly interesting.

Evelyn Cobbold, the English Muslim convert, was clearly aware of the common stereotype of the harem's sensual indolence, and in her *Pilgrimage to Mecca* firmly refuted it.

> As I have been granted the great privilege of being received as a guest in this Mecca household I feel it is up to me to refute the false impressions that still exist in the West about the harem. Not only in this house, but in every harem I have visited in Arabia I have found my host with only one wife. Far from being a sensuous life of ease, these ladies are busy with their household duties; at the same time living a happy, even a gay life, entertaining their friends and having their own amusements and festive occasions. There are no lonely old maids, the system being mostly of a joint family, and the joyous laughter and atmosphere of content that emanates from the harem convinces that 'all is well in the best of possible worlds'.[7]

(Later writers from Muslim-majority countries are also aware of this orientalist legacy, and are at pains to stress the banal, domestic nature of harem life.[8]) One's final impression from these relatively short references is that the female orientalists of the twentieth century had little interest in these issues: perhaps it was considered that the theme of the harem had been exhausted by the earlier writers, perhaps their interests lay elsewhere.

The veil, a topic that has been discussed with such intensity recently, was only occasionally discussed by the orientalists. Melman notes some debate among them concerning whether it was a device that could aid seduction, or whether it freed women from sexual harassment – something of which these observers generally approved.[9] The twentieth-century orientalists usually refer to it in a playful manner. At one point in her narrative concerning her journey to Persia, Sarah Hobson asks a Persian woman to make her a veil.

> I went to her home in the evening, and she hung the long veil over me.
> 'Beautiful,' she said, clapping her hands.
> 'Beautiful,' said her family, and giggled.
> I swayed the material about me, flimsy black cotton speckled with white commas. It was soft, and when I stood near the light, the veil was seductively transparent – I was beginning to understand the advantages of a veil.[10]

Although she eventually decided not to wear it, there is no sense of horror or disgust expressed here. Instead, for Hobson and for other similar orientalists, veil-wearing was just another enjoyable element in the games that they could play with their identities while in the East.

Even the sight of women wearing full, face-covering burqas seems to excite little interest or comment from these travellers. Ella Maillart, travelling through Afghanistan in 1939, records a typical encounter:

> Now and then we passed a few of these hidden women – shrouded silhouettes guiding their steps from behind peepholes embroidered lattice-like before their eyes. Driving, we found them a public danger: they saw little and heard even less. We had to be right upon them before they would jump aside, frightened like cackling hens.[11]

Her observations suggest no sense of empathy with, or outrage about, these women: they merely seem ridiculous as they block her way. Her attitudes are amplified in a second observation.

> Here, where the pattern of life remains unchanged, where the son thinks as his father did, men are still proud to be men. Meanwhile in the West where there is nothing but change, no-one knows what to think, nobody feels secure – least of all the rich – and that even in so-called peace time. Here [in Afghanistan], no more high-heeled sluts in short frocks: you've come to the country where women are not seen, where men are capped with snowy muslin and walk with heavy shoes like gondolas. You've come to a country which has never been subjugated.[12]

As noted in chapter two, travelling to the East provided these orientalists with an opportunity to consider different gender roles. But this does not produce a generalised sense of female solidarity. On the contrary, like Maillart, these writers often seem to relish the chance of playing at being men, and attempting to replicate male attitudes. The veiled spectres that they saw might excite some admiration for their beauty or some astonishment at their strangeness, but not any deep repulsion or anger. Such points indicate the limitations of the orientalists' sense of wonder: the East was there to be stared at, and perhaps admired, but it was not understood as a place inhabited by human beings more-or-less similar to the orientalists themselves, who merited sympathy or even communication.

Saadawi: the epistemological break

It is always foolish to reduce a major interpretative change to a single event, yet sometimes the publication of an important book does seem the clearest

illustration of a cultural or intellectual shift. For many observers, the
publication of Edward Said's *Orientalism* (in 1978) marks an important
change in the history of East/West exchanges; others have suggested some
qualifications to such arguments. Said's study suggested a new, critical
manner in which to view a whole tradition of Western writing in the East.
Of course, there were precedents to his work: the idea that *Orientalism* was
a bolt from the blue makes little sense.[13] Yet it remains true that Said
successfully redefined the term 'orientalist', and even this small etymo-
logical innovation suggests the greatness of his work.

Nawal El Saadawi's *The Hidden Face of Eve* was translated from Arabic
and published in London in 1980. It seems reasonable to suggest that, with
reference to the specific topic of women's writing, *The Hidden Face of Eve*
is probably of greater importance than *Orientalism* in marking a change in
the manner in which the East was discussed.[14] Saadawi graduated as a
doctor in 1955, and had worked extensively in rural Egypt. In the 1960s
and 1970s she published a number of Arabic texts that were critical of
Egyptian government policies, and in particular highlighted the horrific
consequences of female genital mutilation.

When *The Hidden Face of Eve* was published in English, Saadawi wrote
a lengthy preface for the new edition, in which she tried to forestall some
possible misinterpretations of her work. In this text, she explained that she
was not a critic of Islam, but of its distortion. 'Islam in its essence, in its
fundamental teachings, in its birth and development under Mahomet, was
a call to liberate the slave, a call to social equality and public ownership of
wealth. In its earliest form . . . [it was] a Primitive Socialism.'[15] Above all,
she specifically stated that she did not consider Islam as the cause for
female genital mutilation. She warned against the manner in which
Western powers had intervened in the Arab world, and noted how they
could use the admirable concept of 'human rights' in a manner that actually denied political liberation in Middle Eastern societies. She insisted
that a knowledge of sexual abuse in Muslim societies should not be
exploited as part of a Western imperialist strategy, whether by feminists or
others.

[Women in America and Europe] tend to depict our life as a continual
submission to medieval practices such as female circumcision. They
raise a hue and cry in defence of the victims, write long articles and
deliver speeches at congresses. Of course, it is good that female
circumcision be denounced. But by concentrating on such manifesta-
tions there is a risk that the real issues of social and economic change
be evaded or even forgotten, and that effective action be replaced by a
feeling of superior humanity, a glow of satisfaction that may blind the

mind and feelings to the concrete everyday struggle for women's emancipation.[16]

She criticised the superficial manner in which Western lifestyles were presented as models of liberation, and in particular refused any simple assertion that Western women were substantially more liberated than Muslim women. 'Sexual rights as practised in many Western societies do not lead to the emancipation of women, but to an accentuated oppression where women are transformed into commercialized bodies and a source of increasing capitalist profits.'[17] Above all, she insisted that the root cause of women's oppression in Muslim majority countries was not culture, ethnicity or religion:

> We the women in Arab countries realize that we are still slaves, still oppressed, not because we belong to the East, not because we are Arab, or members of Islamic societies, but as a result of the patriarchal class system that has dominated the world since thousands of years.[18]

Despite all these warnings, despite Saadawi's own foreboding concerns that her writing could be abused and exploited, it seems reasonable to conclude her writing contributed to the creation of a new stereotypical interpretation of the East, different in some important ways from that developed by the orientalists, but not any more suitable as a medium for dialogue.

It is interesting to compare the Western reception and interpretation of Said's *Orientalism* and of Saadawi's *Hidden Face of Eve*. Said was seen as difficult and – above all – as rude or aggressive.[19] He was criticising passionate, sincere Western scholars who had devoted their lives to their research, many of them genuinely fascinated by Muslim societies, some of them even willing to use terms such as 'love' to describe their motivations. 'When it comes to the Arabs, I must admit to an incurable romanticism; nay, more than that: to having a lifelong attachment to Araby', commented the veteran orientalist Raphael Patai in 1976.[20] In a single gesture, Said seemed to dismiss their work, to recategorise it as venal propaganda rather than pure, disinterested research. Worse still, he invoked modern theory, referring appreciatively to Michel Foucault, who then seemed a rising star of the French intellectual left. To many traditional scholars, Said was therefore beyond the pale. Bernard Lewis, the prestigious conservative American scholar, found Said's work 'mystifying', as if Said had invented a science-fiction universe.[21] The most favourable response to his work came from the academic left in Britain and America, where his concept of orientalism was intertwined with the various 'posts' (postmodernism, poststructuralism, post-humanism, postcolonialism), often producing a hyper-theoretical discourse that drove Said himself to despair.

Saadawi seemed different. After all, this was not a woman who concentrated on criticising the West: instead, her greatest concern seemed to be criticising the East. The picture she presented of the lack of human rights suffered by many Muslim women was quite distinct from the wonder evoked by generations of orientalists, but it was not completely incompatible. Nineteenth-century male orientalists had written at length, often in sensationalistic terms, about harems: the idea that the East was not a sexually egalitarian society was no surprise for Western readers. The fact that Saadawi was a trained doctor meant that she was speaking a language which was similar to that spoken by the new generation of trained, professional women who travelled in Muslim societies and who were often more critical, more curious than the previous generation of orientalists. The Western vocabulary was changing: the interest in the East was now no longer based in spiritual or religious values; the hippies travelling to Morocco, Afghanistan and Nepal in the 1960s and 1970s were probably the last significant group to go searching for a solution or a cure in the East.[22] Saadawi's research seemed compatible with a more secular, more self-consciously modernising approach.

All of these apparent links to Saadawi's work were also politically useful. The Western world was horrified by the Iranian revolution of 1978–9, which presented a new form of radical Islam that decisively broke with the tradition of secular nationalist radicalism which had grown in the Middle East since 1948. How was this to be criticised and refuted? Saadawi's research seemed to give an answer. Not by reference to female genital mutilation, a practice that is extremely rare in Iran (it is limited to certain minority tribes), but by the wider topic of human rights for women. The theme became an accepted component of American foreign policy, and was well rehearsed by the time that Madeleine Albright visited some female Afghan refugees in Peshawar (Pakistan) in November 1997.

> It's very clear why we're opposed to Taliban. We're opposed to their approach to human rights, to their despicable treatment of women and children and their lack of respect for human dignity, in a way more reminiscent of the past than the future . . .
>
> I know we are all the same, and we have the same feelings – we all suffer when we hurt and we all suffer for each other . . .
>
> I hope I can come visit you again – but come to an Afghanistan where you can live as full equals. We really are all sisters.[23]

The change from the older orientalist discourse is obvious. The image of Islam is no longer linked to some glorious revelation of the secrets of the past, but to female suffering in the present. The standard of women's rights was raised as a crucial issue to de-legitimise governments in Muslim-majority countries such as Iran and Afghanistan. Albright, explicitly and unmistakably, feels for these women. She claims solidarity, even sisterhood with them. But the vector for that solidarity is suffering, and above all the suffering of the other. The role of the West is therefore recast: it is now the scientist, the doctor, the donator, the aid worker (and the hairdresser?) who will guide the poor people of the East to their liberation. There is no hint of Western self-criticism or questioning here; equally, despite the conspicuous display of concern and sisterly solidarity, no possibility of dialogue. The idea that Afghan women might have their own, specific criticisms of their society, or even have something critical to say about Western society, is simply not considered.

Despite her best intentions, Saadawi's work undoubtedly contributed to this recasting of the East. Even the implication of her title was reformulated: Saadawi intended her work to contribute to a process of enlightenment and clarification; instead, the 'hidden face' of the East was recast as a heuristic model, in which the old orientalist concept of the mysterious East was reformulated as being defined by some shameful secret concerning women's lives.

Clearly, Muslim women do suffer from some specific oppression. Whether the new Western interest in their suffering has benefited them is open to question. Arguments along these lines have been used to justify military intervention in Iraq and Afghanistan, and even to encourage a woman like Rodriguez to open her beauty salon in Kabul. It is clear that some women benefited from such initiatives: they have received wages and learnt a profession. It is still unclear whether these actions will really produce any substantial, long-term benefits for women in either country.[24]

The new East: the turn to horror

A new tone emerged in women's writing concerning Muslim societies after the 1980s. These new travellers were no longer the leisured orientalists, travelling for their own pleasure, nor even their lesser sisters, the tourists with guidebooks, but a new generation of trained, qualified women. While their works discuss a wide range of diverse issues, their general shift towards a new sense of criticism and sometimes outright horror is clear. Dervla Murphy's writing stretches over these two generations. *Full Tilt* is a playful and witty account of her journey by bicycle from Ireland to Afghanistan and Pakistan, while *Tales from Two Cities* is a more serious, quasi-anthropological account of what Murphy calls 'brown' and 'black' communities in the UK.[25] In the twenty-two years separating the two works, Murphy's sense of wonder concerning Islam seems to have vanished. The idea that Muslim women are oppressed by Islam now seems to be taken as a self-evident truth:

> their continuing oppression seems an indefensible anachronism near the end of the twentieth century . . . The degree of male chauvinist piggery sanctioned by the Qur'an is considerable . . . [The Islamic family is a] male-worshipping institution . . . The Islamic oppression of women, ostensibly as part of a religious tradition, is also pretty extreme.[26]

Suzy Wighton, the nurse in the Bourj al-Brajneh Palestinian refugee camp, voiced similar frustrations at approximately the same time:

> I feel disturbed by the cruelty of the domestic tension between men and women. I have no patience left for the brutal chauvinism and autocratic patriarchs masquerading as gentlemen, sitting all day in the sun doing *nothing* whilst the women clean, cook, wash, cook, wash, serve, serve, clean and risk their children's lives daily to bring in food. I've no patience at all with men who ask me if it is not *ieb* (culturally wrong) that women smoke, question their fathers and brothers, or make their own choices.[27]

The point I wish to make here is not to question whether Muslim women suffer oppression from male power (the answer is obviously 'yes'), but to note how swiftly the terms of discourse changed. Points that Vita Sackville-West or Ella Maillart would have dismissed as irrelevant or perhaps even as unacceptable, became normal, almost obligatory for the writer. While the shift from the orientalists' uncritical sense of wonder is to be welcomed, this new requirement to describe at length Islam's oppression of women has rarely resulted in any real understanding of Muslim women's experiences.

The production of literature devoted to accounts of women's oppression and misfortune in Muslim countries has grown into a flood in recent years. While clearly present before 9/11, the tragedy of the Twin Towers has undoubtedly stimulated a still greater demand for this form of writing, in part because it seems to justify Western military interventions. Some Muslim and ex-Muslim writers have built publishing careers and even political careers on answering this demand: one could cite Chahdortt Djavann and Ayaan Hirsi Ali as examples of this tendency. In other cases, as we have seen, there is a tension between what the Muslim writer wants to say and what the Western reader wants to hear: thus Rania al-Baz and Zainab Salbi have both voiced frustration about the manner in which their experiences were being cited by the Western media.

One important sign of this shift is the new discussion of the veil.[28] As was noted above, earlier female orientalists would comment on the wearing of the veil, but did not discuss it at length. The significant change in attitudes can be dated to the late twentieth century. Anne Mehdevi travelled to Persia for a second time in 1964, with the aim of meeting her husband's Persian family and repairing their strained relations with them. Her comments on the chador seem to suggest a type of transitional mentality, in between the orientalists' passive appreciation of Eastern customs and the more critical, self-consciously modernising approach of the trained, professional women. Seeing a household servant wearing a chador, she was provoked to write the following comments:

> This traditional garment, the *chador*, was always an affecting sight to me. I could not understand why many Persian women still wore it, as it is now frowned upon as a left-over from the unenlightened past . . . It can be lovely on young girls, framing their shy faces – as feminine as a nun's habit, as dainty and fresh as dawn. On most women, though, the *chador* seemed to me a humiliation. Whenever I saw a poor woman in the back streets of Tehran clutching the ghostly shroud about her face and bent body, turning herself into a shapeless wraith I wanted to turn my eyes away.[29]

One can almost hear her shuffling the different possible interpretations of veiling in this passage. The chador is traditional, therefore not modern, therefore bad. But it can be feminine and pretty, and it can resemble a form of Western dress (the nun's habit); therefore it is possibly good. Finally, however, the chador also is associated with poverty, it disguises the forms of the body in a manner that is not compatible with the demands of Western fashion and so, it is bad. Mehdevi arrives at no final interpretation, and the issue does not feature prominently in her record.

Saadawi's text from 1980 only referred to veiling in passing: while she condemned the recent Iranian moves to make the chador compulsory, she clearly did not think that the meaning of the veil merited any lengthy discussion, for other social and political issues were more important to her. Betty Mahmoody, in *Not Without My Daughter*, refers frequently to the compulsory chador in extremely negative terms, expressing her resentment of having to wear this heavy garment in oppressive heat, finding it smelly and cumbersome, and getting annoyed by the way that pious relatives would constantly berate her for her casual, improper manner of wearing it.[30] But even in this polemic against all things Iranian, the chador features more as a constant irritation, rather than as a major issue.

Veronica Doubleday, an ethnomusicologist, visited Afghanistan in the 1980s, and published her impressions in her *Three Women of Herat* in 1988. Her discussion of veiling is more striking and emphatic than that in *Not Without My Daughter*. On the streets of Herat she sees women who 'moved silently and inconspicuously, closely veiled, impenetrable and faceless. I was appalled by my first sight of the Afghan burqa.'[31] Some months later, however, she makes friends with some Afghan women who persuade her to try on a veil.

> I had thought I was buying something drab and shapeless, but they made me see that the prayer veil was a highly coveted item of fashion . . . The reaction among the Herati women was unanimous: the veil looked beautiful and they were pleased that I had adopted their custom . . . [Yet] I do not approve of the veil, and I see it as a vehicle of oppression.[32]

This passage is significant. Doubleday suggests something quite different from the criticisms presented by Mehdevi, who merely considered that veiling was old-fashioned and perhaps ugly. *Three Women of Herat* suggests that the veil is actually oppressive to women. The veil functions as a barrier that cannot be crossed: despite Doubleday's ability to gain access to so many aspects of women's lives through conversation and dialogue, this seems to be the point at which she considers she has to stop. In the next chapter, we will discuss Muslim women's attitudes to veiling in more detail.

I will now analyse three examples of the new, post 1980s, horror-orientated writing concerning Muslim societies.

Forbidden love
At times, the new terms of discourse have clearly been used in a manner that encourages prejudice. Norma Khouri's *Forbidden Love* tells the tragic story of a young, unmarried Jordanian Muslim woman who was killed by her family because of her secret affair with a Catholic man. Obviously, such actions are inexcusable. It is still disturbing, however, to read Khouri's contextualisation of this murder.

> Jordan is a place where men in sand-coloured business suits hold cell phones to one ear and, in the other, hear the whispers of harsh and ancient laws blowing in from the desert. It is a place where a worldly young queen argues eloquently on CNN for human rights, while a

father in a middle-class suburb slits his daughter's throat for commit-
ting the most innocent breach of old Bedouin codes of honour . . .

Its fierce and primitive [Bedouin] code is always nagging at men's
instincts, reminding them that under the Westernizing veneer, they
are all still Arabs.[33]

This passage sets up a set of unfortunate contrasts, based on simplistic and
inaccurate representations of different cultures: on the one hand, the
West, the modern, the civilised, human rights and – presumably – the
humane; on the other hand, the ancient, the desert, the Bedouin and
dreadful murders. There is a type of continuity with the older orientalist
accounts: Khouri still assumes that Bedouin culture is a sort of quintes-
sence of Arab culture, but rather than admiring Bedouins for this quality,
she criticises their culture for its primitive nature. She even seems to
suggest that an Arab using a mobile phone is somehow less 'Arab' than an
Arab living in a desert. This type of argument resembles the older orientalist argument that Muslims and Arabs were incapable of modernisation,
for their identity rooted them in the past.

9/11 in Saudi Arabia

Qanta Ahmed's account of her work in Saudi Arabia as a surgeon, *In the
Land of Invisible Women*, is considerably more subtle and more perceptive.
As a Western Muslim, Ahmed did not travel to Saudi Arabia to see 'the
other': she went thinking that she was one of them. She is honest enough
to acknowledge her ignorance, to speak of the surprises she encountered
and to note how perplexed she felt. As will be seen in sections below, on
several occasions she changed her opinion about aspects of both Saudi
society and Islam: these are all welcome signs of an open-minded text
which could contribute to a process of dialogue; her book is genuinely a
voyage of discovery. However, Ahmed had the misfortune to be present in
Saudi Arabia at the moment of the 9/11 tragedy.

She saw things that shocked her: her Saudi medical colleges cheering
each time they saw repeated video clips of the Twin Towers falling; two
obstetricians ordered two cakes, one for each of the towers. Most of these
people had benefited from subsidised medical training in the USA, but
still they cheered this act of mass murder.

A veil had been lifted . . . In the days following 9/11, I bore witness to
an extraordinary fabric, uniting the most educated and elite of
Muslims to the weakest and the least educated in shared hatreds. As I
stumbled upon rancid hates and crude appetites, I was reminded of
what I had chosen to forget: the deep-rooted currents of anti-

Americanism and anti-Semitism that here often seemed to run together.[34]

This is a difficult passage to analyse. On the one hand, one understands Ahmed's revulsion at her colleagues: the image of hospital staff applauding at the sight of slaughter is horrific. On the other hand, there remains something disappointing and frustrating in her account. Having made such an effort to educate herself about Saudi norms and cultures, it seems a shame that her powers of analysis seem to abandon her at this point, with so many questions left unanswered: why did her colleagues cheer at this sight? If they are motivated by anti-Americanism and anti-Semitism, then why do these feelings run so strongly in Saudi Arabia?

The Bookseller of Kabul

Åsne Seierstad's *The Bookseller of Kabul* is somewhat different from the previous two examples.[35] Seierstad is a Norwegian war reporter who has written on conflict in Iraq, Chechnya and Afghanistan. She visited Kabul in November 2001 and struck up a friendship with Shah Muhammad Rais, one of the most prominent booksellers in the city who was trying to re-establish his trade following the fall of the Taliban. She stayed for several months in his house, and met his second wife, a teenager far younger than him. She spoke to several family members, and took notes of their conversations. Rais had understood that she was interested and sympathetic to his work in rebuilding the book trade, and expected that anything she wrote would centre on this. In fact, *The Bookseller of Kabul* is more ambitious: it attempts to present a type of 'interior' history of the family, in the form of a series of linked short sketches, rather like James Joyce's *Dubliners*. Some of these passages are extremely well written: 'The call from Ali', an account of a journey to Mazar-i-Sharif by Mansur, one of Rais's sons, is a beautiful, sad tale. But it is extremely difficult to believe that Seierstad could have had direct knowledge of all the details of Mansur's private thoughts: his doubts about his national identity, his feelings about religion and his frustrated desire for fun and excitement. Similar points could be made about the long passages that describe the feelings and experiences of the older and younger wives, and of Rais. A work which starts off as an ostensible attempt to represent the lives of an Afghan family turns into something else: an attempt to write onto the lives of an Afghan family Seierstad's concerns about male power in Afghanistan.

Her work had an unusual sequel: Rais wrote a reply, *Once Upon a Time There was a Bookseller in Kabul*, and took out a case against Seierstad in a Norwegian court, alleging defamation of character.[36] In 2005 the whole family applied for asylum in Norway, arguing that as a result of Seierstad's book, it had become impossible for them to live in Afghanistan. A provisional judgement on *The Bookseller of Kabul* in July 2010 did accept some criticisms of Seierstad's work: the judge found Seierstad guilty of 'negligent journalistic practices' and of invasion of privacy.[37] She was ordered to pay the sum of approximately £26,000 as damages to the first wife. Seierstad and her publisher appealed against this judgement and in December 2011 she was cleared of all charges: a fact that she considered vindicated her book.[38]

This confrontation is a complex one which raises many issues concerning cross-cultural communication: a pessimist might well conclude that the incident shows that such communication is well-nigh impossible. In the absence of clear, verifiable information, it is impossible to say which of the parties involved is the most truthful. However, it is possible to make some comments concerning the form in which Seierstad wrote. Her work clearly resembles some of the previous books cited: like Tehmina Durrani's self-published *My Feudal Lord*, it concerns the contradiction between an apparently liberal male public figure and the manner in which he acted in private.[39] *The Bookseller of Kabul* features no horrific stories of extreme violence, but it does document grinding misery and inequality, and effectively suggests some blatant hypocrisy, if nothing more. The interesting point is Seierstad's confidence. She decides that the important story is not Rais's efforts to revive the Kabul book trade, but his family life. New to Afghanistan, unable to speak any of its languages fluently, she still considers that after a stay of only a few months, she is capable of passing judgement about the most intimate feelings and convictions of a number of adults, and that she has the right to write about this. If we could imagine Seierstad being posted to – for example – south Wales for three months, would she have the same confidence in her ability to read the minds of the people she met? Would she consider that she had the same right to publicise their feelings to a wider public?

If Seierstad had written a less ambitious work in the first person, as the older orientalists did, recording her feelings and experiences rather than those of others, she probably would have been able to rebut any legal challenge. But the post 1980s demand for stories of women's oppression led her to a different type of writing. In legal terms, her most serious mistake was probably to present her work as non-fiction, almost as an exercise in oral history. By claiming this absolute knowledge concerning the private thoughts of a whole family, she weakened the validity of her work.

These three works illustrate how female authors have contributed to a particular Western literary tradition that has developed in recent decades.

Each work is predicated on the idea that there is a repellent 'secret' about Muslim societies, which is not apparent to the casual observer. The author's reaction to their discovery of this 'secret' is, in each case, more than understandable: each of the books recounts attitudes and actions which are repugnant. With all three works, the problem comes when these actions are then presented almost as sociological laws by which to judge not single families or specific work groups, but entire societies and cultures. Read in this manner, their discoveries actually hinder a process of dialogue and mutual understanding, for they each contribute to the development of fixed forms of interpretation or, more simply, clichés about the other.

London-based Bee Rowlatt and Baghdad-based May Witwit have produced an interesting book, *Talking about Jane Austen in Baghdad*, based on their e-mail exchanges. Inadvertently, the book includes an example of where thirty years of cliché-mongering has led the Western world. Rowlatt comments 'I just don't think Islam is much good for women. Seems to be great for men. But what's in it for you, May? Really?'[40] Witwit replies with a whole page of arguments, demonstrating her opinion that Islam is 'greater for women than men', points which will be considered in the next chapter.[41] Rowlatt prefaces her comments with a series of qualifications: 'I know it's controversial and I apologize for making generalizations', but her confidence in her 'knowledge' of Islam is obvious. In fact, her brief comments resemble a miniature version of horror literature discussed above: the polite beginning and then the revelation of the secret. In Rowlatt's case, her confidence in her observation is surprising: she willingly admits that she has no particular knowledge of any Muslim-majority society, she cannot speak Arabic, but she still 'knows' that Islam is 'not much good' for women. The contrast between her breezy confidence in her knowledge and Witwit's rather awkward, page-long reply is instructive: one partner in this exchange has power and confidence; the other is relatively powerless and – while she has real experience of the topic in question – is less certain about how to present her arguments. The power structures created by the traditions of orientalist writing are still present, if in a changed form. Over thirty years ago, Saadawi foresaw this situation: the Western concentration of analysis on the theme of Islam's oppression of women has not assisted Muslim women to articulate their experiences of their faith.

Beyond the horror: the secret dancing

Alongside the now near-obligatory portrayal of woman as Islam's slave, other images of 'secret' women's cultures in Muslim-majority countries circulate. Many of these are markedly more positive in tone. One of the most interesting examples can be found in Jehan Sadat's *A Woman of Egypt*. After a heart attack in 1960, her husband, Anwar Sadat, decided that he needed to lead a less stressful life. He chose an almost traditional solution: he went back to the village of his childhood, Mit Abul-Kum. Jehan Sadat followed him there, and for the first time in her life lived alongside Egyptian villagers. At first, she found this an unattractive proposition.

> The sight of the village women depressed me at first. Older women over forty dressed always in black from head to toe and the women of all ages worked harder than the men. At dawn the women rose to the prayer of the muezzin calling the faithful to the morning prayer, and then prepared the morning meal of white cheese and very sweet black tea for their families. Then there were the dirt floors of their houses to sweep out, the animals to feed, the dough to make for fresh bread, water which the women pumped by hand from the village well and carried back in jugs on their heads. Just in time they then hurried to carry lunch to their husbands in the fields, where, after the meal, they joined the men for the remainder of the day, weeding, hoeing and harvesting crops of cotton, corn, clover and wheat . . . The women seemed like nothing but beasts of burden – or even less, because the men cared more for their cows than they did for their wives.[42]

However, as the weeks go by, Jehan Sadat joined in the conversations of the women. She learnt more about their lives, and began to revise some of her first impressions. 'Compared to many middle-class women in Egypt in the fifties and sixties, the women of the village had far more freedom and independence.' Instead of being isolated in their homes, they worked together and helped each other. They often were responsible for their own small businesses, like raising chickens. Although frequently illiterate, they were not ignorant: they would listen to the radio to stay in touch with outside events. Lastly, despite the appearance of male power in the families, at many points it was the women who made the decisions. Jehan Sadat drew back from romanticising their condition: she notes the persistent problems of grinding poverty, inequality, illiteracy and disease. But in these pages, Egyptian village women move from being stereotypical images of oppression to living people. Jehan Sadat herself concludes: 'How I loved the spirit of the village women. No longer was I lonely when Anwar was away, for wherever I went the women now knew me by name and would rush to hug and kiss me.'[43] The portrayal of Muslim women simply as oppressed slaves usually excludes this humanist quality.

Sadat is not alone in finding these hidden strengths in Arab women. The independent French-Algerian radical, Houria Boutelja, addresses a similar theme when she expresses her exasperation with the flood of analyses that stigmatise Arab society as marked by the oppression of women, and asserts 'there is something feminist in our culture, in OUR references'.[44] When Deborah Kanafini, originally resident in the USA, visited Palestinian women in Bethlehem in 1997 who were criticising the actions of Muslim fundamentalists, there was an interesting exchange of attitudes: 'These women seemed to look up to me, perceiving me as a liberated Western woman, but it was I who was impressed and inspired by them.'[45]

Other observers are still more explicit: even in some wildly contrasting texts, there is a delighted, sometimes ambiguous, fascination with Muslim women's sociability, particularly in parties and dances. Above all, it seems to be the figure of the secret dancer that has mesmerised observers. Pauline Cutting addresses this theme in a benign and non-sensationalistic manner when she describes a wedding festival in the primitive conditions of the Bourj al-Brajneh refugee camp: the incident she relates takes place before the siege of the camp, and in this case men and women mix freely.

> The girls loved to dress up in colourful, flamboyant, modern Western fashions, and dance with a kaiffiyeh, a chequered Palestinian scarf, tied around their hips. They danced wildly to traditional Arabic music played live by a group consisting of Ali the bongo player, a guitar player and a singer, Hassan's cousin. The Arab music was interrupted for 20 minutes by another cousin, an eleven-year-old who brought his own modern post-punk tape so he and his two friends could show off their breakdancing and robot dancing . . .
>
> Ten older women in long dresses and scarves, Hassan's mother and her neighbours, got carried away dancing the *Debke* – a [Palestinian] dance in which the dancers link arms in lines, and involving some fancy footwork and much jumping, stamping and shouting.[46]

Although Cutting specifies that these are mixed events, it is clear that she is most interested in the women's participation. She is surprised, amused and perhaps just a little worried by them. Looking at the older dancers, she remembers her medical role in the camp and thinks to herself 'I'll be seeing some of them tomorrow'.

Qanta Ahmed is more shocked by what she sees. The wife of a worker in her Saudi hospital invites her home for a party at which only 'glittering, extraordinary women' are present:

> After dinner the music began to rock, reverberating with unpent energy in the marble basement. The soundtracks were a mix of cutting-edge Beirut house and traditional Arab melodies . . . Clearing

a space in the middle of the room, the women began to dance. They tied their scarves low around their hip bones, accentuating their movements, the hip-scarves forming a visible line of gyrating iliac crests that moved to a beat. The wider the hips appeared the better they seemed. Unlike the fashion world of the West, where androgyny was king, here womanly, voluptuous figures were admired. The lights remained bright, not turned down. And one by one, each woman took the lead, dancing wildly and without inhibition, so self-confident that even bright lights were no deterrent . . .

No one danced *with* one another; rather they danced *for* one another, the dancing woman surrounded by an enclave of clapping, laughing joviality.[47]

Despite her shock, Ahmed's reaction is clearly positive: she is delighted to find this sensual secret beneath the apparent puritanism of Saudi women.

Betty Mahmoody sees a similar sight at a private party in Tehran in which both men and women are present. She is less able to articulate her feelings: 'The moment we entered the house we heard loud American music and saw the improbable sight of Shiite Moslems dancing to rock-and-roll. The women were dressed in western clothing, which none bothered to cover with chadors.'[48] Compared to the ecstatic scenes evoked by Cutting and Ahmed, Mahmoody's description is disappointing, little more than cultural point-scoring, sneering at Iranians for dancing to their enemy's beats. Where Cutting suggests a type of fusion of past, present and future, of East and West, of young and old through the transcendence of dance and music, even within the drab limitations of life in a refugee camp, Mahmoody can only see an error on the part of the Iranians.

Seierstad's description of Afghan women's behaviour while dancing in a segregated room at a wedding feast is more disturbing than joyful:

Left alone the women display a fierce, almost frightening power. They hit each other's bottoms, pinch each other's breasts, and dance for each other, arms flailing like snakes, hips like Arab belly dancers. Little girls dance as though they were born to seduce and wriggle across the floor with challenging looks and raised eyebrows. Even the old grannies test the water, but give up halfway, before the dance is over.[49]

The dancers here seem like wild animals, savage and aggressive towards each other. Rather than celebrating the union of young, middle-aged and old women in a single event, she insists on their separation from each other, and even – in the reference to the little girls – their domestication into a set of repressive sexual roles.

These four examples, from Saudi Arabia, Iran, Afghanistan and Palestinians in Lebanon, suggest a fascinating shadow-image to the stereotype of the oppressed Muslim woman. The sight of these dances test our authors, revealing them as imaginative, perceptive or dismissive: it is significant that the two best-selling authors (Mahmoody and Seierstad), both severe critics of Muslim cultures, are also the ones who are least able to describe the sight of women dancing, and the most likely to be dismissive or critical of what they see.

The point I wish to make here is not that Muslim women dance therefore they are not oppressed. It is rather to question the manner in which Muslim women's oppression has been positioned by so many authors as the secret which reveals the truth about Muslim societies. First, it is not logical to suggest that there is one secret which is relevant to a whole community of believers. When reduced to Rowlatt's 'not much good for women', the Western stereotype of Islam becomes a silly, lazy generalisation: a moment's thought should be enough to inform anyone that a religion which has existed for more than thirteen centuries and which now has more than a billion believers will take different forms, some providing women with opportunities and support, some more repressive and censorious. Given the material available, it would clearly be possible to create a counter-cliché of the secret dancer as Islam's inner mystery: hardly more accurate than the first cliché, but at least a mode of perception which reveals autonomy and action. Instead, the model for research should be that suggested by Sadat's stay in an Egyptian village: through dialogue, to learn more about the other.

Watching the Western women

A clear sign that the structures of orientalism have been substantially challenged is the presence of so many Muslim and ex-Muslim women among our hundred authors. They potentially provide a challenge to the West's global cultural powers: in practice, some are keen to belong in the West, and often seem to see their writing more as a chance to demonstrate their loyalty to Western values rather than as an opportunity to criticise.[50] Their argument is clear: the West is modern and the modern is liberating, according to writers such as Djavann and Hirsi Ali.

For others, the debate is more difficult: the point here is not so much that they simply hate the West, but that they are faced with some awkward dilemmas. Qanta Ahmed's questioning about her identity and her loyalties while staying in Saudi Arabia is a good example of this. But, more typically, it is migrant Muslims who face particular problems. The 'West' they encounter is rarely the glorious place that they had imagined. As Karen

Armstrong notes, 'When Muslims look at Western society, they see no light, no heart, and no spirituality.'[51] Fatéma Hal was extremely disappointed by the first French place in which she lived: it was a filthy suburb, in which everything was dirty and muddy. It seemed worse than the Algerian slum in which she had grown up. 'The France that I saw all around me was nothing like the land of which I had dreamt. Everything seemed sad: the sky was always grey, the concrete and the roads were always muddy. I just couldn't take it.'[52] Dervla Murphy met three Pakistani women in northern England who seemed to prefer their new lives to living in their old Pakistani villages, but it wasn't easy to decide which was best.

> Three wives . . . confided that for all Bradford's drawbacks – an atrociously depressing and inconvenient climate, less freedom of movement than in the village, loneliness for parents left behind, suspense about unemployment, fear of children going off the rails, resentment of husbands Westernised enough to go out whoring, drinking and gambling, financial demands from Mirpur that couldn't be met – for all these disadvantages they were glad to be in Bradford, away from the tensions and constraints of a joint-family existence with unsympathetic in-laws.[53]

Zaiba Malik, writing about the similar women in the same town in the same period, cites similar evidence but arrives at a different conclusion:

> Economic necessity had cost the Aunties their sanity. They had married young in Pakistan, left their extended families and moved to the UK, a new country with a new religion, new culture, new language and new rules.
>
> Of course there were benefits to coming here – regular employment, access to better health care and education and a higher standard of living. That was why they had come.
>
> But there were also significant disadvantages that weren't so tangible; a loss of self, a feeling of isolation, a sense of insecurity, all of which, over time, manifested themselves in a yearning for the old, an incomprehension of the current and a fear for the future.[54]

The similarities and differences between these two accounts, one by a perceptive outside observer, one by a daughter of the women of 'Bradistan', are thought-provoking. They survey similar issues, and then Murphy arrives at a broadly positive conclusion, while Malik seems less certain, less willing to calculate the weight of the tangible against the intangible.

When Muslim writers present criticisms of Western standards, they often consider issues of sexual behaviour and women's appearance.

Sometimes these are little more than differences in cultural habits. Shappi Khorsandi records that her mother felt ill at the sight of a couple kissing in public.[55] The young Rania al-Baz followed her parents from Saudi Arabia to New York after her father enrolled in an American university. She was shocked when she saw her parents kissing in the street: she considered this 'shameless'; she felt 'horror' and 'fear'.[56] Asra Nomani's liberal, open-minded parents, born in India and living in the USA, took for granted that they should not ever engage in public displays of affection.[57] Labelling such attitudes as 'fundamentalist' or 'backward' does not explain them: in these particular examples, none of the authors or the people they cite can be categorised as fundamentalist Muslims. Rather, these records are lessons in cultural rituals: each society has its own irrational codes, which it regards as 'natural' and moral. Trying to evaluate which is admirable, which is acceptable and which is unacceptably repressive is a complex issue which, thankfully, is beyond the scope of this book. As Hélé Béji notes 'how can you decide whether [Islamic] veiling is a greater insult to women's dignity than pornography?'[58]

On other occasions, however, Muslim women express criticisms of Western society which are something more than merely expressions of contradictory cultural codes. Like Saadawi, they refuse to accept Western cultural norms as desirable images of liberation. The independent Egyptian thinker, Heba Ezzat, makes the following point about the fashionable exposure of the female body.

> You have a right to expose your body, but – what if I don't wish to see it? . . . Is it actually a young woman's choice to do this today at this particular time and place, or is the market trying to reshape and refocus people's concerns on consumerism to suit itself?[59]

Iraqi exile Zainab Salbi finds Western criticisms of Muslim dress codes puzzling: 'Many Western women fail to notice the forces that make them dress as they do, yet they pity Muslim women wearing the hijab, unaware that covering their heads is sometimes a choice that educated women make on their own.'[60] Susan Nathan, after moving from Tel Aviv to the Palestinian-Arab village of Tamra, found that her attitudes to Arab modest dress were changing:

> Nowadays I find it shocking to return to Tel Aviv in the summer and see women, including older women, wearing crop-tops that expose their tummies or blouses revealing their bras. It seems vulgar in the extreme. I regard the Arab women around me as much more digni-fied; they even seem to move in a more upright, graceful manner. I

now find the idea of being covered liberating . . . it frees me from
confrontations with men, the kind of situation I had experienced all
my life without fully realising it. If my body is properly covered, men
have to address what I am saying rather than my body. It was only
after covering myself that I started realising that most of my life I had
been used to men having conversations with my body rather than
with me.[61]

These examples challenge some of the common clichés that circulate
concerning Muslim women's status. While some Muslims do envy the
liberties offered by Western societies, this is often not as simple a choice as
might be thought. As in the examples from Murphy and Malik, quoted
above, Muslim women are often also acutely aware of the misery and
oppression that is present within Western societies. More seriously, some
will also criticise the standards set by the West. Consumer capitalism and
the cult of the body does not appeal to all women; labelling their criticisms
as 'fundamentalist' functions as a means to forestall and reject them, but
this is also an excellent means of refusing dialogue.

These examples also raise a vital issue. They show that it is genuinely
difficult to understand and to assess diverse codes, particularly in a situation within which the Western codes are supported by such a powerful
culture industry. The most common result for Muslim women is the difficult experience of attempting to live within dissonant and contradictory
moral codes. Turning back to *The Hidden Face of Eve*, it is worth stressing
that Saadawi predicted this dilemma:

> To be contradictory is the essence of all logic based on exploitation.
> Thus it is that at the very same time when the pictures of half naked
> women occupy more and more space on our walls, in our films, and in
> our magazines, an increasing number of women and girls are taking
> once more to wearing the veil.[62]

Unfortunately, the most common response to this situation is secrecy.

Secrecy and dialogue

There are a number of obvious responses to this dissonance. One is an ever
shriller declaration of the validity of one particular set of moral codes over
all others: among our hundred authors, writers such as Melanie Phillips
and Oriana Fallaci appoint themselves as guardians of Western values
against the invading Muslim hordes, while some of the Muslim converts –
such as Na'ima Roberts – devote themselves to the patient explanation of

why Islam is correct. Others, such as Shelina Janmohamed or Asra Nomani, attempt to remain true to their inherited cultural values but think in a less dogmatic manner, and are willing to consider criticisms or propose reforms. Another, more ambitious response is the attempt to learn from all values, and to move towards a synthesis. Significantly, none of these hundred writers claims to arrive at such a point but, as will be seen in this chapter's conclusion, Mai Ghoussoub does draw some interesting lessons from living where cultures collide. The most common response to this dissonance, however, is secrecy, particularly about romance and sex.

Secret lives are frequently invoked by the Muslim writers. As was seen in Khouri's *Forbidden Love*, these can have dreadful, tragic consequences. In other examples they can take a highly dramatic form, such as Fadia Basrawi's secret romance with Adnan, a Lebanese boy, in 1970. For two years she kept this secret from her Saudi parents, but then finally told them after her graduation in 1972. Her father's response was predictable: 'NO!!!!!!'[63] To Basrawi's disappointment, her mother sided with her father. The problem was not one of religion or ethnicity: Adnan was a Muslim Arab. It was nationality: he was not Saudi, and therefore unacceptable. The story of Basrawi's eventual marriage has all the ingredients of a Gothic novel: she tricked her parents into letting her travel to England, met Adnan there, and then flew to Beirut for their wedding.

Azadeh Moaveni, an Iranian-American who grew up in the exiled Iranian community in America, experienced a different version of the same dilemma. Her mother tried to fuse the two cultures into one lifestyle. One day, her mother delicately told the teenager Azadeh that if she wanted to talk to her about her boyfriend, then she would listen: 'Not to lecture you, but because I want to be your friend and advise you.' Azadeh was so enchanted by the idea of having a 'modern mother' that she told all. Her mother's reaction was predictable:

> Immediately red splotches appeared all over her face, and she began crying, in huge, gulping sobs, emitting a string of incoherent denials and interrogations: 'May dirt fall on my head! . . . You're too young, why did we ever come to this . . . ruined country! When?? For how long?[64]

Azadeh's reaction? 'The episode cemented a conclusion I had long been approaching: Being Iranian amounted to psychological torture.'

Ghada Karmi faced similar problems. As a teenage Palestinian exile living in London in the 1950s, she was amazed when she heard her parents discussing with real fury the news that a friend's daughter was going to marry a non-Muslim. When she told her parents that she could not understand their anger, her father dismissed her concerns with, 'You should know these things without having to be told': an unanswerable moral imperative. The result, predictably, was the opposite of what her parents intended:

> I had a sense of revulsion and horror. 'I am nothing to do with these people,' I finally decided. 'They're intolerant and primitive and I do not belong to them.' I comforted myself with the knowledge that I was part of a higher order of being, liberal, free, English, where such bigotry would not be tolerated.[65]

While at university she fell in love with John, a British student, but felt unable to tell her parents. Like Basrawi, she waited until after her graduation to inform her parents of her intention to marry, which she communicated in a long letter. John and Ghada then went to her parents' home. While John's arguments concerning Ghada's personal happiness meant little to her father, he was prepared to compromise and respect his daughter's wishes. It was her mother who objected most strongly:

> Unexpectedly, she addressed [John].
> 'Please,' she appealed in a pitiable voice and suddenly burst into tears. 'Please, please,' she kept repeating as the tears streamed down her face. 'You no for Ghada, no.' I tried to get her to stop, but she shook me off and went up to John and made as if to touch him, begging and pleading. If ever there was a moment in her life when she wished she had spoken English, I am sure it was then. The meeting turned out infinitely worse than I had imagined.[66]

The subsequent wedding felt more like a funeral, and Ghada's mother did carry out her threat to leave home, but returned after a few days.

Secrecy in these cases signifies a failed dialogue or an absence of dialogue. It is worth stressing that Karmi's mother's outburst really did hurt Karmi; Azadeh's disappointment at not really being able to talk to her mother is sincere – their pain is real. Both find that the contradictions between the two codes cannot be negotiated. Subterfuge then becomes the only possible strategy left to these young women.

Love as dialogue

Not all these works, however, are so pessimistic. Amid the rising tide of schism, separation and choosing sides, there are some heroic parents who do what parents are supposed to do: support their daughters in extraordinary circumstances. When hippy Marguerite van Geldermalsen wrote to her parents to tell them of her sudden marriage to Bedouin Mohammad, their reply is a textbook illustration of liberalism and tolerance: 'We think we have given you a good upbringing with plenty of opportunity to learn to think for yourself, so we trust you know well enough what you are doing. And we are here for you anyway, anytime.'[67] American Muslim Asra Nomani thought that her parents might disapprove of her premarital sexuality, subsequent pregnancy and the fact that she would become a single parent. She returned to their house: 'My mother and father hugged me and my swollen belly without a word of reprimand. "We love you. We love our grandson."'[68] When Lebanese Muslim Hala Jaber announced her intention to marry Steve, she met with some serious, but intelligent, opposition from her father. Didn't mixed marriages usually end in divorce? Would Steve be able to understand Hala's Arab political concerns? If Hala heard an Arabic-language song that she really liked, would Steve ever be able to understand it?

> I gently told my father it was thanks to him that I could not be the traditional Arab Muslim woman he had presumed I would become. I could not settle for this because he had spent too much on my education, devoted too much time to developing my mind, put too much effort into encouraging me to seek something more in life.

Very unusually, Jaber describes a moment of dialogue: 'My softly spoken father, who had never once raised his voice to me, accepted what I had said. As I thought it all through for the final time before my wedding, his acceptance re-assured me.'[69]

Willow Wilson was extremely worried about telling her parents about her conversion to Islam. Their reaction was cautious: 'My parents were supportive in a weary and slightly self-recriminating way, as if my decision to do something this terrible resulted from a defect in their parenting. They didn't say so, but guilt flowed between the lines.'[70]

Wilson's long-suffering parents were then confronted with another, greater shock. Their wayward daughter had not only chosen to live in Cairo, had not only converted to Islam, but had chosen to marry Omar, a Muslim. Both families grew extremely tense about a first meeting. Wilson was reduced to issuing edicts: don't mention Israel. Don't mention Churchill. In fact, don't make any reference to the Second World War. Omar's parents' worries are revealing: they were concerned that Willow's parents might fear Cairo; they were

> very aware of how frightening their city was to westerners – the noise, the pollution, the women without faces, the soldiers with

semiautomatic rifles. [Omar and his parents] were resigned to it; had been brought up with the knowledge that they were seen as exotic at best and at worst, barbaric. If they have been hurt or sad, I could have reassured them, but resignation was unassailable.[71]

Yet the meeting of the two families, and the announcement of their engagement, was a success. Willow's parents did their best to adapt. When a party was arranged, Willow's father arrived dressed in a galibayya and with his head in a turban. Under other circumstances, this could have been seen as a rather condescending piece of fancy-dress play-acting, such as the orientalists loved. On this occasion, however, it meant something else. Omar's father, who was dressed in a suit and tie, was delighted, and burst into laughter.

> With that, the atmosphere was established; no one was quite an American or quite an Egyptian . . . What happened was something so fragile and brave that it is difficult to put it into words; my family and Omar's family agreed to love one another for no other reason than that we had asked them to. Nothing else would ever be quite so important; it no longer deeply mattered to me whose rules I followed, Arab or American or eastern or western, and the words themselves faded in significance. I had caught hold, and seen others catch hold, of something that could not be touched by geography . . . To live beyond the threshold of identity, to do so in the name of a peace that has not yet occurred but that is infinitely possible – this is exhilarating, necessary and within reach.[72]

And so, there was one marriage of East and West, and it is pleasant to be able to record at least one successful union (in every sense of the word).

In most cases, however, things were not so simple. Deborah Rodriguez, the American hairdresser in Kabul, records her sudden (and rather mysterious) marriage to an Afghan named Samer, who she nicknames 'Sam'. The problems that face them are immense: unable to speak each other's languages, they can only communicate by phone for about a minute before both find they have exhausted their vocabulary. When Sam goes on the hajj pilgrimage to Mecca, and returns he has changed: he prays five times a day, and scowls whenever Rodriguez smokes or drinks. An Afghan female friend gives her the necessary advice: 'all the hajjis came back like this and it wouldn't last long'.[73] On another occasion, the two are walking to the Kabul market, when an Afghan man calls out something. Sam rushes through the crowd, grabs him, smashes him against a wall, and repeatedly punches him extremely hard. 'I stood in the middle of the crowd screaming at him to stop.' Sam finally returns and says 'We leave now'. By way of explanation, he tells Debby, 'He call you a prostitute and me your pimp.' A moment later, he adds that in future they will not be able to walk together to the market, because Sam might have to kill someone. Rodriguez begins to realise that Sam's past as a guerrilla fighter is more important than she had thought.[74]

Other small incidents reveal the gap between them. When they visit the few Western restaurants in Kabul, Sam is turned away at the door.[75] Rodriguez takes weeks to realise that she should not kiss Sam after he has gone through the ritual washing that is required for prayers: if she does, Sam will have to begin the ritual all over again.[76] Sam can't understand why Debby often wants to hold hands, hug or kiss. 'Is not time for sex!' is his response: she has to explain the idea of 'a snuggle'.[77]

There is an interesting contrast here between Rodriguez's attitudes to Afghan women and her attitude to Sam. At first sight, she seems far more affectionate and admiring of the women: her work even ends by acknowledging Afghan women's 'honesty, friendship, love'.[78] However, for all this admiration, Afghan women seem markedly passive in her hands: they receive copies of *Vogue* and Clairol products, better highlights and proper perms, and then they are transformed. Her relationship with Sam seems uneasy and tense, a 'cross-cultural collision' as she terms it.[79] In the last pages of her book, she makes it clear that she is not even sure that their marriage will last. And, yet, when compared with her descriptions of her simple, problem-free relationships with Afghan women, one cannot help thinking that Sam emerges far more as a real person, while the passive Afghan women seem mere ciphers. Rodriguez is forced to talk with Sam, despite their language limitations; she's forced to learn from him. This tense, uneasy and possibly unsuccessful relationship looks far more like a dialogue than the easy references to the Afghan women she so admires.

Conclusion

Mai Ghoussoub, from a Lebanese Christian family, contributes an interesting anecdote concerning conflicting cultural codes. Her mother used to love to tell her the story of her birth. Mai was her second child, and her mother used the same gynaecologist who had delivered her first daughter. After the birth, Dr Razook walked out, looking tense and disappointed. The look on his face terrified Mai's father. In fact, nothing was wrong with the birth: the only problem was that the doctor felt disappointed that he had delivered two girls. Mai's parents were both delighted, and they considered that the difference in their attitudes seemed to sum up the difference between two cultures. Ghoussoub comments:

[My parents] dreamed of bringing up free, responsible individuals – individuals who were nonetheless constantly reminded that they were the custodians of their family's honour, especially if they stood on the female side of the gender border; individuals who had to watch constantly for 'what the neighbours say' about them, their parents, their uncles, cousins and other relatives.[80]

Ghoussoub grew up between 'two epochs, two modes of behaviour, two value systems'; she was criticised by her neighbours for playing with boys in the street when she was nine and, as her parents had no answer to these criticisms, Mai was banned from street games. In the 1960s, 'I learned to live with these conflicting attitudes. Jugglers we became.' Even as a wave of radicalism passed through Lebanon's students, and they read Engels, de Beauvoir, Kollontai and Reich, people would still shout in protest if they saw female demonstrators lifted up onto the shoulders of men. 'Hypocrisy', Ghoussoub had thought, and felt frustration with her parents and their generation. Then came the years of Lebanon's civil war, and Ghoussoub found her attitudes were changing. 'What we called hypocrisy before the war was the best form of compromise people had found for living together. The taboo preventing one spelling out one's dislike for the other had been a good discipline.' This is far from the union of East and West which Willow Wilson thought she had glimpsed briefly at her engagement party. But, equally, it is an attitude that is quite different from the orientalists' willingness to believe that 'East is East'; it is an attitude that is far more positive and active than the secrecy adopted by so many young Muslim women; it is an attitude closer to the rough-and-ready dialogue that Deborah Rodriguez constructed with Sam.

Travelling in Manistan is difficult. Despite some pleasant interludes, the dominant impression is that of the isolation that these women face while making difficult journeys. Sometimes their parents support them, sometimes they make links with local women, more often they travel alone. Claims to female solidarity usually seem hollow or irrelevant.

Is there nothing which unites women from across the world? As was seen in the last chapter, Rodriguez sketches out an argument concerning the universal validity concerning certain female traits and – for a moment – Janmohamed seems to echo her ideas when she writes 'I loved looking beautiful: all women do, it is part of being a woman.'[81] The problem with these arguments is precisely the one that Rodriguez so conspicuously ignores: different cultures have different interpretations of female beauty. Can a veiled woman be beautiful? Djavann, Mahmoody, Phillips would all very emphatically answer 'no'. Women from Afghanistan, Iran and Saudi Arabia have different opinions. More importantly, such feelings are often superficial: while initiatives such as Rodriguez's beauty salon may provide a type of bridge, allowing the powerless a means to access the culture of the powerful, they do not form a structure of dialogue between equals. While Raymonda Tawil was waiting for her case to be heard by an Israeli military official, a young female Israeli soldier began to sweep the room. Tawil observed: 'She is young, little more than a child. But in her khaki uniform, she represents all Israeli women: proud, emancipated, and free.'[82] The fact that Tawil admired this woman did not lead to any sense of solidarity: they went on to argue bitterly about Palestinian-Israeli politics.

Very few of our authors attempt to construct generalised, politically aware arguments concerning global female experience. It is significant that the most resonant politically based argument for female solidarity cited in this chapter is that produced by Madeleine Allbright. Saadawi has clearly been considering these issues, but sees their problems. The majority of our authors are held in their camps by the bonds of culture, religion and ethnicity.

Given these constraints, the most powerful example of cross-cultural solidarity is love.[83] (This nearly always means heterosexual love: three or four of our authors refer in passing to the existence of lesbianism, but do not discuss it any detail. The single exception is Annemarie Schwarzenbach who does describe her lesbian affair in Persia in *La mort en Perse*.[84]) Women such as Jaber, Rodriguez and Wilson are in the front line: these are the people who are actively overcoming borders and barriers that prevent dialogue. In their marriages, the cultural inequalities are clearer than ever.

CHAPTER FIVE

Islam: Return Journeys

'Muslim women have many stories to tell.'
Shelina Zahra Janmohamed[1]

Like Muslim pilgrims at Mecca, our authors circle around Islam. Unlike the pilgrims, they do not pace regularly: their steps do not produce that entrancing, astonishing sight of an even, molecular movement formed by the thousands of people walking ritually round the Kaaba. Instead, our authors move in irregular, unpredictable patterns, pulled towards and then pushed away, spiralling in and then falling out, some feeling an almost gravitational attraction, some vigorously contesting it, others blithely ignoring Islam's obvious presence.

This chapter will evaluate our hundred authors' varying attitudes to Islam. After noting the obvious point that one can find examples of almost every possible stance, from extreme devotion, through indifference, to extreme antipathy, this chapter will concentrate on the history of these patterns, analysing Islam's increasing importance in these hundred works.

The rise of Islam

As was noted in the introduction, one can almost date these works by the labels that they use to describe their journeys. Over the decades, references to Islam grow both more frequent and more prominent. Juliette de Baïracli Levy writes in 1959 of her journey to 'Galilee'; in 2005 Sadek Hajji and Stéphanie Marteau travel through the land they term 'Muslim France'.[2] Zaiba Malik notes a similar process taking place among the Pakistanis living in Bradford: 'by the mid-1980s, "the community" that had previously described itself as "black" or "Pakistani" or "Asian" now described itself as "Muslim". Religion took precedence over colour and nationality.'[3]

The older generations of writers, who used terms such as 'Orient', 'desert' and 'Holy Land' to describe their destinations, did not necessarily see Islam as an important aspect of their destination. When Kathleen Kenyon wrote that 'Palestine is the home of the most famous book in the world', she did not think it necessary to spell out that she was referring to the Bible: this point seemed obvious, and the attraction and overriding importance of the region as a site of Christian identity also seemed self-evident.[4] The Muslim presence in the Holy Land often seemed an anomaly, the sort of contradiction which – it was hoped – the Zionist initiative might resolve by restoring a sense of biblical logic and chronology to the region. When they came to consider the region's inhabitants, the orientalists were more likely to define them by race, as Arabs, rather than by religion. Thus Pamela Bright in *A Poor Man's Riches* and Martha Gellhorn in 'The Arabs of Palestine' were both sharply critical of Palestinian refugees, but contextualised their criticisms largely by reference to Arab race and culture, rather than by reference to Islam.[5] To some extent, their caution about the use of religious vocabulary is justified: among the Palestinians there is a substantial Christian minority, and across the Middle East there are also many minority faiths such as the Druze, Alawi, Izidi (or Yazidi) and Zoroastrians, as well the representatives of Islam, Christianity and Judaism.

Betty Mahmoody's *Not Without My Daughter* suggests a moment of transition, rather than a turning point. Religion is certainly an issue that she considers frequently: her attitude to Islam is curious, often confused, often critical, but not blankly hostile. She resented those Iranians who cling 'to their own zealous brand of the Ayatollah Khomeini's fanatical Shiite sect of Islam', but not all Muslims.[6] Mahmoody accepted that Islam shares many features with Judeo-Christian traditions; while held in Iran, she read the Koran and attempted to cite it to support her case; while in despair, and desperately seeking for a means to escape, she followed a specific form of Islamic prayer ritual, apparently sincerely and without hypocrisy; when she finally managed to escape, she considered this as an answer to her prayer and commented, triumphantly, 'we *did* worship the same God'.[7] While bitter, hostile and contemptuous about Iran, her attitude to Islam was less obviously antagonistic.

It is among the later, post-9/11 authors that attitudes finally crystallise. To the misapplication of some of the themes of Saadawi's *Hidden Face of Eve* is added a clear, explicit hostility to Islam; a hostility which now appears so obvious, so indisputable that there is no need to debate the issue.[8] In order to learn what is wrong with Islam, all the reader needs to do is to 'look at the images that TV brings us every day', notes Oriana Fallaci.[9] The basis of Islam is 'fear', writes Ayaan Hirsi Ali.[10] Melanie Phillips introduces a qualification or two: in her *Londonistan* she draws back from deciding 'whether or not Islam is intrinsically a religion of violent conquest or whether it has been hijacked by a revisionist ideology'.[11] However, she does feel confident in stating that 'jihadi Islamism' is now the dominant tendency within British Islam, with no attempt to demonstrate her interpretation by reference to lifestyles or beliefs of British Muslims. These works clearly echo Samuel Huntington's 'Clash of civilizations' thesis:

they assert that religion, rather than ethnicity or culture, is the feature that defines peoples in the modern world, and that there is some essence of Islam that is violent, anti-Western and radically incompatible with modernity. One immediate result of this new attitude was an aggressive, hostile questioning of women in the USA or Europe wearing any form of Islamic veil.[12]

The point I wish to stress here is the newness of such attitudes. Older authors saw Islam as just one feature among many within Middle Eastern society, and saw the veil sometimes as old-fashioned, sometimes as charming and pretty, but rarely as a challenge to Western civilisation. While the new hostility to Islam is led by conservative authors, who often write in defence of traditional values, their political concepts are – in reality – extremely innovative. There can be no doubt that they have achieved some success: in place of 'Arab' or 'oriental', 'Muslim' and 'Islam' have become key analytic categories. However, this success may well be temporary. The critical comments by Ken Booth and Tim Dunne seem justified: instead of a clash of civilisations, 'what we have instead is a confusion of misunderstandings, crude stereotypes, and parallel absences of self-knowledge'.[13] The monolithic concept of Islam to which some of the more recent works subscribe is clearly so inaccurate that it is difficult to sustain it in any serious analysis. The new movements and cultures that have been revealed by the Arab Spring of 2011, with their intoxicating blend of ethical protest, patriotism, democratising aspirations and Muslim values, cannot be contained within the simple binary categories of the clash of civilisations.

There is another way of understanding the 'Clash of civilizations' thesis that may well have more relevance to this study. This could be illustrated by a reference from Béji's *Islam Pride*. Discussing both the new visibility of Islamic veiling and an apparent resurgence in Islam, Béji suggests that these points are linked to the hopelessness felt by the most humble, the crushed and lowest in Western society.[14] As is so often the case with such arguments, Béji provides no examples or evidence: it is simply assumed that 'everyone knows' that this is the case. In fact, there is a considerable quantity of evidence that suggests something quite contrary. In Turkey, the rise of a new form of political Islam (which has developed alongside a new popularity for veiling) is clearly linked to an aspiration to social mobility, not to the despair felt by the crushed; the new Islamism is a religion of the rising middle classes, not of the despairing proletariat.[15] Faïza Guène's remarkable semi-autobiographical novel, *Kiffe Kiffe Demain*, is set among the demoralised, impoverished inhabitants of a housing estate on the edge of Paris: rather than being a site for a radical religious resurgence, what strikes the reader in her descriptions is the near absence of all forms of organised culture, whether religious, political or intellectual in nature.[16]

There is little evidence here that a new Islamism is spreading as a faith of the poor: the Muslim religious practices that Guène describes seem perfunctory and incapable of arousing any deep emotions. Given these examples, it is therefore significant that a number of commentators have mistakenly linked Islamism to the hopelessness of the sub-proletariat.

When one looks closely at the references to social crisis by the new polemists, one is struck by how frequently Islam, or the presence of Muslims, is taken as a constituent element of social crisis. For Phillips, Muslims in Britain threaten an established national identity; for Djavann, the presence of veil-wearing women in French schools stops a process of education and enlightenment; Hirsi Ali sees an over-representation of Muslim men in Western prisons and Muslim women in shelters for abused women.[17] In each case, the author argues that Islam represents not simply a challenge but a new, growing threat within these countries to established social norms. In these references, one can see a type of displacement taking place. Rather than debating the declining attraction of British national identity, it is easier to identify a foreign threat, and then blame this outsider for any problems; rather than considering why French schools seem to be becoming more tense, less inclusive, less harmonious places, it is easier to blame a few hundred veil-wearing schoolgirls for their ills; rather than analysing the factors that lead to family breakdown, it is easier to blame a malign Muslim violence. In each case, the reference to Islam seems to stand in for undesirable features of modernity and globalisation. This interpretation of Islam as enemy can also recreate the classic stance of paranoid politics: the critics of Islam claim to speak for the victims of a stronger enemy, and therefore ruthless measures can be justified in their defence. (Such attitudes resemble the political anti-Semitism of the late nineteenth and early twentieth century.) These references to Islam are also a means of implicitly acknowledging the changes that globalisation has brought to the status of the West, which is no longer the undisputed dominant power in a globalised world. A swift reference to the terrifying rise of political Islam can set this new context, without engaging in any form of meaningful dialogue with the other players; it is a means of imagining a globalisation without contributing to the construction of global culture.

New Muslims

Our hundred authors suggest forms of religious identity that are considerably more complex than the structures suggested by the simplistic concepts of the 'Clash of civilizations' thesis. Even categorising them raises some important issues: obviously, one can begin by classifying them as Muslims and non-Muslims. But these categories miss important

distinctions. Qanta Ahmed was a sincere Muslim who experienced a spiritual awakening after her pilgrimage to Mecca; after 9/11 she identified
with the West, against Saudi Arabia. Joumana Haddad proclaims herself
'an angry Arab woman', but stays relatively discrete about her religious
identity. She states that – in many ways – she feels more at home in the
Saint-Germain quarter in Paris, in northern Italian cities and in Cartegena
in Columbia than in her native Beirut. When it finally becomes clear that
she has a Christian background, she refuses to pick sides, boldly stating
that 'I have seen the worst from both sides'.[18] While she is not a practising
Muslim, she writes with a clear, deep knowledge of Islamic practices.
Where does she fit in the 'Clash of civilizations'? Several of our authors –
for example Djavann and Hirsi Ali – are also proud of their status as
ex-Muslims, and clearly identify with Western values. Muslims who have
lived in Western cities all their lives – such as Zaiba Malik, Shelina
Janmohamed or Faïza Guène – obviously have a different understanding
of Islam from those who grew up in Muslim-majority societies. Our last
'grey area' among our hundred authors are the ten or so who indicate a
close, even personal, knowledge of Islam, but never actually declare in
their texts whether or not they are practising Muslims. It is interesting that
even the prominent and celebrated author, Azar Nafisi, who is so often
taken as an expert on Muslim women's experience, falls into this category.
Possibly, for some, the question of religious identity is genuinely complex,
and they find it difficult to give a simple, yes-or-no response. More
frequently, as in the case of Nafisi, the stance looks convenient: it allows
her to write at once as a native and as an orientalist.

Islam from the inside

A number of our authors discuss their religious conversions. There is a
strange asymmetry present here: those who lose their Islamic faith tend to
summarise this point in a single sentence, while those who convert to Islam
can spend a whole book discussing the experience. Houria Boutelja is
typical of the first tendency. In a single sentence, she states that while a
teenager she broke with her parents' ideals, represented by religion,
virginity and Ramadan.[19] Malika Oufkir discusses a similar experience in
an equally concise form: 'We had rejected Islam, which had brought us
nothing good, and opted for Catholicism instead.'[20] While such prominent
ex-Muslims as Djavann and Hirsi Ali speak at length about how they
suffered in Muslim-majority societies, it is interesting that they only seem
to speak of before and after: never of the transition between the two.

Conversion to Islam is at the centre of the works by Willow Wilson and
Na'ima Roberts; alongside them, Carol Anway describes her daughter's

conversion to Islam at length, Evelyn Cobbold contributes a chapter which recounts how – despite being born into a Christian family – she had 'always been a Muslim'; Qanta Ahmed and Asra Nomani both experience something akin to a spiritual reawakening when they visit Mecca, and Zaiba Malik conducts a protracted, life-long debate concerning the nature of her Muslim faith.[21] All these works are marked by a clear desire to talk in detail about their religious experiences and attitudes, which contrasts with the concise, ultra-summary forms adopted by those who leave Islam.

The disparity between the narratives of conversion to and conversion from Islam is odd, and hard to explain. Looking back, one can easily find examples of older works that discuss at length the painful process of losing faith, such as James Joyce's *Portrait of the Artist as a Young Man* and Bertrand Russell's *Why I Am Not a Christian*. In the modern context, one surmises that converting to Islam is seen as exceptional, and therefore in need of explanation, while losing Islamic faith is seen as normal, and therefore not worth writing about at length. Furthermore, some of the ex-Muslims are writing in order to demonstrate how fully they have assimilated into Western society and its norms. For them, denouncing the evils of Islam and admiring the liberties of the West are both means of demonstrating their assimilation; discussing the agonies of the loss of Islamic faith would not perform this task. It is relevant that Djavann's longest discussion of her assimilation into French culture is far more concerned with questions of literature and language than with religion: a focus that allows her constantly to voice her admiration of all things French.[22]

Critics of Islam point to many unattractive and repellent aspects of modern Muslim practices. Pardis Mahdavi provides a memorable example, if not the most serious: she cites an Iranian poster, showing the figure of Ayatollah Khomeini and an inspiring slogan: 'The Islamic revolution is not about fun, it is about morality: in fact, there is no fun to be had in the Islamic Republic.'[23]

However, within these hundred works there are many other opinions concerning the nature of Islam. Here, our authors show an ability to pick and choose, to construct *their* Islam. Willow Wilson cites an interesting illustration of this approach, relating to the period when she shared a flat with another American woman in a rundown part of Cairo. Full of a convert's zeal, Wilson announces to her flatmate that 'Islam is antiauthoritarian sex-positive monotheism.' Her flatmate is stunned by her words, and vehemently disagrees.

> 'You see the way women are treated here. You walk in the streets. It's like being a hunted animal! If that's sex-positive I'm the freaking pope.'

'I'm not arguing with that' [replies Wilson]. 'It's disgusting and hypocritical and wrong. And I don't think there's a single Muslim cleric out there who'd disagree with you. This is not Islam. This is a society in freefall. This place is a *mess*. Egypt is at a lower point today, *today*, than it has been in its entire history.'[24]

Wilson's distinction between Islamic ideals and Muslim practices is an important one: for her, becoming a Muslim is not the equivalent of a new nationality, but something that leads her away from the existing societies and nation states, and into another zone.

Surprisingly, there is one point at which the writings of modern Muslims and those of the older orientalists seem to converge: both generations speak of the beauty of Islam in similar terms. Walking towards a shrine in the Iranian city of Qom, Sarah Hobson was suddenly struck by the splendour of the sights before her:

> I felt what can be termed only as awe. The brilliance of the sanctuary, the dark figures of Muslims who moved beneath without frenzy, the gentle chanting of prayers – all contributed to an atmosphere of peace and certainty, the certainty of God and the need to worship him.[25]

Rona Randall uses similar language to describe the Al-Aqsa mosque in Jerusalem: 'It really is impossible to describe the beauty of this noble mosque – the second most sacred in all the Muslim world . . . It is harmonious and lovely, without a single jarring note.'[26] Marguerite van Geldermalsen contributes a marvellously hippy-ish passage, in which she remembers sitting over a valley at Petra (Jordan) as the sun rose and hearing her Bedouin husband recite passages from the Koran: 'I didn't need to understand a word – it was made for this world, especially for such mornings as we watched in awesome wonder as the valley awakened and the sunlight slipped down the rock face in our view.'[27]

Sincere Muslims often seem to reach for a similar vocabulary to express their relationship with Islam. Evelyn Cobbold, listening to the cry of a muezzin calling Muslims to prayer in Port Said, notes 'I wonder how anyone can listen to that call unmoved'.[28] Jehan Sadat was struck by the language of the Koran.

> Even at the age of thirteen, I heard in the rich melodic Arabic of the Quran something transcendent and, indeed, divine . . . The beauty of the language used in the Quran is almost inexpressible. The public recitation of its flawlessly constructed rhythms, rhymes and assonances is an art in the Arab world, and those best at it are as famous here as classical musicians are in the West.[29]

Shelina Janmohamed speaks in similar terms:

> Poetry is designed to inspire love, and Islam is about falling in love
> with the Creator of the Universe. The Arabic is simple and rhythmic
> and has layers of meaning that reveal themselves to you each time you
> return. The Arabs of the time were so taken aback by the elegance and
> mystery of the words, they called the Prophet Muhammad a
> magician.[30]

While there are clearly similarities and compatibilities between the two
visions, there is also an important difference. Predictably, the orientalists
view Islam as outsiders: they might feel 'awe', but this is a passive emotion,
associated with something that they see from afar. Thus Geldermalsen is
content to hear without understanding. The Muslims talk about the beauty
of the language as an aid to understanding and participation in a ritual or a
culture. For them, the beauty of Islam is not a quality sufficient in itself.

We meet an apparent paradox as we turn to consider forms of participation in Islam. On the one hand, Islam has a sort of recognised status as a
'rules and regulations' religion: the Koran contains fewer stories, and far
fewer miracles, than the Bible, but it also contains many more instructions
concerning how to live one's life. This clarity is often cited by believers and
converts as one of the most attractive aspects of Islam. Wilson speaks of
becoming 'part of a mathematical algorithm linking earthly and heavenly
bodies' through following Islamic rituals: a stripped-down, rationalist
image of religious practice.[31] And yet, on the other hand, Muslims
constantly make reference to the individual choices that they make
concerning their religion. The Palestinian Shireen Anabtawi suggests this
type of idea in her dialogue with Israeli Daniela Norris. Norris expresses
surprise when she learns that Anabtawi is a practising Muslim, commenting
that she had understood that such rituals led to radicalism, and 'You don't
look radical to me!' Anabtawi replies 'I consider myself to be a religious
Muslim, though perhaps it is hard to tell from looking at me. It doesn't
always show on the outside.'[32] In part, this is simply a rather euphemistic
discussion concerning veiling: one gathers that Anabtawi does not veil. But
her reply says something more: she regards herself as a 'religious Muslim'
not because she prays five times a day (she never confirms whether or not
she follows this ritual), nor because of some validation from an external
authority, but simply because she thinks she is. These brief comments
suggest a type of rational individualism within Islam, shared by many
Muslims, alongside the 'rules and regulations' dimension.

This leads to a wide variety of attitudes towards Islamic veiling, even
among sincere Muslim women. Here, a qualification is needed. There is

no doubt that this issue has been massively misinterpreted and over-discussed, and that its importance has been sensationalised by the Western media. For example, Melanie Phillips's *Londonistan*, a book that presents an argument concerning Britain's laxity towards international terrorism, is illustrated by a picture of veiled women on the cover. Phillips moves quickly to discuss the presence of veiled women: she questions whether veiling is a 'religious requirement or a political statement of antagonism towards the British state'. Whichever is the correct interpretation, Phillips reports that one feels 'a niggling feeling of insecurity and unease' at the sight of veiled women on London's streets.[33] 'The veil is the emotional focus', accurately observe Dounia Bouzar and Saïda Kada, referring to the intense French debate over the status of Muslims in French society.[34] After her return from Saudi Arabia to the USA, Carmen Bin Ladin found that the first question that people asked her was always 'Do you wear the veil?' She 'used to get a kick out of how astonished and appalled they were' when she answered yes.[35] Shelina Janmohamed's words are a necessary corrective to this appalled fascination: 'It's just a little piece of cloth . . . It's not the end of civilisation as we know it.'[36] In some commentaries, it is clear that the obsessive focus on the veil has obscured discussion of more important issues such as women's rights to employment, freedom of speech and legal equality. Zainab Salbi makes an interesting observation concerning an early American toleration of Saddam Hussein's rule:

> American obsession with the way women dress helped dupe Americans into believing that because Iraqi women looked more like them, they also had greater freedoms. Behind this façade there was almost no freedom to travel or speak or pray, zero tolerance for any public views at all that conflicted with Saddam Hussein's.[37]

In other words, the confidence of American authorities that they knew what the veil meant and that they could therefore relate most easily to a society in which veiling was largely absent, misled them. What should be 'just a little piece of cloth' has been misinterpreted as the representation of a vast religious culture. The question of 'what veiling means' therefore inevitably becomes a discussion of 'how has veiling been interpreted': both questions are too large to be discussed in this work.[38] Instead, in the passages below, I will analyse how women among our hundred authors have experienced veil-wearing. In this section, I will concentrate on those who have relatively positive or ambivalent attitudes towards veiling.

Qanta Ahmed, working as a surgeon in Saudi Arabia, was not required to veil in her hospital, but did have to wear a long, almost completely enveloping *abbayah* when she went outside the hospital compound.

Initially, she found this uncomfortable. However, she soon realised that there were advantages to wearing one:

> Immediately, I felt safer. This veil would deflect intrusive male gazes. I was shielded, impregnable, and most importantly of all completely concealed. The abbayah was easy to move in, not at all restrictive of my movements . . . I was enthralled at my complete submission . . . My social suicide had begun . . . Inside the abbayah, I felt oddly free . . . In some respects, the abbayah was a powerful tool of women's liberation from clerical male misogyny.[39]

Obviously, these comments are ambivalent: Ahmed is honest enough to record her complex, contradictory feelings, rather than adopt a more simple attitude of acceptance or rejection. She certainly is not saying that she approves of the compulsory, enforced veiling of women by the Saudi state. Instead, her comments suggest that she sees that within the context of a repressive society which denies women many rights, wearing an *abbayah* could have advantages as well as disadvantages. Ahmed, however, is then surprised by the attitude of Zubaidah, a good-looking, educated Saudi woman, dedicated to her work. They get to talk at a party attended only by women. 'I veil because I choose it!' states Zubaidah forcefully. 'As I looked at Zubaidah's shining eyes, which glowed with idealism and spiritual enlightenment, I believed her. There was no doubt that Zubaidah's enthusiasm for veiling was genuine, her passion for her beliefs not fanatical but quietly steely.'[40]

Outside Muslim-majority societies such as Saudi Arabia and Iran where veiling is compulsory, one finds a different set of attitudes towards the veil. One basic – but often ignored point – is that there is not one veil: this 'little piece of cloth' can take many forms and carry many meanings. Visiting Ramallah, Anne Brunswic is honest enough to note that veiling seems to be governed by some subtle social considerations which she does not understand. Some points, however, are clear to her:

> There are veils and veils. There is a chasm between the well made-up young middle-class woman, wearing jewellery, tight jeans and high heels, plus a brightly-coloured veil, held in place with a wonderful broach, and her black-veiled cousin, hidden beneath a dark black coat that reaches to her feet. At least this woman shows her face: you can also find women who only show their eyes, others whose face and hands are entirely covered. Experience, however, has taught me that the veil tells you nothing about the ideas of the lady who wears it.[41]

Allegra Stratton learns a similar lesson outside Beirut:

We were still gridlocked in the traffic. Tapping the window of her BMW, Darah pointed at two girls crossing the street in front of us. They were cigarillo thin and Coco Chanel chic. Both wore black-nylon boot-cut hipster trousers and high heels, carried baguette handbags and wrapped around their heads were black sheer head-scarves as tight as the rest of their outfits . . .

A few girls lined up nearby were obviously waiting for a lesson. If their bottom halves were a uniform of the same blue stone-washed jeans, then their hijab seemed to display their personality: the Arab equivalent of the witty T-shirt aphorism across the boobs. Two tied their veils – one fuchsia, the other a lighter pink – at the side of their heads like side ponytails; another's was so loose it was barely a hijab – more a sheer accessory with diamanté studs.[42]

This relatively obvious point, that veils take different forms, clearly refutes the arguments presented by authors such as Melanie Phillips, who seek to uncover the political message that the veil conceals. In reality, veiling cannot be reduced to a single political tendency.

The debate between Dounia Bouzar and Saïda Kada, both French Muslims, outlines some implications of veil-wearing. Bouzar presents a typical critique: while she is a Muslim, she considers veil-wearing to be unhelpful in France, for it amounts to 'defining oneself first of all as a Muslim. It therefore creates a distance, a separation.' Kada's reply is interesting:

My veil is a springboard . . . It is an extension of myself. When you communicate with someone, you give a part of yourself, and take something from the other. Exchange is based upon sharing, and can only be fruitful if each participant is accepted for what they are.[43]

For Bouzar, the veil hinders dialogue; for Kada, it is a necessary pre-condition to genuine dialogue.

Among the writers who voluntarily wear the veil, one finds clear references to the choices that the wearer has made. Veiling is clearly, for most of them, not the equivalent of a uniform which annihilates individuality. Willow Wilson contributes a memorable passage concerning the first day she wore a veil at her school in Cairo. She spent some time considering this issue: she was afraid of both the reactions of Muslims and non-Muslims. The factor that seems to have been decisive for her was that she wanted to signal her faith to the outside world.

The first scarf I ever bought and wore was apple red, a color that ensured my ultraconservative [Muslim] colleagues would be as shocked as my non-Muslim ones . . . The moment of tension had passed. I kept up this attitude throughout the day; when people were surprised, I was cheerful and neutral, which left some puzzled, some amused, some alarmed, and some delighted. I had achieved what I set out to do, which was to avoid philosophical conversations with those who were not Muslim, and clichéd spiritual raptures with those who were.[44]

Shelina Janmohamed speaks with an obvious affection about the pink hijab that she wears on the streets of London:

My *hijab* is pink, the colour of an April sunset or a dusk summer rose. It is a long, flowing piece of silk fading into a bold purple that reminds me of royal brocades and sacred discoveries. It is fragranced lightly with the scent of bukhoor, so that it surrounds me wherever I go, gentle but not overpowering.[45]

Her identification with her veil is evident.

Na'ima Roberts discusses in some detail the dilemmas faced by converted women trying to dress in an Islamic manner. Unusually, she seems to accept without question that some form of head-covering is obligatory for any sincere Muslim women, refusing to leave the issue open to individual decisions. However, she then outlines a zone of self-determination. She criticises Muslim women who decide that 'our clothing should be longer, wider, darker, in a word, frumpier'. She labels this tendency as 'New Muslim Tramp syndrome'. Roberts sees this as a mistake, for 'looking good and maintaining oneself [has] to be a matter of self-respect'. Instead, she recommends that Muslim women should learn from the differing fashion styles worn in the various Muslim communities: Chinese *cheongsam*, *kurta* pyjamas, hooded *jalibiyyah*, Somali *dira*.[46]

There is an absolute difference of opinion here. Critics of Islam focus on veiling as a crucial issue. They will normally ignore the distinction between compulsory veiling and voluntary veiling, and underestimate the extent to which veiling can be experienced as a form of individual expression. Voluntary veil-wearers see their veils as part of themselves, not as a uniform, which may suggest a connection stretching over the countries of the world, but not a means by which to annihilate individuality, difference and distinction.

Mecca

The ability of Islam to connect the believer to a wider world is suggested by some of our authors' records of trips to Mecca. Four of our authors describe in detail their journeys to Mecca: Evelyn Cobbold, Asra Nomani and Qanta Ahmed go on the hajj, the pilgrimage that every Muslim is meant to make at least once in their lives, while Jehan Sadat does the *umrah*, the lesser form of pilgrimage which takes place outside the official dates set for the hajj.

Going to Mecca necessarily means travelling to Saudi Arabia. Among our hundred authors, there is a constant refusal of the Wahhabi interpretation of Islam practised and enforced in Saudi Arabia. For Fadia Basrawi, it functions as a form of repressive social control in Saudi society: 'Wahhabi Shari'a became a handy bully that pushed a work force for the oil producers into obedient shape by brutally stamping out any forms of dissent.'[47] Qanta Ahmed's memoir concerning her residence in Saudi Arabia contains frequent reference to the censorious brutality of the muttawa (morality police), willing to humiliate and even arrest non-married men and women who mix at the same social gathering. Carmen Bin Ladin dismisses Wahhabism as a ferocious enforcement of an ancient, Bedouin social code.[48] Curiously, however, despite the Saudi possession of the most holy sites in Islam, Wahhabi Islam is never presented by any of these authors as the 'real' Islam. Even the most fervent critics of Islam look to other examples, usually from Iran or Somalia.

Each of the four authors finds the trip exhausting, and each describes some of the apparent contradictions they encounter, perhaps best summed up by the references to KFC's thriving trade in Mecca (discussed in chapter three). More importantly, each experiences a type of revelation; each is clearly moved. Nomani even goes on to entitle her book *Standing Alone in Mecca*. Of the four, Cobbold is the least expressive, and much of her narrative is reduced to technical explanations and Koranic references. The last sentences of her work state that, after her hajj, she treasured 'the abiding sense of joy and fulfilment that possesses the soul. What have the past days held out but endless interest, wonder and beauty? To me an amazing new world has been revealed.'[49] Unfortunately, she provides very few details of this 'amazing new world' that arouses her sense of 'interest, wonder and beauty'. In reality, was she disappointed by what she saw? Or is it simply that words failed her?

Nomani, Ahmed and Sadat are more expressive and revealing. The most important lesson is probably that uttered by Nomani's father, who accompanied her on the hajj: '*This* is *ummah*.'[50] (*Umma* or *ummah* is the Islamic concept of a worldwide community of believers.) He finds the crowds at

Mecca a physical embodiment of this religious concept. For these authors, the journey to Mecca reveals something vital about the nature of Islam, for they travel to the 'epicentre of Islam' and at this spot they are able to survey the variety of Muslim cultures and identities that make up the *umma*.[51] However, like Willow Wilson refusing to see the streets of Cairo as representative of Islamic ideals, our three pilgrims do not accept every detail of their experience in Mecca as representing Islam. They pick and choose, separating the banal, the inconvenient and the annoying from the genuinely spiritual aspects of their hajj. Sitting in Tent 50007 with sixty other women, Ahmed is both horrified and disappointed by the prejudices she sees among her fellow pilgrims. The rich Saudi women despise the poor Egyptians; the poor Egyptians resent the pretensions of the rich Saudis. Some of the Saudis signal 'to the maids to bring them another soda with a contemptuous and dismissive wave, not even articulating the words'. Ahmed herself suffers due to a misplaced prejudice: she is dark-skinned and the Saudis assume that she can only be a poor Pakistani maid. Their attitudes suddenly change when they realise her true, exalted status: she is a doctor! Then they want to talk to her.[52] Each of our pilgrims records similarly unattractive sights and incidents, and each grumble about the complex, cumbersome organisation which attempts to host the million and more pilgrims who arrive.

Perhaps it is Nomani who provides the most imaginative and original introduction to the 'real' Mecca, deliberately and continually challenging her (assumed) American reader's expectations by constantly comparing the sights of the hajj to everyday American experiences:

> [Mecca] felt quite familiar. I could have been entering any other urban capital of the world. It was a mix of traditional ways and Western trappings . . .
>
> I was surprised at the freedom here [walking towards the Kaaba]. I could have been approaching the steps of New York Public Library. I felt no inhibitions or restrictions as a woman approaching this daunting creation . . .
>
> It was madness near the Ka'bah as pilgrims threw themselves against its walls to try to kiss the stone. It took such faith and devotion to fling [oneself] forward. The situation at the Ka'bah reminded me of the time I wiggled my way into the mosh pit at a No Doubt concert to sing with Gwen Stefani, 'I'm just a girl'. I loved mosh pits, but I didn't get the scene in front of me.[53]

The diversity of the pilgrims is striking. All our writer-pilgrims note the sudden disappearance of the usual Saudi barriers between men and women mixing: while the regulations of the pilgrimage force women to accept male direction in order to arrive in Mecca, and while there remain some restrictions on women's movements outside the holy places, inside them, men and women mix as approximate equals.

Ahmed recalls praying in front of the Kaaba. She realises that behind her are two Americans, whose accents she can identify as from the southern states. To her right, there is a man from Kosovo, in front of her, men from Ghana; to her left, a half-English, half-Egyptian woman:

> In this diversity, finally I belonged. Islam was many-faceted and I was simply one. Our diversity had obliterated . . . Wahabiism . . . This was Islam: Hajj! Not the Muttawa with their nightsticks and nihilism. Equality in the eyes of our Maker, whether we be men or women, rich or poor, able-bodied or deformed, black or white, was all that mattered. The frenzied, fascist supremacy of Wahabiism had simply been washed away by a torrent of truth: the multiracial, spiritually hybrid Muslims now flooding Mecca.[54]

Sadat, travelling to Mecca about forty years before Ahmed, uses remarkably similar language:

> Nowhere have I felt the power of belief so strongly. Praying along with others, I was at once humbled and uplifted. Before God there are no distinctions between races, classes, or even sexes. In the Haram, women were forbidden to cover their noses and mouths with veils or their hands with gloves. In the true spirit of Islam, carpet weavers from Pakistan were bowing down beside oil executives from Bahrain, engineers and architects from Egypt, factory workers from Russia and Indonesia. Housewives from Afghanistan were praying next to teachers from Sri Lanka, doctors from Iran and the wives of Arab sultans and emirs. There were pilgrims, too, from America. On one Umrah I saw the boxer Muhammad Ali leaving Haram as I entered it . . . To actually see the Kaaba with my own eyes, to be close to the one object that binds Muslims all over the world, was a profound sensation.[55]

Nomani's narrative is more distant, and her relationship with Islam, even at Mecca, more problematic. Standing in front of the 'mosh pit' of the Kaaba, she doesn't 'get the scene'. While her father is stunned by the immensity and diversity of the crowd, Nomani feels intimidated: at first, she experiences no oceanic sense of belonging to a greater collectivity in these vast public rituals. Her moment of revelation is quite different, and takes the form of a 'Not Without My Son' experience. She brought her baby son, Shibli, with her on the hajj, constantly aware that as an unmarried mother she was contradicting a number of Islamic precepts and Saudi regulations. While performing the ritual walks between the points of Safa and Marwah, she realises that her son is restless and needs feeding. She ducks behind a wall, but cannot take off her tightly wrapped chemise. Her father cuts through her clothes.

> I drew Shibli to me. His desperate lips found the milk within me, flowing to him like holy water onto his parched lips. I felt as if I was connected to Shibli with the eternal bond that linked Hajar to Ishmael. It was the life force of creation that touched everyone and everything around us, before us and after us. To me, it was what we call God. It was what we call Allah . . .
>
> That moment meant so much to me. I was in Mecca, a criminal in this land for having given birth without a wedding ring on my finger. And I was nursing my son at the holy mosque of Mecca, overlooking the sacred Ka'bah. This was nature's law expressing itself, more powerfully than man's law . . . I recognized the great lineage I had in Islam.[56]

After this individual, highly maternal moment, Nomani then experiences a sense of unity with the million or more pilgrims as they pray together before the Kaaba.

These experiences are open to a number of different interpretations: one could simply classify them as 'spiritual', and therefore choose to keep them separate from other experiences or dimensions of being. Or, as I would prefer to do, one could note some similarities between these forms of experiences and others. In chapter three I discussed modernity, and cited Doris Lessing's ideas concerning 'a world-mind, a world ethic'.[57] It is clear that these three pilgrim-writers encounter something like this at Mecca: they find the means to think on a world scale, and they see this as at the heart of their religious identity. In other words, for these authors, rather than Islam functioning as a particular, separate mode of thought, Islam can become a form of modernity, enabling Muslims to act within a global context.

Islam and modernity

The idea of Islam as a form of modernity challenges many deeply rooted Western prejudices. As was seen in chapter three, many orientalists and other commentators almost automatically consider Muslim cultures as 'medieval': a misleading term that does not help outsiders to understand the Muslim world. In reality, there are some good reasons for classifying Islam in exactly the opposite manner: for considering it as 'modern' rather than 'medieval'. First, in the most obvious sense, it is the most recent of the three great monotheisms, and whoever designed it seems to have deliberately tried to improve on the structures provided by the previous two. Islam's stress on the written word, its attempts to abolish a priestly stratum and to replace it with a direct, one-to-one relationship between believer and deity all suggest distinctively modern rather than medieval traits. Such interpretations are not new: they have been noted by standard commentaries for decades. Cobbold, writing in the 1930s, compared Islamic structures to those of the League of Nations.[58] More than thirty years ago, Ernest Gellner, the prestigious British sociologist, observed that:

> By various obvious criteria – universalism, scripturalism, spiritual egalitarianism, the extension of full participation in the sacred community not to one, to some, but to *all*, and the rational systemization of social life – Islam is, of the three great Western monotheisms, the one closest to modernity.[59]

Many Muslims would automatically agree with Baroness Warsi's ideal: that 'Faith and Reason go hand in hand'.[60]

Furthermore, Islam reveals another great strength under the new challenges created by the structures of globalisation.[61] Unlike Christianity, Islam has rarely been closely fused with the nation-state.[62] (Iran could be cited as an exception to this observation, but Shia Islam as practised in Iran is certainly not typical of Islam as a whole.) Bouzar speaks of a new generation of French Muslims who are inspired by what she terms a 'de-localized Islam', free of ethnic and national traits; Ruba Salih notes the attraction of 'a transnational and modern Islam cleared from local variations and traditional performances' to Moroccan migrant women in Italy.[63] This 'non-national' status can make it far easier for Islam to function today. For perhaps three centuries, from the eighteenth to the twentieth century, the close links between Christian churches and nation states appeared as clear signs of Christianity's modernity. Today, as nation states are increasingly unable to protect or to guide their populations, Islam's relative independence from nation states now appears as a strength rather than a weakness, and arguably one which will prove more important in future decades.

Thus the sensations experienced by our pilgrims at Mecca should not be seen as a form of conservative obscurantism, a mystical turning away

from the real world or – worse still – a validation of the oppressive structures of Saudi society. These women are all logical, intelligent, perceptive
writers; they make some carefully considered choices; if they say that they
experienced something special while staying in Mecca, we should at least
listen to their words and consider what they might signify.

Conclusion

The return journeys that we have discussed have often taken the form of
long, disjointed, rambling voyages: in some cases, they are still unfinished.
The material they present could be read as an extended discussion of the
location of the epicentre of Islam. Several possible places have been
suggested. The works by our pilgrims suggest the orthodox, traditional
answer: Mecca. The works by the Iranian-Americans implies another
answer: Tehran, which is presented as the cutting-edge of Islam as a political force in the modern world. A third answer, not discussed in this
chapter, might be that Israel/Palestine forms the true border of the 'Clash
of civilizations', and the interaction between Israeli authorities and subject
Palestinians is the most accurate representation of that contest.

All these answers have a certain validity, but each ignores the true nature
of a globalised world. As Bauman noted, the frontier is now all around us.[64]
Mecca no doubt constitutes a privileged locus of Islamic identity, but one
can also easily study Islam by talking to passers-by at Cardiff central
station. Carol Anway has probably never visited Cardiff, but she echoes
this argument in the dedication of her work: 'One of these Muslim women
may be your classmate, your co-worker, your grocer, your neighbour, your
cousin, your niece, your grandchild, and yes, maybe even your daughter.'[65]
Muslims are no longer strange, distant, alien creatures who needed to be
studied by privileged researchers who journey far: they are our
neighbours.

CHAPTER SIX

Towards Dialogue?

'Dialogue, worth its name, is thick and heavy, grounded in a sense of love and emotional bonding to the community combined with an ethical commitment to its fulfilment.'

Kinnvall and Nesbitt-Larking[1]

The peaceful universalism experienced by our writers at Mecca project one image of Islam. A quite different one was projected by the attacks of 9/11 and 7/7. This chapter will consider some of the most important studies by women on Muslim societies published after 9/11. In the second half of the chapter, we will concentrate on some highly innovative works that begin to break with the first-person narrative format that has dominated women's writing to date.

From 9/11 to *Reading Lolita*

In works written after the attacks of 9/11 and 7/7, all our writers are forthright in their condemnations: there is no hint of apology or qualification in their writing. Phillips's comment that what she terms 'jihadi Islamism' is dominant among British Muslims is simply not supported by the evidence reviewed here.[2] Zaiba Malik's work takes the form of a kind of dialogue with the British terrorists of 2005, which is initiated when she realises that one of the terrorists was actually born in the same street as her. Her response is to reconsider the Islam of her father, and to contrast this with the religious imagery that inspired the bombers; she concludes 'I don't recognise your god, who is violent, vengeful and malicious.'[3]

Veil-wearing British Muslim Shelina Janmohamed speaks with feeling about how her life changed after 9/11. Her opposition to the attacks and revulsion are obvious; like Malik, she refuses to accept that the terrorists were acting according to Islamic principles, for 'even the very name "Islam" means peace'.[4] But her feelings do not prevent her from being blamed, by association, for the attack. The atmosphere in her office changed:

I could sense that people at work wanted to know what I thought, and whether what they had heard about Islam was true or not, but they seemed afraid to ask. I heard their whispers, trying to unravel the different ideas that were portrayed about Muslims on television and then trying to reconcile them with their experiences of me, the resident office Muslim.[5]

Yet it was difficult for her to speak:

> No matter how much we condemned the atrocious acts, we were informed that we were actually supporting them. We were told that we ought to condemn them more fervently and more passionately. So we condemned them some more, and then we were told that we were insincere . . . Speaking out just attracted more attention, more vitriol, more hatred. But keeping quiet was not an option . . . [Public opinion] identified me as too repressed to know my own mind; so repressed, in fact, that I wasn't allowed to speak for myself in these debates.[6]

The lessons offered by Rowan Williams were ignored. In one of the most intelligent reflections on 9/11, he argued that this tragic event could constitute a breathing space, and that those with power should try 'to act so that something might possibly change, as opposed to acting so as to persuade ourselves that we're not powerless'.[7] Instead, in the days after 9/11, one of Janmohamed's friends was punched on her way home and her nose was broken.[8]

9/11 did not produce a sudden change in East/West relations: as we have seen, tensions and prejudices existed long before September 2001. Its most important effect was to suggest a radical change in the sense of political borders. 'Don't ask where the frontierland is', observed Zygmunt Bauman in an article on 9/11, 'it is all around you, in your town, on the streets you walk'.[9] This shift in the nature of the border meant that Janmohamed's pink hijab was transformed from the colourful headgear of an eccentric – but otherwise likeable – colleague into something which suddenly appeared to many to be the enemy's flag, flying in London. We have already considered a number of the possible reactions to this situation: the conservative one, suggested by writers such as Fallaci, Phillips and Djavann, is to demand the restoration of border controls, to recreate a clear, strict sense of divided camps. The weakness of such arguments is obvious: first, it is by no means certain that those old borders were ever as impervious as these conservatives like to imagine. Processes of interchange and fusion seem to have been a norm in most societies.[10] Secondly, those clear, mono-ethnic, mono-cultural camps, for which writers such as Phillips show such nostalgia, are clearly no longer practical in a globalised world. Often they could only be created by caricaturing 'the other' to form an image of some united image of a despicable and unwelcome presence.[11] Some other solution is needed.

It is in this post-9/11 context that Azar Nafisi's *Reading Lolita in Tehran* was published, and quickly acquired a certain sort of celebrity. Her work was rapidly followed by a number of comparable works by Iranian-Americans, such as Azadeh Moaveni's *Lipstick Jihad* and Pardis Mahdavi's *Passionate Uprisings*.[12] These works have been extremely influential in providing a mental map of the post-9/11 landscape. They share some important features: their authors grew up in exiled Iranian families in the USA, but were – arguably – more American than Iranian. They were relatively wealthy, and each held relatively secure, sometimes high-ranking academic positions. Their works suggested a new approach to the discussion of Muslim societies, which was then taken up by others. For example, Nahal Tajadod, author of *Passeport à l'iranienne* (An Iranian Sort of Passport), came from a different but comparable background: French-Iranian rather than American-Iranian, and with connections to the world of film rather than universities.[13] Her work, however, shared some important features of the Iranian-American publications: it was sophisticated, witty, well written, often centred on everyday aspects of women's lives, and devoid of any obvious, explicit political message.

Alongside these works, another type of Iranian exile publication emerged. Nahid Rachlin's *Persian Girls* and Afschineh Latifi's *Even After All This Time* speak of a different sort of experience: these are not women born in the USA, but women who travel from Iran to the USA when young.[14] If Nafisi, Moaveni, Mahdavi and Tajadod can be classified as representing a bourgeois form of exile, Rachlin and – in particular – Latifi are closer to a proletarian exile, in which the departure from Iran produces a rapid and radical fall in social status, to the point where piecework for McDonalds can appear as liberation. One wonders to what extent readers were aware of the significant differences between these works: certainly the cover images of *Persian Girls* and *Even After All This Time* resemble the now-classic stereotypes of the Muslim exile memoir: delicate lettering, veiled women or girls and promises of mesmerising revelations of horror and heroic stories of survival within.

Of all these works, it is undoubtedly *Reading Lolita in Tehran* which has been the most successful and most influential: this was the book which Laura Bush listed as nineteenth in her list of 'twenty-five works to read before you're twenty-five'.[15] It is an odd work to acquire notoriety: one wonders whether, like *The Satanic Verses*, it is more a book that people have heard about rather than one they have read. Its differences from most of the other works in our sample of a hundred are obvious: it is an imaginative, well-written and far more sophisticated text than most of the autobiographical memoirs that we have considered (after all, Nafisi was a professor of English literature). Rather than using the simple 'flash-forward, flash-back' technique by which many of our authors introduce their narratives, Nafisi uses parallel narratives. *Reading Lolita* includes long passages of literary analysis, which provokes frequent complaints from readers who were expecting a simpler, more straightforward denunciation of Iranian repression or an autobiographical tale of misery and exile. This literary focus draws the work away from explicit political discourse, putting Nafisi in the happy position where she can have her cake and eat it. Thus the right-wing, anti-Palestinian *Middle East Quarterly* can enthusiastically review *Reading Lolita* as 'a riveting story of hope, disillusionment, and hope rekindled' and the left-wing, pro-Palestinian *New Internationalist* includes *Reading Lolita* in their list of five key sources through which to hear the 'multiplicity of Iranian voices'.[16] (The *New Internationalist* is rather more grudging in its praises than the *Middle East Quarterly*: it comments that 'the first section will probably tell you more about Nabokov than you ever wished to know, but it is well worth persevering'.) Nafisi's own sympathies seem to be closer to the *Middle East Quarterly* than to the *New Internationalist*: it has published long excerpts from her work and interviewed her.

Where Betty Mahmoody's *Not Without My Daughter* told a simple tale of the misfortunes suffered by an American abroad, *Reading Lolita* takes the reader on a more complex journey.[17] At first sight, it seems to be solidly located within Iranian society: we meet Iranian students and academics, men and women who, unlike *Not Without My Daughter*, do not take the form of grotesque Swift-ian caricatures but are reasonably believable and often sympathetic portrayals. These scenes provide clear, memorable examples of the humiliating and repressive actions carried out by the various Iranian security forces to restrict women's lives. Many appreciative readers seemed to have stopped at this point: *Reading Lolita* 'is an accurate description of what women have to go through in such communities and how even a simple walk in the park can become an act of rebellion', writes one reviewer on the Amazon website.[18] But it is clear that this work is more than an example of documentary reportage: the title alone tells us that. The second dimension to the work concerns an escape from Iranian repression into a type of fem-utopia: the safety and affection provided by a women's reading group, created by Nafisi when it became impossible for her to continue her work at Tehran University as a professor of English literature. 'How well could one teach when the main concern of university officials was not the quality of one's work but the color of one's lips, the subversive potential of a single strand of hair?'[19] The reading group provided the escape: 'we were in that room to protect ourselves from the reality outside'.[20] As this seems to be chaired or directed by Nafisi herself, there is a strong continuity here with her work in the university.[21] The scenes concerning the reading group and the stories of her work in the university then provide the platform for Nafisi's extended analyses of and meditations on a select number of literary texts: *Lolita*, *The Great Gatsby*, *Daisy Miller* and *Pride and Prejudice*. Sometimes these discussions lead to some surprising incidents. For example, in a passage concerning the period when she was employed as a lecturer in Tehran, Nafisi talks of her frustration with the critical comments by both her leftist and Islamist students concerning *The Great Gatsby*, and then recounts her solution: she invited all her students to put the novel on trial.[22] The extent of literary commentary in *Reading Lolita* provokes questions: is this really the best way to document life in an oppressive society? And why has a work of this extended, highly literary nature achieved such prominence?

The third dimension of the book, Nafisi herself, is left in a strangely hazy form. Certainly, this is not a work with the type of simple, raw emotional power that sometimes flares up in *Not Without My Daughter*. One notes another continuity with the work of the orientalists here. Nafisi plays games with her identity and personality in the same manner: they described (or seemed to describe) landscapes and picturesque people; she analyses (or seems to analyse) texts. The end product is remarkably similar: an autobiographically inclined text which is somehow not quite an autobiography.

Despite general praise and commendation for the work, there have been some criticisms. The radical American-Iranian literature expert, Hamid Dabashi, has contributed a particularly trenchant rejection of the work:

> With one strike, Azar Nafisi has achieved three simultaneous objectives: (1) systematically and unfailingly denigrating an entire culture of revolutionary resistance to a history of savage colonialism; (2) doing so by blatantly advancing the presumed cultural foregrounding of a predatory empire; and (3) while at the very same time catering to the most retrograde and reactionary forces within the United States, waging an all-out war against a pride of place by various immigrant communities and racialised minorities seeking curricular recognition on university campuses and in the American society at large . . . [It exudes] a visceral hatred of everything Iranian . . .
>
> Rarely has an Oriental servant of a white-identified, imperial design managed to pack so many services to imperial hubris abroad and racist elitism at home – all in one act.[23]

Dabashi bases much of his analysis on the cover image, which shows two good-looking, black-veiled, young Iranian women reading together, which

– argues Dabashi – provokes a voyeuristic thrill in the Western reader, for the combination of title and image suggests that they are reading *Lolita*.

While I sympathise with Dabashi's political perspective, this seems a strangely incomplete critique; more a way of de-legitimising the work, than of understanding it. Certainly, Dabashi sidesteps one of the most important aspects of the work, which have clearly attracted the interest and sympathy of Western readers: its detailed examples of the daily harassment faced by women in the Islamic republic. Moreover, Nafisi's work is more delicate, more elusive than Mahmoody's *Not Without My Daughter*: characterising it as marked by a 'visceral hatred of everything Iranian' is a wild exaggeration, as Nafisi speaks with affection and sympathy for her Iranian students. In order to criticise the work, we need to think more carefully about its contents.

The chronology of *Reading Lolita* is strange. This is a work published in 2003, two years after 9/11, whose narrative commences in 1979 (the Iranian revolution), includes a flashback to Nafisi's own formative years in the USA in the 1960s and 1970s, makes some reference to the grim experiences of the Iran–Iraq war (1980–8) but then seems to fade out somewhere in the 1990s. Curiously, Nafisi leaves Iran just as a significant experiment in liberalisation starts, symbolised by the election of Seyed Mohammad Khatami as president of the Islamic republic in August 1997. In other words, Nafisi portrays the fixed, stultified Iran of the 1980s in a book published towards the end of a period of some real, if limited, social and political reform in Iran; she presents an American audience, desperate to find the source of 9/11, with an image of an intransigent Islamic republic that is approximately twenty years out of date. Certainly, there is nothing in her book that suggests to her American audience the potential of an Iranian reform movement.

These types of dissonances point to the works' greatest weaknesses: not so much what they say as what they imply. If one made such criticisms of Betty Mahmoody's work, then it could well be legitimate to respond that as a naive, inexperienced writer, Mahmoody probably had little idea of the manner in which her work would be read. Furthermore, as was the case with Saadawi's *The Hidden Face of Eve*, sometimes books have an effect that is quite contrary to their author's intentions.[24] Such objections cannot be applied to *Reading Lolita in Tehran*. Nafisi was a specialist in literature: she ought to be fully aware of the implications of her own work. As one reads the work more closely, one notes its odd features. First, there is the implication that Iranians are simply crushed by a totalitarian juggernaut, which leaves them with no possibility of resistance, only – like Orwell's Winston Smith – of escape into a fantasy of dissidence. Nafisi's students are not the dim people that seem to populate Deborah Rodriguez's

beauty school – but they often seem to play a similar role: a chorus to vali-
date the role of the Western expert. Rodriguez distributes *Vogue* and
Clairol products, Nafisi hands out Austen and Nabokov, but the final result
seems to be much the same. Secondly, there is the implication that it is the
great current of Western literature that, somehow, constitutes the unique
vehicle for the liberation of Iranian women. Other reformers, such as the
human rights activist and lawyer Shirin Ebadi, have sought to build radical
reformist platforms based on the norms of Iranian culture, including
Islamic legal norms. Thirdly, like Rodriguez, like Mahmoody, Nafisi's
premise is that no dialogue is necessary: the idea that Muslim women
might have the capacity or the desire to criticise Western norms, or might
have their own criticisms of Iranian power structures, is ruled out by the
structure of the work. Nothing in *Reading Lolita* troubles the conscience
of the West: Nafisi makes only very brief reference to the legacy of British
and American imperialist adventures in Persia. These three considerations
lead to a fourth, perhaps more fundamental, criticism: why is Nafisi read
as a voice of Iranian women? Her background, her training and her
academic status mark her out as an extremely unusual writer: one well
worth listening to, but unlikely to be representative of anyone. Significantly,
while some Western writing does have a resonance among dissident circles
in Iran, *Reading Lolita* has attracted little attention.[25] In particular, by
stressing so forcefully the fixed, unchanging and unchangeable nature of
the Islamic republic, Nafisi implicitly plays down the success of Iranian
women's groups in achieving some significant, if limited, reforms.[26]

The Iranian-American works which immediately followed *Reading
Lolita* adopted a different tone. Azadeh Moaveni's *Lipstick Jihad* and
Pardis Mahdavi's *Passionate Uprisings* are both descriptions of struggle.
They celebrate, or commemorate, the reform years of Khatami's presi-
dency: like *Reading Lolita*, they follow women's daily lives; unlike *Reading
Lolita*, they at least suggest the possibility of small victories. Mahdavi cites
the telling words of a Tehran beautician:

> I remember fifteen years ago they were beating up women and taking
> everyone who wore nail polish to jail . . . Now look at us; we can do
> what we want. I can wear orange toe polish, and that's that. If any
> member of the morality police tries to touch me, I will scream at him,
> and everyone will support me. I can wear my nail polish, and lipstick
> too! That means something. That means we are getting to them, that
> we *do* have power, that they are more afraid of us than we were of
> them ten years ago![27]

The difference between this description and the stultified society
described by Nafisi is clear. However, the significance of such advances is

difficult to judge. Mahdavi clearly overestimates the importance of the data she has uncovered: her claim that 'their resistance is threatening the entire social and moral order of the Islamic Republic' is an exaggeration.[28] It is hard to think of any political structure which has been overturned by orange toe polish, and it seems unlikely that Iran will provide the first example of such a transformation. While Iranian female activists are certainly right to demand the end of police harassment of their lives, and while such small liberties are worthy of documentation and celebration, Mahdavi seems to ignore the most obvious interpretation of her material: the social, cultural and sexual experimentation that she witnesses is not a revolution, but a substitute for a revolution; it creates a small zone of personal autonomy, instead of a significant change in power structures.

The two later authors also equivocate on whether this type of small-scale activism should be read as Westernisation. Sometimes, their material certainly seems to suggest precisely this. One interviewee tells Mahdavi: 'We don't like Persian music; we prefer European techno or hip-hop.'[29] Moaveni encounters fashionable Tehran girls who 'worked furiously to imitate music videos and Hollywood movies to every last detail.'[30] She finds young people

> Transfixed with the United States . . . American products were growing more popular each day . . . young people, tired of the constrained social life prescribed by the regime, associated brand-name icons of American culture, Coke and Barbie, with the freedoms they were denied . . . Young people from all walks of life loved American-style burger outlets.[31]

The authors do not consider whether they are simply seeing one side of a process of fusion: does hip-hop mean the same thing in Tehran as it does in Los Angeles? Is it not possible that Iranians are using Western products to create a different sense of meaning for themselves?

I have spent some time analysing *Reading Lolita*, *Lipstick Jihad* and *Passionate Uprisings* because these works suggest the most recent interpretative framework through which Muslim societies are judged. As Susan Sontag's comments on the back of *Reading Lolita* state, Nafisi's work describes 'radical Islam's war against women'. The three works outline or imply a number of key themes: that Iran provides a typical case of Islam in practice; that Islam is necessarily misogynistic; that reform of Muslim societies can only take place under the direct or indirect leadership of the West. There are some continuities with the classical themes of orientalism:

principally in the suggestion of Muslim backwardness and Western modernity. But there are also some important differences. The authors are no longer Western ladies of leisure, who travel for pleasure; they are people with mixed identities, who write partly in order to demonstrate – or perhaps to negotiate – their membership of one camp. The sense of awe, playfulness and fun that marked the orientalist narratives has gone; these are often grim narratives that speak of repression and suffering; the moments of pleasure and relaxation only take place against a backdrop of ugly oppression. Lastly, the new authors discuss women's sociability and cultures in a far more detailed, sometimes more sympathetic, manner than the older orientalists.

Compare this collective vision with that provided by our three modern pilgrims to Mecca: Asra Nomani, Qanta Ahmed and Jehan Sadat. None of these three women are blind, uncritical believers; none of them could possibly be termed a fundamentalist. Each of them is passionately concerned about the nature of Islam, and each suggests reforms and improvements. Without doubt, each of them is fully able to discuss Islam from the inside, and each shows an ability to communicate abstract ideas and to engage the reader's attention. But, in the years after 9/11, it has been writers like Nafisi, Moaveni and Mahdavi who have grabbed the Western public's attention and who are – in general – uncritically accepted as the proper sources for an informed knowledge of the nature of Muslim society. The works of the modern pilgrims demand dialogue: they refuse to present the Western readership with what it wants to hear; they demand that their religious principles be accepted as a beginning point of a dialogue; they insist that Muslim criticisms of Western lifestyles and cultures must also be considered. The works of the American-Iranians are considerably less demanding of a Western audience: in their works Muslims are aliens, largely to be considered from outside; frequently their work leaves their readers with the impression that Muslims are either irrational, anti-Western fanatics or virtuous victims, hungry for Western culture.

The argument that I wish to present here is not that *Reading Lolita*, *Lipstick Jihad* and *Passionate Uprisings* are worthless texts, but that they are misunderstood texts. Too often they have been treated as the authentic voice of Iranian women: instead, they represent something much more specific. Taken collectively, they form a type of meditation on identity by a particular strand of American-Iranian exiles. They have some documentary value: certainly, within their pages there are some memorable examples of the daily harassment that women experience in Iran, and some evidence of strategies of resistance. But these works are weaker in contextualising and in analysing these contestations. There can be no doubt that they have proved to be convenient vehicles for American foreign policy: the authors can rightly be criticised for not considering how their works could be distorted.

Four journeys on the road to dialogue

Of our hundred texts, four are consciously designed as dialogues. These were all written within the last decade, and this new presence may point to a recognition of the limitations of the first-person, semi-autobiographical narrative, and a transcendence of the limitations set by the previously used literary forms, namely travel-writing, memoirs and polemics.

Significantly, only two of these dialogue texts can be considered successful. One of the most difficult works to read and evaluate is Laura Blumenfeld's *Revenge: a Story of Hope*. Like Emma Williams's *It's Easier to Reach Heaven than the End of the Street*, this is a work by an author who was tricked by history: Blumenfeld was provoked to write her book after a failed gun attack on her American father, a rabbi, which took place when he visited Jerusalem in 1998.[32] The work takes for granted the validity of the Israeli–Palestinian peace process and is – in a sense – a meditation on how individuals might contribute to it. But after Blumenfeld's completion of her manuscript, the Israeli–Palestinian peace process was in tatters, and 9/11 had occurred. The work ends with a triumphant scene of apparent reconciliation: her father's attacker, having been judged guilty and held in an Israeli jail, has his case reviewed by an Israeli court and Blumenfeld – to her surprise – finds herself supporting him, arguing that the attacker has already suffered enough punishment; her mother even stands up in court to state that she forgives him, and the attacker kisses her mother. These elements form a surprising and touching moment: an apt ending for a work that is structured around an extended series of meetings, conversations and discussions. But this work's story is not as simple as it might seem. No one could doubt the efforts that Blumenfeld has put into her quest, the difficulties that she has experienced and the sincerity with which she writes. Yet, unfortunately, her work seems incomplete. The remarkable scenes of written communication, then direct, face-to-face conversations with her father's attacker are actually constrained by Blumenfeld's commentary: when her attacker puts forward a political justification for his actions, the reader is repeatedly told that this is 'just' political jargon, a sign that he is unrepentant and unwilling to see her father 'as a man'.[33] The possibility that there might be any legitimacy to the many Palestinian criticisms of the Israeli presence is constantly denied. Blumenfeld often seems to be an unresponsive observer of the highly politicised landscape within which her work is situated, making no comment as she travels through a criss-crossing maze of visible and invisible borders. Thus, visiting Ramallah, she comments: 'As we approached the army checkpoint, Jewish apartment blocks gave way to Arab stone houses. Sidewalks disappeared, eaten away by sandy shoulders. Hebrew signs surrendered to Arabic billboards. The land opened up to craggy hills and olive trees.'[34] Where other travellers, such as Anne Brunswic, Susan Nathan and Emma Williams, were shocked by the physical evidence of inequality which they saw etched into the landscape, Blumenfeld sees an unremarkable normality. There is no attempt to consider how this landscape might look to a Palestinian, or to represent the diverse elements which meet in this troubled little land. The dialogue within her work is similarly constrained: while there is an element of real debate between herself, her family, her legally trained acquaintances and an array of Israeli legal, political and moral authorities, Arabs and Muslims are only represented in the most cursory manner. The attacker's Palestinian family are shown to be naive fools, Muslim learned opinion is reduced to a walk-on role by a lecherous 78-year-old Bedouin sheikh (who could have stepped out of *Lawrence of Arabia*) and two conversations with authorities on Islamic law in the city of Qom (in Iran). Why does she go to Iran? Palestinian Muslims are not Shia; the obvious place to go for an authoritative consultation would be the much closer al-Azhar University in Cairo, a world-renown centre of Islamic philosophy and one with close connections to Muslim traditions in Palestine.[35] Blumenfeld's journey to Qom appears to be another reflection of the American obsession with Iran, which miscasts this unusual society as the political and religious centre of the Islamic world.

Perhaps such critical comments suggest impossibly high criteria for reconciliation and dialogue; perhaps one should simply accept that some traumatised people will never be able to contribute fully to such processes; perhaps, in general, these hundred works draw the reader to a pessimistic conclusion.

Similar problems mar the otherwise promising work *Talking about Jane Austen in Baghdad*, which presents the e-mail exchanges between Bee Rowlatt, a British journalist employed by the BBC, and May Witwit, an Arab lecturer in English literature at Baghdad University.[36] Their communication begin almost by chance, which then grows into a cycle of communication which both women obviously appreciate: their growing friendship is a clear and attractive theme within the work. The flaw in their exchanges, to which neither woman refers explicitly, is the power inequality between them. Witwit, in her own words, is living in hell, and will do almost anything to get out; Rowlatt lives in a comfortable London suburb.

Witwit constantly demonstrates her acquired knowledge of English-language culture: she writes, with force and precision, in English; she teaches the novels of Jane Austen; she reads *The Tale of Two Cities* and *Men are from Mars, Women are from Venus*; she refers to her Ph.D. thesis on the theme of love in the poetry of Geoffrey Chaucer; she quotes Shakespeare; she even expresses delight when she learns that they are both Librans. Rowlatt expresses sympathy with Witwit's position in a collapsing Baghdad, but shows almost no interest in Iraqi, Arab or Muslim culture. In their exchanges, one mode of culture had value, while the other seems valueless. As is the case with *Not Without My Daughter*, one could almost ask whether the work was intended as a Swift-ian satire on Western indifference and arrogance. Certainly, if the evidence presented in *Talking about Jane Austen* was used as the basis for the nationality test for those applying for UK citizenship, then very few immigrants would ever be able to enter this green and pleasant land.

Une voilée, l'autre pas (One Veiled Woman, the Other Not) is more promising.[37] This work was produced during the French moral panic concerning the presence of a few hundred veiled schoolgirls in French state schools. It has an unusual, possibly unique, structure: two women, both with some experience in public debate, consider a wide variety of contemporary accounts of veiling which record quite different experiences, mostly from women living in France. Following each example, they debate the issues raised. Mostly, they reach some point of consensus; sometimes their concerns and values are contradictory; occasionally they openly disagree. Unlike the dialogues in *Revenge* and *Reading Jane Austen*, there is equality between the two women: the idea that both have something valid to contribute forms the basis of the work. Obviously, no final answer emerges from this collection of texts: how could it? Compared with the emotional power of *Not Without My Daughter* or the elegant writing of *Reading Lolita in Tehran*, this may well seem a difficult, rather abstract, work. However, if one is searching for an open-minded and genuinely informative account of Muslim women's lives in France, then its strengths are obvious.

Lastly, there is *Crossing Qalandiya: Exchanges across the Israeli/ Palestinian Divide*, by Daniela Norris and Shireen Anabtawi. The two women are members of opposing communities: Norris is a non-practising Jewish Israeli and Anabtawi a practising Muslim and Palestinian Arab. Qalandiya is an important checkpoint run by the Israeli security forces outside the central Palestinian town of Ramallah: it is a dismal place with which most Palestinians are unfortunately familiar. Like *Reading Jane Austen*, *Crossing Qalandiya* presents an exchange of letters between two different women who grow to like each other. They write in the only language they share: English. In *Crossing Qalandiya* there is one constant irony: 'It is so strange that you live less than one hour's drive away. If I were a little braver, I would just get in the car and drive to meet you, but things are not that simple, are they?'[38] While it would be possible for them to visit each other's homes, this does not happen. They first met in Geneva, and then Norris took the initiative of contacting Anabtawi. One reason for doing this may seem surprising: Norris is thirty-six and has lived all her life in Israel, and in that time, she has never once met a Palestinian. Within the pages of the work, quite appropriately, they do not physically meet for a second time. Unlike *Reading Jane Austen*, *Crossing Qalandiya* presumes a basic equality between the two women or, more exactly, an equal moral worth and cultural validity: both show a keen, sympathetic interest in the other's life, culture and attitudes. At the same time, they are also aware of the inequality that lies between them. Anabtawi produces a powerful image of the physical constraints that hinder her life: she dreams of driving a car in fourth gear.[39] In this work, therefore, the issue of 'equality' is approached in a subtle and sensitive manner: the two women accept each other as equals in terms of their worth, but also recognise the inequality in their positions within a hierarchical social structure.

As with *Une voilée, l'autre pas*, there are differences of opinion. They discuss some serious issues: terrorism and other forms of political violence, the permanent Israeli clampdown on Palestinian lives, Islam, the politics of Israeli-Jewish history. Sometimes the exchanges between the two women are quite sharp. Discussing Palestinian political violence, Anabtawi remarks: 'Of course violence is negative – but we did not invent this kind of action. Perhaps we even learnt some of it from you, Israelis . . . ?'[40] But there are also some examples of acts of friendship: they exchange recipes, they discuss the joys and the frustrations of their family lives, they describe celebrations and meals. 'I will send you a CD with some of my favourite songs', remarks Anabtawi at one point, 'I know you won't understand the words, but at least you can listen to the melodies.'[41] Both women record how their exchange has made them rethink the camps to which they belong. Sometimes they show real sensitivity to each other: when Anabtawi describes the sexual conservatism of Palestinian society which makes it difficult for one of her female relatives to travel to Europe alone, rather than launching into the predictable polemic about the ingrained, conservative sexism of Arab society, Norris pauses to consider whether there is anything similar in Israel. She remembers the refuseniks, the Israelis who refuse to carry out military duties: 'In a way, this is not so different from the bad reputation young women in your society risk if they hang out with male friends. There can be finger-pointing and accusation, and even discrimination when they try and get jobs in the future.'[42] This is an important point: Norris does not ignore the sexism that stunts Palestinian women's lives, but she draws back from arguing that Israeli society is fault-less or prejudice-free; she openly recognises the faults and weaknesses in her own society.

As with *Une voilée, l'autre pas*, there's no conclusion to *Crossing Qalandiya*. The two women are left physically separated; the Palestinian–Israeli conflict continues; the contact zone remains a tense, awkward place. But the work achieves something. Two women learn more about each other's lives; to some extent, they learn to see the other from the inside, and the boundaries between 'self' and 'other' grow just a little more porous.

Conclusion

The format discussed above is probably the best vehicle for works that genuinely aim to encourage dialogue. The first-person narrative format has been exhausted: in the new cultural context set by globalisation, it too easily becomes a device to protect the self from apparent threats from outsiders; the weakness of the other contender – the edited collection of interviews – is that they usually leave the reader with a series of disparate snapshots, but nothing more. Once these have been validated as the 'voice of the voiceless', it then becomes almost impossible to criticise them. These new works, explicitly and deliberately constructed as open-ended dialogues, without an obvious centre, without a narrator or interviewer to direct the reader to concentrate on specific themes, predicated on the equal value of the participants, are potentially a valuable contribution to the construction of genuine dialogue between cultures.

Conclusion

'The best part of the story is still to come.'
Scheherazade[1]

The hundred books that have been studied here are all concerned with travel. Their authors do not head in the same direction: they move in uneven spirals, and their words ricochet back and forth over the new, irregularly formed barriers that proliferate in a globalising world. Rather than pointing in any specific direction, these works provide diverse perspectives which illuminate many different problems and obstacles. One possible objection to this book might be that these works are simply too varied to analyse as a single bloc. However, in the past chapters it has been shown that these works do map out some consistent themes that have developed over past decades. Our final impression is that these works suggest a crossroads.

A hundred answers

This work has been based on a sample of a hundred texts. At this point, it is probably worth stressing, once more, some limitations: these hundred works are all produced within a curiously ignored literary sub-sphere that has developed within the cultural marketplace formed by Western capitals. These works clearly do not represent all women's opinions: radical Muslims, advocating a complete rejection of Western values and a 'return' to an imagined seventh-century purity, are not present; nor have women's voices from the Far East (including the world's largest Muslim country, Indonesia) or from central Asia been represented. The frontiers of this literary sub-sphere remain unclear, and readers may well question the inclusion of particular authors and the exclusion of others. I see this study as merely a first, preliminary exploration: more detailed studies may well suggest revisions and corrections.

It is clear that these works, despite their obvious divergences, share common features. A history of their common development is certainly viable: trends and shifts are registered in multiple examples, and patterns of approaches and concerns developing over the decades can be identified. Apart from a few highly unusual exceptions such as Freya Stark, these women are not literally 'explorers' of new territories. The curious and distinctive qualities of their writing lie elsewhere: they travel to 'known' lands, but by writing in a self-consciously feminine fashion – as female authors addressing an assumed female audience – they raise specific questions which previous, largely male, authors have ignored; they illuminate issues in a new manner. These authors show how globalisation is interacting with private lives; how identities are growing at once more complex and richer; how ill-prepared the dominant cultures of Western nations are to meet these challenges. No single political attitude can be read into them: while female identity encourages authors to adopt particular literary forms, it does not lead to any specific political commitment. These hundred works' literary and political qualities are open to debate: alongside assured and proficient writers such as Azar Nafisi, there are many examples of amateurs and beginners. Admirable qualities can be found in most of these works: they present interesting details of memorable personal experiences; they document people who are normally un-documented; they speculate about important issues that will concern larger and larger numbers in an increasingly globalised world. The extent to which they contribute to a global process of dialogue can be questioned: in general, these books often seem to aim to interrogate other cultures without constructing dialogue. Their authors are sometimes motivated more by their desire to demonstrate their membership of a specific camp, rather than a wish to open dialogue with another culture or society.

At the crossroads

Standing at the crossroads formed by the meeting of these diverse cultures are three responses. Some authors seem content to note the variety of routes, and to indicate possible directions and implications. Other works are marked with a far greater sense of urgency: they argue that we must take a particular route, and warn of the dangers that will follow if we head the wrong way. A third response is a simple statement of doubt, a sense of bewilderment at the choices that face the world. This last attitude is reminiscent of the categories established by Roland Robertson who, twenty years ago, identified the current phase of globalisation as 'the phase of uncertainty'.[2] The development of the hundred works that we have consulted seems to illustrate this attitude: we move from the confident certainties of the older orientalists to the more agonised efforts by migrant Muslims to find their place in the West, and finally to the corresponding panic by Western polemicists concerning the shape and identity of their society. Here, our metaphor of 'the crossroads' begins to break down. Mary Pratt's phrase may well be more accurate: in her study of eighteenth-century explorers and travel writers she identified 'contact zones' or 'social spaces where disparate cultures meet, clash, and grapple with each other, often in highly asymmetrical relations of domination and subordination'.[3] The final picture from these hundred works is that the 'contact zone' has now reached almost all localities: it is no longer restricted to particular frontier areas. The result has not been a free-floating, equal exchange of ideas or the fruitful development of open-minded cultures that synthesise and fuse diverse elements, or even the streamlining of a colourful diversity into a grey global uniformity. Instead, globalisation throws together once distant cultures into unexpectedly intimate contacts in a manner that many find unexpected and alarming. For many of the most modern travellers, there is now no familiar home to which they can return; their 'home' has been apparently transformed by the presence of the other, and their reaction is usually a pained assertion of embattled identities, fighting to ward off apparent threats.

In the introduction to this work I briefly referred to the music of Anouar Brahem, whose work embodies an easy, assured, non-threatening form of cultural fusion. It is now clear that the hundred works surveyed in this book cannot be seen as literary equivalents of Brahem's work. More frequently, our authors prefer to choose camps rather than to fuse cultures. The older generation of the orientalists were certainly capable of adopting a positive, welcoming attitude to other cultures, although they were less competent in understanding and contextualising them. More modern writers such as Djavann, Phillips, Falluci and Hirsi Ali urgently wish to identify an enemy, to repulse an influence, to strengthen defences and – above all – to belong to a camp. Very few of our hundred authors make any claim to synthesise cultures and influences: instead, the more itinerant writers are actually more likely to state that they do not feel at home anywhere. Travelling alone in a globalised world is, for them, usually a frightening and unwelcome experience. In a more limited sense, however, these works suggest a certain, qualified, homogenisation of disparate elements. In a subterranean, quiet manner, these female authors have developed semi-autobiographical, first-person narratives into a form that illuminates certain key issues that concern the contemporary world; the family resemblances between these works, some accidental, some delib-erate, point to a growing sense of familiarity with certain issues; the ideas and reflections that they produce have circulated among a surprisingly wide Western readership. The evidence of their texts suggests, in general, that there are major obstacles to processes such as fusion, hybridity and dialogue. Globalisation certainly means that contact zones are now virtu-ally omnipresent, but the form that contacts normally take has not grown noticeably more sophisticated since the days of Wharton's dash through

Morocco in 1917. Iranian authorities still regularly denounce 'Westoxicification', while serious political commentators in the West still question whether veiled women can ever become full citizens, preferring the simpler thesis of the 'Clash of civilizations': that these representatives of other cultures cannot be accommodated within the political structures of Western nations.

Prominent, and even popular, examples of cross-cultural contacts do exist in the contemporary world, but they rarely take the form of serious dialogue. Adel Iskandar's spirited essay on Shakira Mebarak Ripoll (better known simply as 'Shakira') points out how an Arab, even a Muslim, identity can be successfully deployed within a Western-orientated commercial strategy, expressed through some vigorous examples of belly-dancing, and then quietly dropped as Shakira dyes her hair blonde and twists round into a new mode.[4] Djavann and Hirsi Ali have both exploited the status of 'ex-Muslim' in a similar way: when presented in the form of a repetitive litany of the evils and abuses to be found in the Muslim worlds, a representation of Muslim cultures is acceptable, almost comforting, to a Western readership.[5] After considering such examples, it would then be possible to argue that the Muslim contribution to this newly developed literary subsphere is simply the equivalent of a surrender to the norms and cultures of the West, in which foreign terms have been translated into a supine, non-threatening form, and their respective authors are effectively integrated as collaborators with the dominant cultural forces. Certainly, it is important to note how the least challenging works are – in general – the most successful: the comfort that Djavann brings to a nostalgic French identity and Nafisi to a worried American public is obvious. However, the Muslim and ex-Muslim contributions to this literary sub-zone cannot be reduced to a simple form of collaboration. As has been shown, the authors themselves show an increasing political sophistication, and some explicitly construct their works as criticisms of Western prejudices and misconceptions. They raise serious questions concerning racism, citizenship and identity; on occasion, they demand that their readers begin to think critically about their own cultures. Obviously, readers' responses to this wide variety of different voices are unclear.

There is a similar ambiguity concerning these authors' female identity. The development of this female-orientated literary zone is certainly a welcome by-product of recent debates. But is this just a form of cover? Does it allow the author to present highly ideological themes in a manner that readers will read as non-threatening and politically neutral? Or is there a type of proto-feminist assertion in these works? By questioning the practices and the realities of globalisation from a self-consciously female viewpoint, are they inevitably, despite their instincts and aims, led to question entrenched power structures? My answer to such questions can only be tentative: there are a great variety of different voices in these works. Alongside the dominant tone of conformism and conservatism, some new, more critical tendencies seem to be emerging.

To some extent, the debates conducted in these books run parallel to the recent debates concerning multiculturalism. Some caution is needed when approaching this topic: while a tremendous amount of time has been spent differentiating between – for example – the self-consciously 'integrationist' and 'republican' policies of France and the allegedly 'multicultural' policies of the UK, it has to be acknowledged that the results of these apparently quite different forms often seem remarkably similar: a mishmash of open hostility, sullen indifference and misplaced benevolence, within which a rising tide of xenophobic aggression identifies specific targets such as veiled women as symbols of unacceptably alien cultures. Much of the rather abstract, theoretical debate on the implications of such models seems to have little bearing on the practices of daily life: thus, for example, the criticisms that multiculturalism might lead to an uncritical acceptance of abuses of human rights in the name of a refusal to criticise others, simply do not make sense.[6] There have clearly been problems with the manner in which specific multicultural policies have been interpreted: in particular, the way that multiculturalism has been frequently reduced in the UK to a multi-faith focus, ignoring the diversity and the complex stresses within minority communities.[7] Despite my use of the term 'Muslim' in the title of this work, I am not convinced that such religious terms provide the best conceptual vocabulary for exploring communities and cultures in a globalised world. Instead, a multifaceted and constantly evolving approach is probably needed. The independent French radical movement, the Parti des Indigènes de la République (the party of the natives of the republic), which combines a clear sympathy for Muslim cultures, a keen awareness of social equality, a perceptive, sometimes astringent, critique of dominant cultural norms and a bold assertion of political autonomy, may well be the best model for future political movements addressing these issues.[8]

Arriving at a final conclusion on the value of multiculturalism, which may well have a different meaning in different social and national contexts, is therefore difficult: arguably, given that the preservation of apparently pure national cultures is well-nigh impossible within a context created by globalisation, something like multiculturalism may well be a useful instrument for accommodating different cultures within the same locality.[9] Certainly, the incidents recorded in many of the memoirs by migrant Muslim women demonstrate the sheer weight of the obstacles which block the progress of newcomers to many Western societies, often despite official

policies which suggest a stance of acceptance and welcome. If multiculturalism leads to a more positive approach, within which immigrants' and
minorities' specific needs and aspirations are identified, and their voices
are listened to, then it should be welcomed.

Goodbye to orientalism

There are some obvious flaws to many of our hundred works. Sometimes
these have been created by external, political factors. The obsession with
Iran, which is placed as the centre of the Islamic world, has clearly stimulated the production of some of these books, and the heavy weight of these
political concerns have distorted the more delicate narrative of personal
development and identity which should have been at the centre of these
works. The community of Iranian-Americans has certainly produced some
talented writers, but few bridge-builders. If we are searching for interlocu-
tors, then Lebanese writers may well be in a better position to claim special
advantages: belonging to a society in which there is an ever-increasing
number of recognised religious-ethnic-political communities, they are
familiar with some of the basic issues of cross-cultural dialogues, they are
often fluent in several languages, they have a rich, rounded picture of the
strengths and weaknesses of Muslim cultures and – if nothing else – they
have learnt the dreadful lesson of the years of conflict, which shows what
can happen when all dialogue fails.

The most significant flaw, however, is the reliance on variants of nineteenth-century autobiographical forms. The format of the single author
going out to discover the unexplored land no longer makes any sense; its
use as a means to debate identity and culture usually fails, as the exterior,
alien and foreign easily become transformed into unwelcome threats. The
single author can no longer function as the unchallenged and legitimate
representative of a single culture, for the cultures of globalisation have
produced richer, more complex identities, in which all already echo with
the sounds of the others. Those who seek to deny this point rapidly adopt a
defensive, almost paranoid tone, ransacking the box of historical clichés
for images of pure, integral identities, which are then contrasted with the
apparent impurity of globalised cultures. The obvious solution to this
question of literary narrative is to construct works as dialogues with the
other: a prospect which many of our authors clearly view with fear and
disgust. A key change would be a preliminary change in attitude: to accept
the limits of one's knowledge, to acknowledge one's own ignorance,
preconceptions and confusion – a stance that would draw authors far away
from the confidence of the older orientalists.

These relatively simple devices, if taken up sincerely, in this new context of cultural globalisation, might finally provide an answer to Said's question of how to construct libertarian, non-repressive and non-manipulative perspective. Then, at last, we would be able to place orientalism where it belongs: in the history books.

Notes

Notes to Introduction

[1] Information in this paragraph is taken from Elizabeth Kinder, 'A complex life', *FolkRoots* 334 (April 2011), 29–31, and Carlos Galilea, 'Voces femeninas del Magreb', *El País*, 11 June 2011, 20–1.

[2] W. T. J. Mitchell, 'Translator translated (interview with cultural theorist Homi Bhabha)', *prelectur.stanford.edu/lecturers/bhabha/interview.html*, accessed 18 June 2007; originally published in *Artforum*, 33, 7 (1995), 80–4. See also Jonathan Rutherford, 'The Third Space: interview with Homi Bhabha', in Jonathan Rutherford (ed.), *Identity: Community, Culture, Difference* (London: Lawrence and Wishart, 1990), pp. 207–21, and Homi K. Bhabha, *The Location of Culture* (London: Routledge, 1994), p. 37.

[3] Billie Melman, *Women's Orients: English Women and the Middle East, 1718–1918* (2nd edn; Houndsmill: MacMillan, 1995), p. 2.

[4] Ibid., p. 12.

[5] Ibid., pp. 60–2.

[6] See, for example, his remarks in *Orientalism* (Harmondsworth: Penguin, 1978), pp. 26, 285–90.

[7] Gayatri Chakravorty Spivak, 'Can the subaltern speak?', in Bill Ashcroft, Gareth Griffiths and Helen Tiffin (eds), *The Post-colonial Studies Reader* (2nd edn; London and New York: Routledge, 2006), pp. 28–37.

[8] Said, *Orientalism*, p. 24.

[9] Azar Nafisi, *Reading Lolita in Tehran: a Memoir in Books* (New York: Random House, 2003); Bee Rowlatt and May Witwit, *Talking about Jane Austen in Baghdad* (London: Penguin Books, 2010); Haddad, Joumana, *I Killed Scheherazade: Confessions of an Angry Arab Woman* (London: Saqi Books, 2010).

[10] Carol L. Anway, *Daughters of Another Path: Experiences of American Women Choosing Islam* (Lee's Summit, Mo.: Yawna Publications, 1996), p. 5.

[11] G. Willow Wilson, *The Butterfly Mosque: a Young Woman's Journey to Love and Islam* (London: Atlantic Books, 2010), p. 43.

[12] Raymonda Hawa Tawil, *My Home, My Prison* (New York: Holt, Rinehart and Winston, 1979); Haleh Esfandiari, *My Prison, My Home: One Woman's Story of Captivity in Iran* (London: Harper Collins, 2010).

[13] Edith Wharton, *In Morocco* (1920; London: I. B. Tauris, 2006); Hala Jaber, *The Flying Carpet to Baghdad: One Woman's Fight for Two Orphans of War* (London: Pan, 2010).

[14] Freya Stark, *A Winter in Arabia* (1940; London: Arrow Books, 1991), p. 29.

Notes to Chapter 1

[1] Bee Rowlatt and May Witwit, *Talking about Jane Austen in Baghdad* (London: Penguin Books, 2010), p. vii.

2 Sattareh Farman Farmaian, *Daughter of Persia: a Woman's Journey from her Father's Harem through the Islamic Revolution* (London: Corgi, 1992); Deborah Kanafani, *Unveiled: How an American Woman Found Her Way through Politics, Love and Obedience in the Middle East* (New York: Free Press, 2008).

3 Susan Nathan, *The Other Side of Israel: My Journey Across the Jewish-Arab Divide* (New York: Doubleday, 2005), p. 15.

4 Shirin Ebadi with Azadeh Moaveni, *Iran Awakening: From Prison to Peace Prize: One Woman's Struggle at the Crossroads of History* (London: Rider, 2006).

5 Nawal El Saadawi, *The Hidden Face of Eve: Women in the Arab World*, trans. Dr Sherif Hetata (London: Zed Books, 1980).

6 Sadek Hajji and Stéphanie Marteau, *Voyage dans la France musulmane* (Paris: Plon, 2005).

7 Ruth Frances Woodsmall, *Women and the New East* (Washington: The Middle East Institute, 1960); Kathleen M. Kenyon, *Archaeology in the Holy Land* (1960; London: Ernest Benn, 1979).

8 Pauline Cutting, *Children of the Siege* (London: Heinemann, 1988).

9 Chahdortt Djavann, *Bas les voiles!* (Paris: Gallimard, 2003).

10 Melanie Phillips, *Londonistan: How Britain is Creating a Terror State Within* (London: Gibson Square, 2006).

11 Ayaan Hirsi Ali, *The Caged Virgin: A Muslim Woman's Cry for Reason* (London: Simon and Schuster, 2006), p. 81.

12 For example, Dounia Bouzar and Saïda Kada, *L'une voilée, l'autre pas: le témoignage de deux musulmanes françaises* (Paris: Albin Michel, 2003); Ismahane Chouder, Malika Latrèche and Pierre Tevanian (eds), *Les filles voilées parlent* (Floch: La Fabrique, 2008); Carla Fibla García-Sala and Fadi N. Skaik, *Resistiendo en Gaza: Historias palestinas* (Barcelona: Península, 2010); Anne Nivat, *Lendemains de guerre en Afghanistan et en Irak* (Paris: Athème Fayard, 2004).

13 Nivat, *Lendemains*, p. 16.

14 Dina Matar, *What It Means to be Palestinian: Stories of Palestinian Peoplehood* (London: I. B. Tauris, 2011), p. xi.

15 Pardis Mahdavi, *Passionate Uprisings: Iran's Sexual Revolution* (Stanford, Calif.: Stanford University Press, 2009).

16 Zlata Filipović, *Zlata's Diary*, trans. Christina Pribichevicj-Zorić (London: Viking, 1994).

17 Laura Blumenfeld, *Revenge: a Story of Hope* (London: Picador, 2002).

18 Shappi Khorsandi, *A Beginner's Guide to Acting English* (n.p.: Ebury Press, 2009).

19 Zaiba Malik, *We are a Muslim, Please* (London: Windmill Books, 2011); Shelina Zahra Janmohamed, *Love in a Headscarf: Muslim Woman Seeks the One* (London: Aurum, 2009).

20 Quotation from the back cover of Salwa Al Neimi, *La preuve par le miel*, trans. Oscar Heliani (Paris: Robert Laffont, 2008). See also Nedjma, *L'Amande, récit intime* (Paris: Plon, 2004).

21 Waris Dirie and Cathleen Miller, *Desert Flower: the Extraordinary Life of a Desert Nomad* (London: Virago, 1998).

22 Jehan Sadat, *A Woman of Egypt* (London: Bloomsbury, 1987).

23 Daniela Norris and Shireen Anabtawi, *Crossing Qalandiya: Exchanges across the Israeli/Palestinian Divide* (London: Reportage, 2010).

24 Joumana Haddad, *I Killed Scheherazade: Confessions of an Angry Arab Woman* (London: Saqi Books, 2010).

25 Mary Louise Pratt, *Imperial Eyes: Travel Writing and Transculturation* (London and New York: Routledge, 1992), p. 78.
26 Vita Sackville-West, *Passenger to Teheran* (1926; London: Tauris Parke, 2007), p. 31.
27 On the politics of blogging in a Muslim context, see the perceptive work by Annabelle Sreberny and Gholan Khiabany, *Blogistan: the Internet and Politics in Iran* (London: I. B. Tauris, 2010).
28 Carol L. Anway, *Daughters of Another Path: Experiences of American Women Choosing Islam* (Lee's Summit, Mo.: Yawna Publications, 1996), pp. 45–6.
29 Na'ima B. Roberts, *From my Sisters' Lips: a Unique Celebration of Muslim Womanhood* (London: Bantam Books, 2005), p. 25.
30 Betty Mahmoody with William Hoffer, *Not Without My Daughter* (London: Corgi Books, 1988), p. 149.
31 Dirie and Miller, *Desert Flower*; Wassyla Tamzali, *Une femme en colère: lettre d'Alger aux Européens désabusés* (Paris: Gallimard, 2009); Carmen Bin Ladin, *The Veiled Kingdom* (London: Virago, 2004), p. 1; El-Hanan Cheikh, *Toute une histoire*, trans. Stéphanie Dujois (Paris: Actes Sud, 2010); Latifa, with Chékéha Hachemi, *My Forbidden Face: Growing Up under the Taliban: a Young Woman's Story*, trans. Lisa Appignanesi (London: Virago, 2002), unpaginated introduction; Ruth Frances Woodsmall, *Women and the New East* (Washington: The Middle East Institute, 1960), p. x.
32 Tehmina Durrani, *My Feudal Lord* (Lahore: self-published, 1991), p. i.
33 Qanta A. Ahmed, MD, *In the Land of Invisible Women: a Female Doctor's Journey in the Saudi Kingdom* (Naperville, Ill.: Sourcebooks, 2008); Rania al-Baz, *Défigurée: quand un crime passionnel devient affaire d'Etat* (Paris: Michel Lafon, 2005); Fadia Basrawi, *Brownies and Kalashnikovs: a Saudi Woman's Memoir of American Arabia and Wartime Beirut* (Reading: South Street Press, 2009); Chouder, Latrèche and Tevanian (eds), *Les filles voilées parlent*; Veronica Doubleday, *Three Women of Herat* (London: Jonathan Cape, 1988).
34 Pamela Bright, *A Poor Man's Riches* (Liverpool: MacGibbon and Kee, 1966); Suzy Wighton, *One Day at a Time: Diaries from a Palestinian Camp* (London: Hutchinson, 1990); Deborah Rodriguez, *The Kabul Beauty School: the Art of Friendship and Freedom* (London: Hodder & Stoughton, 2008); Hala Jaber, *The Flying Carpet to Baghdad: One Woman's Fight for Two Orphans of War* (London: Pan, 2010).
35 Virginia Woolf, *Collected Essays*, vol. II (London: Hogarth Press, 1966), p. 144.
36 Colette Modiano, *Turkish Coffee and the Fertile Crescent: Wanderings through the Lebanon, Mesopotamia, Israel, Jordan and Syria* (London: Michael Joseph, 1974), p. 11.
37 Dervla Murphy, *Tales from Two Cities: Travel of Another Sort* (London: John Murray, 1987).
38 Asra Q. Nomani, *Standing Alone in Mecca: an American Woman's Struggle for the Soul of Islam* (San Francisco: HarperSanFrancisco, 2005).
39 Oriana Fallaci, *The Rage and the Pride* (New York: Rizzoli, 2001); Mai Ghoussoub, *Selected Writings*, ed. Rebecca O'Connor (London: Saqi, 2008), p. 22. The second example refers explicitly to a specific essay concerning the atrocities at Abu Ghraib prison.
40 Mahmoody, *Not Without My Daughter*, p. 223.
41 Fedwa Malti-Douglas, *Medicines of the Soul: Female Bodies and Sacred Geographies in a Transnational Islam* (Berkeley: University of California Press, 2001), p. xvii.

42 Marguerite van Geldermalsen, *Married to a Bedouin* (London: Virago, 2006).

43 Fadia Faqir, 'Cultural illiteracy', *The Author* (spring 2011), 18–19. I would like to thank my colleague, Professor Diana Wallace, for drawing this text to my attention.

44 See, for example, Siobhan Lambert-Hurley, 'Afterword: Muslim women write their journeys abroad' in her edition of *A Princess's Pilgrimage: Nawab Sikander Begum's 'A Pilgrimage to Mecca'* (Mansfield: Kube, 2007), pp. 155–72; Rozina Visram, *Asians in Britain: 400 Years of History* (London: Pluto Press, 2002), includes a section on Indian writing on Britain: see pp. 105–22.

45 See the pertinent remarks in Catarina Kinnvall and Paul Nesbitt-Larking, *The Political Psychology of Globalization: Muslims in the West* (Oxford: Oxford University Press, 2011), p. 43.

46 On the stultification of contemporary Arab culture, see Ibrahim M. Abu-Rabi', *Contemporary Arab Thought: Studies in Post-1967 Arab Intellectual History* (London: Pluto, 2004), particularly pp. 126–49.

47 *Not Without My Daughter*, pp. 7 and 47.

48 Edith Wharton, *In Morocco* (1920; London: I. B. Tauris, 2006), pp. 12 and 10.

49 Sackville-West, *Passenger*, p. 31.

50 Rona Randall, *Jordan and the Holy Land* (London: Frederick Muller, 1968), p. 5.

51 Dervla Murphy, *Full Tilt: Ireland to India with a Bicycle* (London: Eland, 1965), pp. 70 and 86.

52 Odette du Puigaudeau, *Tagent: Au coeur du pays maure, 1936–1938* (n.p.: Phébus, 1993), p. 90.

53 Fallaci, *Rage and Pride*, pp. 93 and 89.

54 Phillips, *Londonistan*, pp. 31–2.

55 Kathleen Paul, 'Communities of Britishness: migration in the last gasp of empire', in Stuart Ward (ed.), *British Culture and the End of Empire* (Manchester: Manchester University Press, 2001), pp. 180–99.

56 On this point, see Margaret A. Majumdar, *Postcoloniality: the French Dimension* (New York: Berghahn Books, 2007).

57 Thomas Carlyle, *Chartism* (London: James Fraser, 1840), p. 5.

58 Edward Said, *Orientalism* (Harmondsworth: Penguin, 1978); Billie Melman, *Women's Orients: English Women and the Middle East, 1718–1918* (2nd edn; Houndsmill: MacMillan, 1995).

59 One particularly useful contribution to this process was Reina Lewis, *Gendering Orientalism: Race and Femininity and Representation* (London: Routledge, 1996).

60 Sara Mills, *Discourses of Difference: an Analysis of Women's Travel Writing and Colonialism* (London: Routledge, 1991).

61 Also useful in a more indirect manner was Pratt, *Imperial Eyes*.

62 *http://www.whslibrary.com/firstladyrecommends.htm*, accessed 18 August 2009.

63 Mills, *Discourses*, p. 32.

64 However, Pratt does consider Creole responses to colonial travel writing.

65 Farzaneh Milani, 'On women's captivity in the Islamic world', *Merip*, 246 (2008), *http://www.merip.org/mer/mer246*, accessed 4 June 2008.

66 For example, Hamid Dabashi, 'Native informers and the American empire', *El-Ahram Weekly Online*, 1 June 2006, *http://weekly.ahram.org.eg/2006/797/special.htm*, accessed 2 March 2011. 'Vindication for bookseller of Kabul as court orders author to pay damages', *Irish Times*, 29 July 2010, *http://www.irishtimes.com/newspaper/world/2010/0729/1224275692778.html*,

accessed 2 September 2010; Adel Iskandar, '"Whenever, Wherever!" The discourse of Orientalist transnationalism in the construction of Shakira', *Ambassadors*, 6, 2 (2003), available at *http://ambassadors.net.archives/issue14/selected_studies4.htm*, accessed 15 November 2010.

[67] Charles Taylor, 'The politics of recognition', in Amy Gutmann (ed.), *Multiculturalism: Examining the Politics of Recognition* (Princeton: Princeton University Press, 1994), pp. 25–73.

[68] Patrick West, *The Poverty of Multiculturalism* (London: Civitas, 2005), and Rumy Hasan, *Multiculturalism: Some Inconvenient Truths* (London: Politico's, 2010).

[69] Peter Kivisto, *Multiculturalism in a Global Society* (Oxford: Blackwell, 2002); Will Kymlicka, *Multicultural Odysseys: Navigating the New International Politics of Diversity* (Oxford: Oxford University Press, 2007); Emma Tarlo, *Visibly Muslim: Fashion, Politics, Faith* (Oxford: Berg, 2010).

Notes to Chapter 2

[1] Daniela Norris and Shireen Anabtawi, *Crossing Qalandiya: Exchanges across the Israeli/Palestinian Divide* (London: Reportage, 2010), p. 138.

[2] The same dilemma is recounted in Gelareh Asayeh, 'I grew up thinking I was white', in Lila Azam Zanganeh (ed.), *My Sister, Guard Your Veil; My Brother, Guard Your Eyes: Uncensored Iranian Voices* (Boston, Mass.: Beacon Press, 2006), pp. 12–19. For a thoughtful consideration of how migration can change ethnic identities, see R. Radhakrishnan, 'Ethnicity in an age of diaspora', in Jana Evans Braziel and Anita Mannur (eds), *Theorizing Diaspora: a Reader* (Oxford: Blackwell, 2003), pp. 119–31.

[3] Annemarie Schwarzenbach, *La mort en Perse*, trans. Dominique Laure Miermont (1935; Paris: Editions Payot & Rivages, 2001), p. 105.

[4] Ella K. Maillart, *The Cruel Way* (1947; London: Virago Press, 1986); Vita Sackville-West, *Passenger to Teheran* (1926; London: Tauris Parke, 2007).

[5] Sackville-West, *Passenger to Teheran*, p. 31

[6] Azar Nafisi, *Reading Lolita in Tehran: a Memoir in Books* (New York: Random House, 2003).

[7] Lady Evelyn Cobbold, *Pilgrimage to Mecca* (1934; London: Arabian Publishing, 2009); Na'ima B. Roberts, *From My Sisters' Lips: a Unique Celebration of Muslim Womanhood* (London: Bantam Books, 2005) .

[8] Anne Brunswic, *Bienvenue en Palestine: Chroniques d'une saison à Ramallah* (new edn; Arles: Actes Sud, 2004).

[9] Cobbold, *Pilgrimage to Mecca*, p. 117.

[10] Freya Stark, *A Winter in Arabia* (1940; London: Arrow Books, 1991), p. 218.

[11] Maillart, *The Cruel Way*, p. 37.

[12] Ibid., pp. 37 and 90–1.

[13] Lesley Hamilton, *Where the Mountains Roar: in Search of the Sinai Desert* (London: Victor Gollancz, 1980), p. 40. Emphasis in the original.

[14] Dervla Murphy, *Full Tilt: Ireland to India with a Bicycle* (London: Eland, 1965), p. 55

[15] On the politics of tourism and travel, see Hsu-Ming Teo, 'Wandering in the wake of empire: British travel and tourism in the post-imperial world', in Stuart Ward (ed.), *British Culture and the End of Empire* (Manchester: Manchester University Press, 2001), pp. 163–79.

[16] Jehan Sadat, *A Woman of Egypt* (London: Bloomsbury, 1987); Haleh Esfandiari,

My Prison, My Home: One Woman's Story of Captivity in Iran (London: Harper Collins, 2010).

17 Nojoud Ali with Delphine Minoui, *Moi Nojoud, 10 ans, divorcée* (Paris: France Loisirs, 2009), p. 17.

18 Zoë Ferraris, *City of Veils* (London: Little, Brown, 2010), p. 51. Emphasis in the original.

19 Latifa, with Chékéha Hachemi, *My Forbidden Face: Growing Up under the Taliban: a Young Woman's Story*, trans. Lisa Appignanesi (London: Virago, 2002), p. 158.

20 Bee Rowlatt and May Witwit, *Talking about Jane Austen in Baghdad* (London: Penguin Books, 2010).

21 Christina Lamb, *The Sewing Circles of Herat: My Afghan Years* (London: HarperCollins, 2002), p. 49.

22 Hamilton, *Where the Mountains Roar*, pp. 4–21.

23 Adina Hoffman, *House of Windows: Portraits from a Jerusalem Neighborhood* (London: Arcadia Books, 2001), p. 144.

24 Shelina Zahra Janmohamed, *Love in a Headscarf: Muslim Woman Seeks the One* (London: Aurum, 2009), p. 193.

25 Sadat, *A Woman of Egypt*, p. 5.

26 Colette Modiano, *Turkish Coffee and the Fertile Crescent: Wanderings through the Lebanon, Mesopotamia, Israel, Jordan and Syria* (London: Michael Joseph, 1974), p. 56.

27 Murphy, *Full Tilt*, p. 60.

28 Nafisi, *Reading Lolita in Tehran*, p. 19.

29 Nawal El Saadawi, *The Hidden Face of Eve: Women in the Arab World*, trans. Dr Sherif Hetata (London: Zed Books, 1980), p. 133.

30 Joumana Haddad, *I Killed Scheherazade: Confessions of an Angry Arab Woman* (London: Saqi Books, 2010), pp. 146–7.

31 Stella Rimington, *Open Secret: the Autobiography of the Former Director-General of MI5* (London: Hutchinson, 2001), p. 75.

32 Juliette de Baïracli Levy, *Summer in Galilee* (London: Faber and Faber, 1959), p. 11.

33 Hamilton, *Where the Mountains Roar*, p. xi.

34 Murphy, *Full Tilt*, p. ix.

35 Maillart, *The Cruel Way*, pp. 2–4.

36 Ibid., p. 10.

37 Veronica Doubleday, *Three Women of Herat* (London: Jonathan Cape, 1988), p. 3.

38 Hala Jaber, *The Flying Carpet to Baghdad: One Woman's Fight for Two Orphans of War* (London: Pan, 2010), p. 13.

39 Elizabeth Hamilton, *Put Off Thy Shoes: a Journey to Israel and Jordan* (London: Andre Deutsch, 1957), p. 13.

40 Rona Randall, *Jordan and the Holy Land* (London: Frederick Muller, 1968), p. 6.

41 Melanie Phillips, *Londonistan: How Britain is Creating a Terror State Within* (London: Gibson Square, 2006), p. 71.

42 Rowlatt and Witwit, *Talking about Jane Austen in Baghdad*, p. 109.

43 Ayaan Hirsi Ali, *The Caged Virgin: a Muslim Woman's Cry for Reason* (London: Simon and Schuster, 2006), p. xvi.

44 Waris Dirie and Cathleen Miller, *Desert Flower: the Extraordinary Life of a Desert Nomad* (London: Virago, 1998), p. 85.

45   See Jon Beverley, 'The margin at the centre', in S. Smith and J. Watson (eds), *Decolonizing the Subject* (Minneapolis: University of Minnesota Press, 1992), pp. 91–114.

46   Suzy Wighton, *One Day at a Time: Diaries from a Palestinian Camp* (London: Hutchinson, 1990), p. ix.

47   Anne Nivat, *Lendemains de guerre en Afghanistan et en Irak* (Paris: Athème Fayard, 2004), p. 16.

48   Jaber, *Flying Carpet*, p. 6.

49   Norma Khouri, *Forbidden Love: Love and Betrayal in Modern-day Jordan* (London: Doubleday, 2003), p. 4.

50   Rowlatt and Witwit, *Talking about Jane Austen*, p. vii.

51   Pauline Cutting, *Children of the Siege* (London: Heinemann, 1988), p. 161; Emma Williams, *It's Easier to Reach Heaven than the End of the Street: a Jerusalem Memoir* (London: Bloomsbury, 2006), p. 21.

52   Haddad, *Scheherazade*, p. 25. On this point, see the useful review of Spanish press coverage of Muslim women in Gema Martín-Muñoz, 'Islam's women under Western eyes' (2 October 2002), *http://www.opendemocracy.net/faith-europe_islam/article_498.jsp*, accessed 13 March 2006.

53   Sayeeda Warsi, 'The 2011 University of Leicester Sir Sigmund Sternberg Lecture', 20 January 2011, *http://www.sayeedawarsi.com/2011/01/university-of-leicester-sir-sigmund-sternberg-lecture/*, accessed 23 January 2011.

54   Janmohamed, *Love in a Headscarf*, p. xiii.

55   Frantz Fanon, *Peau noire, masques blancs* (1952 ; Paris: Seuil, 1975), p. 107.

56   Dounia Bouzar and Saïda Kada, *L'une voilée, l'autre pas: le témoignage de deux musulmanes françaises* (Paris: Albin Michel, 2003), p. 13.

57   Ismahane Chouder, Malika Latrèche and Pierre Tevanian (eds), *Les filles voilées parlent* (Floch: La Fabrique, 2008), p. 8.

58   Christelle Hamel and Christine Delphy, 'On vous a tant aimé.e.s! Entretien avec Houria Boutelja', *Nouvelles Questions Féministes*, 25, 1 (2006), 122–35.

59   Carol L. Anway, *Daughters of Another Path: Experiences of American Women Choosing Islam* (Lee's Summit, Mo.: Yawna Publications, 1996), p. 2.

60   Hélé Béji, *Islam Pride: Derrière le voile* (Paris: Gallimard, 2011).

61   Oriana Fallaci, *The Rage and the Pride* (New York: Rizzoli, 2001), pp. 17–20.

62   Stark, *A Winter in Arabia*, p. 241.

63   Murphy, *Full Tilt*, pp. 9 and 94.

64   Betty Mahmoody with William Hoffer, *Not Without My Daughter* (London: Corgi Books, 1988); Esfandiari, *My Prison, My Home*; Laura Blumenfeld, *Revenge: a Story of Hope* (London: Picador, 2002).

65   Fadia Basrawi, *Brownies and Kalashnikovs: a Saudi Woman's Memoir of American Arabia and Wartime Beirut* (Reading: South Street Press, 2009), p. 13; Ghada Karmi, *In Search of Fatima: a Palestinian Story* (London: Verso, 2002), p. 190; Shappi Khorsandi, *A Beginner's Guide to Acting English* (n.p.: Ebury Press, 2009), p. 107; Afschineh Latifi with Pablo F. Fenjives, *Even After All This Time: a Story of Love, Revolution, and Leaving Iran* (London: Fusion, 2005), p. 133.

66   Rania al-Baz, *Défigurée: quand un crime passionnel devient affaire d'Etat* (Paris: Michel Lafont, 2005).

67   Zlata Filipović, *Zlata's Diary*, trans. Christina Pribichevicj-Zorić (London: Viking, 1994), pp. 56, 78 and 114.

68   Rowlatt and Witwit, *Talking About Jane Austen*, p. 60.

69   Malika Oufkir with Michele Fitoussi, *La Prisonnière*, trans. Ros Schwartz (London: Doubleday, 2000).

70 Shirin Ebadi with Azadeh Moaveni, *Iran Awakening: From Prison to Peace Prize: One Woman's Struggle at the Crossroads of History* (London: Rider, 2006).
71 Marguerite van Geldermalsen, *Married to a Bedouin* (London: Virago, 2006).
72 Zaiba Malik, *We are a Muslim, Please* (London: Windmill Books, 2011).
73 Sattareh Farman Farmaian, *Daughter of Persia: a Woman's Journey from her Father's Harem through the Islamic Revolution* (London: Corgi, 1992); Fatéma Hal, *Fille des frontières: récit* (Paris: Philippe Rey, 2011).
74 Chahdortt Djavann, *Comment peut-on être français* (Paris: Flammarion, 2006).
75 Basrawi, *Brownies and Kalashnikovs*, p. 25
76 Malik, *We are a Muslim, Please*, p. 134.
77 Ibid., p. 133.
78 Janmohamed, *Love in a Headscarf*, pp. 190–1.
79 Azadeh Moaveni, *Lipstick Jihad: a Memoir of Growing Up Iranian in America and American in Iran* (New York: Public Affairs, 2005), pp. 26 and 28.
80 Karmi, *In Search of Fatima*, p. 247.
81 Khorsandi, *A Beginner's Guide to Acting English*, p. 47.
82 Latifi, *Even After All This Time*, pp. 117–18.
83 Oufkir with Fitoussi, *La Prisonnière*, p. 260.
84 On Arab forms of prejudice, see Haider Ibahim Ali, 'The other's image: the sociology of difference', in Tahar Labib (ed.), *Imagining the Arab Other: How Arabs and Non-Arabs View Each Other* (London and New York: I. B. Tauris, 2008), pp. 17–34.
85 Zainab Salbi with Laurie Beckland, *Between Two Worlds: Escape into Tyranny; Growing Up in the Shadow of Saddam* (New York: Gotham, 2005), p. 191.
86 al-Baz, *Défigurée*, p. 44.
87 Ibid., pp. 55 and 60.
88 Pamela Bright, *A Poor Man's Riches* (Liverpool: MacGibbon and Kee, 1966), p. 14.
89 Ibid., pp. 22, 23, 37, 40, 56, 82 and 74.
90 On the theme of travel, fantasy and orientalism, see the useful contribution by John Barrell, 'Death on the Nile: fantasy and the literature of tourism, 1840–60', in Catherine Hall (ed.), *Cultures of Empire: Colonizers in Britain and the Empire in the Nineteenth and Twentieth Centuries* (Manchester: Manchester University Press, 2000), pp. 187–206.
91 van Geldermalsen, *Married to a Bedouin*, p. 119.
92 Bouzar and Kada, *L'une voilée*, p. 23.
93 Billie Melman, *Women's Orients: English Women and the Middle East, 1718–1918* (2nd edn; Houndsmill: MacMillan, 1995), pp. 5–8; Sara Mills, *Discourses of Difference: an Analysis of Women's Travel Writing and Colonialism* (London: Routledge, 1991), pp. 2–5.
94 Maillart, *Cruel Way*, pp. 36 and 98.
95 Sarah Hobson, *Through Persia in Disguise* (London: John Murray, 1973).
96 See her novel *The Map of Love* (London: Bloomsbury, 1999).
97 Stark, *Winter in Arabia*, p. 266. On Western women's attitudes to colonised women, see the useful article by Janaki Nair, 'Uncovering the *zenena*: visions of Indian womanhood in Englishwomen's writings, 1813–1940', in Catherine Hall (ed.), *Cultures of Empire: Colonizers in Britain and the Empire in the Nineteenth and Twentieth Centuries* (Manchester: Manchester University Press, 2000), pp. 224–45.
98 Murphy, *Full Tilt*, p. 70.

[99] Åsne Seierstad, *The Bookseller of Kabul*, trans. Ingrid Christophersen (London: Little, Brown, 2003), p. 5.

[100] Lamb, *Sewing Circles*, p. 36.

[101] Hadani Ditmars, *Dancing in the No-fly Zone: a Woman's Journey through Iraq* (Adlestrop: Arris Books, 2006), p. 42.

[102] Jaber, *Flying Carpet*, pp. 150 and 37.

[103] Doubleday, *Three Women of Herat*, p. 9.

[104] Lamb, *Sewing Circles*, p. 100.

[105] Malik, *We are a Muslim*, p. 111.

[106] Basrawi, *Brownies and Kalashnikovs*, p. 35.

[107] Karmi, *In Search of Fatima*, p. 208.

[108] Latifi, *Even After All This Time*, pp. 86, 94 and 114.

[109] Salbi, *Between Two Worlds*, pp. 190–1.

[110] Malik, *We are a Muslim*, p. 135. Radhakrishnan, 'Ethnicity in an age of diaspora', pp. 119–31.

[111] van Geldermalsen, *Married to a Bedouin*, p. 38.

[112] Nahal Tajadod, *Passeport à l'iranienne* (Paris: JC Lattès, 2007), p. 90.

[113] Ibid., p. 112.

[114] Tehmina Durrani, *My Feudal Lord* (Lahore: self-published, 1991), p. 2.

[115] Haddad, *Scheherazade*, p. 61.

[116] Carmen Bin Ladin, *The Veiled Kingdom* (London: Virago, 2004), p. 11.

[117] Farmaian, *Daughter of Persia*, p. 11.

[118] Salbi, *Between Two Worlds*, p. 290.

[119] See the useful comments on this point in Emma Tarlo, *Visibly Muslim: Fashion, Politics, Faith* (Oxford: Berg, 2010), p. 103 and *passim*.

[120] Malik, *We are a Muslim*, p. 254.

[121] Djavann, *Comment peut-on être français*, p. 71.

Notes to Chapter 3

[1] Raymonda Hawa Tawil, *My Home, My Prison* (New York: Holt, Rinehart and Winston, 1979), p. 130.

[2] Edith Wharton, *In Morocco* (1920; London: I. B. Tauris, 2006), pp. 10 and 15.

[3] Voltaire, *Lettres philosophiques* (1734; Paris: Flammarion, 1964), p. 47. 'Mohammadan' was a common European eighteenth-century term for Muslim: today, it is a term which most Muslims refuse, as it seems to imply that their faith is a mere cult of a single personality. It is unlikely that Voltaire intended the term to be pejorative.

[4] There is a wealth of literature on this theme. Three works that I have found particularly useful are Roland Robertson, *Globalization: Social Theory and Global Culture* (London: Sage, 1992); Zygmunt Bauman, *Globalization: the Human Consequences* (Cambridge: Polity, 1998); Arjun Appadurai, *Modernity at Large: Cultural Dimensions of Globalization* (Minneapolis: University of Minnesota Press, 1996). With specific reference to the Arab and Muslim worlds, see the contrasting views in Aziz Al-Azmeh, *Islams and Modernities* (2nd edn; London: Verso, 1996), and Clinton Bennett, *Muslims and Modernity: an Introduction to the Issues and Debates* (London: Continuum, 2005).

[5] Doris Lessing, 'Preface', *The Golden Notebook* (London: Flamingo, 1993), p. 14.

[6] Vita Sackville-West, *Passenger to Teheran* (1926; London: Tauris Parke, 2007), p. 102.

7 Ella K. Maillart, *The Cruel Way* (1947; London: Virago, 1986), p. 138.
8 Carmen Bin Ladin, *The Veiled Kingdom* (London: Virago, 2004), p. 206.
9 Annemarie Schwarzenbach, *La mort en Perse*, trans. Dominique Laure Miermont (1935; Paris: Editions Payot & Rivages, 2001), p. 73.
10 Dervla Murphy, *Full Tilt: Ireland to India with a Bicycle* (London: Eland, 1965), p. 67.
11 Juliette de Baïracli Levy, *Summer in Galilee* (London: Faber and Faber, 1959), p. 26.
12 Laura Blumenfeld, *Revenge: a Story of Hope* (London: Picador, 2002), p. 215.
13 Pamela Bright, *A Poor Man's Riches* (Liverpool: MacGibon and Kee, 1966), p. 12.
14 Veronica Doubleday, *Three Women of Herat* (London: Jonathan Cape, 1988), p. 2.
15 On the difficulty of applying the term to Muslim societies, see the useful study by Kathleen Davis, 'Time behind the veil: the media, the Middle Ages and orientalism now', in Jeffrey Jerome Cohen (ed.), *The Postcolonial Middle Ages* (Houndmills: MacMillan, 2000), pp. 105–22.
16 Freya Stark, *A Winter in Arabia* (1940; London: Arrow Books, 1991), pp. 231–2.
17 Ladin, *Veiled Kingdom*, p. 99. The potential political effects of these technological changes have been debated by many authors. See, for example, Ibrahim M. Abu-Rabi', *Contemporary Arab Thought: Studies in Post-1967 Arab Intellectual History* (London: Pluto, 2004).
18 Qanta A. Ahmed, MD, *In the Land of Invisible Women: a Female Doctor's Journey in the Saudi Kingdom* (Naperville, Ill.: Sourcebooks, 2008), p. 202.
19 Wharton, *In Morocco*, pp. 16 and 10.
20 Lesley Hamilton, *Where the Mountains Roar: in Search of the Sinai Desert* (London: Victor Gollancz, 1980), p. 3.
21 Murphy, *Full Tilt*, p. 65.
22 Sarah Hobson, *Through Persia in Disguise* (London: John Murray, 1973), p. 101.
23 Chahdortt Djavann, *Je viens d'ailleurs* (Paris: Autrement, 2002); Leïla Sebbar, *Mes Algéries en France* (Saint-Pourçain-sur-Sioule: Bleu Autour, 2004); Wassyla Tamzali, *Une femme en colère: lettre d'Alger aux Européens désabusés* (Paris: Gallimard, 2009); Hélé Béji, *Islam Pride: Derrière le voile* (Paris: Gallimard, 2011).
24 Ayaan Hirsi Ali, *The Caged Virgin: a Muslim Woman's Cry for Reason* (London: Simon and Schuster, 2006), p. xiii.
25 Pauline Cutting, *Children of the Siege* (London: Heinemann, 1988), p. 3.
26 Rona Randall, *Jordan and the Holy Land* (London: Frederick Muller, 1968), pp. 3 and 56.
27 Ibid., p. 81.
28 Ghada Karmi, *In Search of Fatima: a Palestinian Story* (London: Verso, 2002), p. 7.
29 Gisèle Halimi, *Milk for the Orange Tree*, trans. D. S. Blair (London: Quartet, 1990).
30 Waris Dirie and Cathleen Miller, *Desert Flower: the Extraordinary Life of a Desert Nomad* (London: Virago, 1998), p. 92. The classic study of this point is E. P. Thompson, 'Time, work-discipline, and industrial capitalism', *Past and Present* 38, 1 (1967), 56–97.
31 Azar Nafisi, *Reading Lolita in Tehran: a Memoir in Books* (New York: Random House, 2003), p. 61

[32] On this point concerning cultural translation, see John Tomlinson, '"Watching Dallas": the imperialist text and audience research', in Frank J. Lechner and John Boli (eds), *The Globalization Reader* (London: Blackwell, 2000), pp. 307–15, and Mark LeVine, *Heavy Metal Islam: Rock, Resistance and the Struggle for the Soul of Islam* (New York: Three Rivers Press, 2008).

[33] Tawil, *My Home, My Prison*, p. 76.

[34] Bin Ladin, *Veiled Kingdom*, p. 84.

[35] Hala Jaber, *The Flying Carpet to Baghdad: One Woman's Fight for Two Orphans of War* (London: Pan, 2010), pp. 188–9.

[36] Emma Williams, *It's Easier to Reach Heaven than the End of the Street: a Jerusalem Memoir* (London: Bloomsbury, 2006), pp. 29–30.

[37] A polemic against the circulation of such images can be found in the opening pages of Tamzali, *Une femme en colère*, pp. 15–21.

[38] Nawal El Saadawi, *The Hidden Face of Eve: Women in the Arab World*, trans. Dr Sherif Hetata (London: Zed Books, 1980); Betty Mahmoody with William Hoffer, *Not Without My Daughter* (London: Corgi Books, 1988).

[39] Karmi, *In Search of Fatima*, p. 18.

[40] Ibid., p. 20.

[41] Ibid., pp. 23–4.

[42] One can find a similar use of English-language terms in Régis Debray, *Eloge des frontières* (Paris: Gallimard, 2010).

[43] Béji, *Islam Pride*, p. 11.

[44] Ibid., pp. 12–13.

[45] Ibid., pp. 28–9.

[46] Ibid., pp. 50–1.

[47] Deborah Rodriguez, *The Kabul Beauty School: the Art of Friendship and Freedom* (London: Hodder & Stoughton, 2008), p. 40.

[48] Ibid., p. 53.

[49] Ibid., pp. 34–5.

[50] Ibid., p. 60.

[51] Ibid., p. 53.

[52] Ibid., p. 90.

[53] Ibid., p. 4.

[54] Ibid., pp. 5 and 158.

[55] Ibid., p. 281.

[56] On this point, see Nur Masalha, *The Bible and Zionism: Invented Traditions, Archaeology and Post-colonialism in Palestine-Israel* (London: Zed Books, 2007), and Shlomo Sand, *The Invention of the Jewish People*, trans. Yael Lotan (London: Verso, 2009).

[57] Colette Modiano, *Turkish Coffee and the Fertile Crescent: Wanderings through the Lebanon, Mesopotamia, Israel, Jordan and Syria* (London: Michael Joseph, 1974), p. 138.

[58] Hamilton, *Where the Mountains Roar*, p. 148.

[59] Martha Gellhorn, 'The Arabs of Palestine', in her *The View from the Ground* (Cambridge: Granta Books, 1989), pp. 197–244 (p. 239); originally published in the *Atlantic Monthly*, October 1961.

[60] On this point, see Krystof Pomian, 'Franks et Gauls', in P. Nora (ed.), *Les Lieux de Mémoire*, II (Paris: Quarto/Gallimard, 1997), pp. 2245–300; Olivier Buchsenschutz and Alain Schnapp, 'Alésia', in P. Nora (ed.), *Les Lieux de Mémoire*, III (Paris: Quarto/Gallimard, 1997), pp. 4103–40; Michael Dietler, 'A tale of three sites', *World Archaeology*, 30, 1 (1998), 72–89.

[61] On these points, see Alden T. Vaughan, 'From white man to redskin: changing Anglo-American perceptions of the American Indian', *American Historical Review*, 87, 4 (1982), 917–53. I would like to thank my colleague, Dr Brian Ireland, for his assistance with this point.

[62] See my 'France, Orientalism and Algeria: fifty-four articles from the *Revue des Deux Mondes*, 1846–1852', *Journal of Algerian Studies*, 3 (1998), 48–70.

[63] One can find similar arguments in Christopher Caldwell, *Reflections on the Revolution in Europe: Immigration, Islam and the West* (London: Penguin, 2010); Melanie Phillips, *Londonistan: How Britain is Creating a Terror State Within* (London: Gibson Square, 2006).

[64] Phillips, *Londonistan*, p. 96.

[65] Ibid., p. 11.

[66] Ibid., pp. 163–8.

[67] On this point, see my 'An extremism of the center: Jean-Pierre Chevènement, French presidential candidate, 2002', *French Politics, Culture and Society*, 22, 1 (2004), 76–97, and *French Muslims: New Voices in Contemporary France* (Cardiff: University of Wales Press, 2010).

[68] On the possible relevance of postmodernity to Islamic studies, see the interesting set of essays in Akbar S. Ahmed and Hasting Donnan (eds), *Islam, Globalization and Postmodernity* (London: Routledge, 1994).

[69] In the interests of balance, mention should also be made of G. Willow Wilson, *The Butterfly Mosque: a Young Woman's Journey to Love and Islam* (London: Atlantic Books, 2010), which presents a more tempered, nuanced and genuinely perceptive account of a conversion experience.

[70] On this point, see the prescient articles by Hicham Ben Abdallah El Alaoui, 'Retour vers le futur dans le monde arabe', *Monde Diplomatique*, 665 (August 2009), 10–11, and 'Les intellectuels arabes entres Etats et intégrisme', *Monde Diplomatique*, 677 (August 2010), 1, 20–1.

[71] Randall, *Jordan*, p. 3.

[72] Fadia Basrawi, *Brownies and Kalashnikovs: a Saudi Woman's Memoir of American Arabia and Wartime Beirut* (Reading: South Street Press, 2009), pp. 3–5.

[73] Susan Nathan, *The Other Side of Israel: My Journey Across the Jewish-Arab Divide* (New York: Doubleday, 2005), p. 80.

[74] Karmi, *In Search of Fatima*, pp. 5–6.

[75] Ahmed, *In the Land of Invisible Women*, p. 9.

[76] Djavann, *Je viens d'ailleurs*, p. 70.

[77] Dirie and Miller, *Desert Flower*, p. 88.

[78] Tawil, *My Home, My Prison*, pp. 38–9.

[79] Sattareh Farman Farmaian, *Daughter of Persia: a Woman's Journey from her Father's Harem through the Islamic Revolution* (London: Corgi, 1992), p. 89.

[80] Nahid Rachlin, *Persian Girls: a Memoir* (New York: Penguin, 2006), p. 142.

[81] Karmi, *In Search of Fatima*, pp. 192–4.

[82] Afschineh Latifi with Pablo F. Fenjives, *Even After All This Time: a Story of Love, Revolution, and Leaving Iran* (London: Fusion, 2005), p. 116.

[83] Basrawi, *Brownies and Kalashnikovs*, pp. 22–3.

[84] Rachlin, *Persian Girls*, pp. 144–5.

[85] Nafisi, *Reading Lolita in Tehran*, p. 172.

[86] Latifi, *Even After All This Time*, pp. 139–41.

[87] Karmi, *In Search of Fatima*, pp. 216–17.

[88] Rachlin, *Persian Girls*, p. 73.

[89] Tawil, *My Home, My Prison*, p. 43.

[90] Haddad, *Scheherazade*, pp. 33–4, 47.

[91] Mai Ghoussoub, *Selected Writings*, ed. Rebecca O'Connor (London: Saqi, 2008), p. 39.

[92] *Brownies and Kalashnikovs*, pp. 36–7.

[93] Latifa, with Chékéha Hachemi, *My Forbidden Face: Growing Up under the Taliban: a Young Woman's Story*, trans. Lisa Appignanesi (London: Virago, 2002), pp. 18 and 155.

[94] Tawil, *My Home, My Prison*, p. 24.

[95] Deborah Kanafani, *Unveiled: How an American Woman Found Her Way through Politics, Love and Obedience in the Middle East* (New York: Free Press, 2008), p. x.

[96] Zainab Salbi with Laurie Beckland, *Between Two Worlds: Escape into Tyranny; Growing Up in the Shadow of Saddam* (New York: Gotham, 2005), p. 290.

[97] Jaber, *The Flying Carpet to Baghdad*, p. 37.

[98] Ghoussoub, *Selected Writings*, p. 39.

[99] Latifa, *My Forbidden Face*, pp. 178–9.

[100] Latifi, *Even After All This Time*, p. 267.

[101] Karmi, *In Search of Fatima*, p. 422.

[102] Latifi, *Even After All This Time*, p. 211.

[103] Bauman, *Globalization*, p. 59.

[104] Karmi, *In Search of Fatima*, p. 205.

[105] See the discussion in Stuart Ward, '"No Nation could be broker": the satire boom and the demise of Britain's world role', in Stuart Ward (ed.), *British Culture and the End of Empire* (Manchester: Manchester University Press, 2001), pp. 91–110. For an example of a study of Arab humour, see Ali Chibani, 'Au miroir brouillé du petit écran', *Monde Diplomatique* (February 2009), 9.

Notes to Chapter 4

[1] Joumana Haddad, *I Killed Scheherazade: Confessions of an Angry Arab Woman* (London: Saqi Books, 2010), p. 72.

[2] Shelina Zahra Janmohamed, *Love in a Headscarf: Muslim Woman Seeks the One* (London: Aurum, 2009), p. xi.

[3] Deborah Rodriguez, *The Kabul Beauty School: the Art of Friendship and Freedom* (London: Hodder & Stoughton, 2008), p. 137.

[4] Billie Melman, *Women's Orients: English Women and the Middle East, 1718–1918* (2nd edn; Houndsmill: MacMillan, 1995), p. 42.

[5] Vita Sackville-West, *Passenger to Teheran* (1926; London: Tauris Parke, 2007).

[6] Edith Wharton, *In Morocco* (1920; London: I. B. Tauris, 2006), pp. 152 and 159.

[7] Lady Evelyn Cobbold, *Pilgrimage to Mecca* (1934; London: Arabian Publishing, 2009), p. 224.

[8] See, for example, Fatima Mernissi, *The Harem Within* (London: Doubleday, 1994), pp. 34–6, and Sattareh Farman Farmaian, *Daughter of Persia: a Woman's Journey from her Father's Harem through the Islamic Revolution* (London: Corgi, 1992), pp. 15–21.

[9] Melman, *Women's Orients*, p. 121.

[10] Sarah Hobson, *Through Persia in Disguise* (London: John Murray, 1973), p. 28.

[11] Ella K. Maillart, *The Cruel Way* (1947; London: Virago Press, 1986), pp. 128–9.

[12] Ibid., p. 117.

[13] Some diverse interpretations are presented and discussed in A. L. Macfie (ed.), *Orientalism: A Reader* (Edinburgh: Edinburgh University Press, 2000).

14 Another relevant work which marks a shift in attitudes is Raymonda Hawa Tawil, *My Home, My Prison* (New York: Holt, Rinehart and Winston, 1979). While Tawil's explicit frustration with male authority structures in Palestinian society caused some shock in Palestinian circles, this work does not appear to have had the same success as Nawal El Saadawi, *The Hidden Face of Eve: Women in the Arab World*, trans. Dr Sherif Hetata (London: Zed Books, 1980).

15 Ibid., p. iii.

16 Ibid., p. xiv.

17 Ibid., p. x.

18 Ibid., p. xv.

19 On reactions to Said, see Gyan Prakash, 'Orientalism now', *History and Theory*, 34, 3 (1995), 199–212.

20 Raphael Patai, *The Arab Mind* (rev. edn; New York: Hatherleigh Press, 2002), p. 1.

21 Bernard Lewis, 'The question of orientalism', in A. L. Macfie (ed.), *Orientalism: a Reader* (Edinburgh: Edinburgh University Press, 2000), pp. 249–70 (p. 259).

22 For a lively, if perhaps not entirely accurate, evocation of the hippie trail, see Rory MacLean, *Magic Bus: On the Hippie Trail from Istanbul to India* (Harmondsworth: Penguin, 2007).

23 Steven Erlanger, 'In Afghan refugee camp, Albright hammers Taliban', *New York Times*, 19 November 1997, http://www.nytimes.com/1997/11/19/world/in-afghan-refugee-camp-albright-hammers-taliban.html, accessed 10 August 2011.

24 See the interesting discussion of this point by Chandra Talpade Mohanty, '"Under Western Eyes" revisited: feminist solidarity through anticapitalist struggle', *Signs*, 28, 2 (2002), 499–535.

25 Dervla Murphy, *Full Tilt: Ireland to India with a Bicycle* (London: Eland, 1965); Dervla Murphy, *Tales from Two Cities: Travel of Another Sort* (London: John Murray, 1987).

26 Murphy, *Tales from Two Cities*, pp. 21 and 27.

27 Suzy Wighton, *One Day at a Time: Diaries from a Palestinian Camp* (London: Hutchinson, 1990), p. 224. Emphasis in the original.

28 On changing Western attitudes to the veil, see Katherine Bullock, *Rethinking Muslim Women and the Veil: Challenging Historical & Modern Stereotypes* (2nd edn; Herndon: International Institute of Islamic Thought, 2002), pp. 85–135.

29 Anne Sinclair Mehdevi, *Persia Revisited* (London: Michael Joseph, 1964), p. 66.

30 Betty Mahmoody with William Hoffer, *Not Without My Daughter* (London: Corgi Books, 1988).

31 Veronica Doubleday, *Three Women of Herat* (London: Jonathan Cape, 1988), p. 3.

32 Ibid., pp. 64–5. A frustrating point in this description is that Doubleday never explains what she means by 'burqa', 'prayer veil' and 'chador', and therefore the reader is never certain of what she is discussing.

33 Norma Khouri, *Forbidden Love: Love and Betrayal in Modern-day Jordan* (London: Doubleday, 2003), pp. 1–2.

34 Qanta A. Ahmed, MD, *In the Land of Invisible Women: a Female Doctor's Journey in the Saudi Kingdom* (Naperville, Ill.: Sourcebooks, 2008), pp. 400–11.

35 Åsne Seierstad, *The Bookseller of Kabul*, trans. Ingrid Christophersen (London: Little, Brown, 2003).

[36] Shah Muhammad Rais, *Once Upon a Time There Was a Bookseller in Kabul* (n.p.: Shah M. Book Co., 2007).

[37] Amelia Hill, 'Bookseller of Kabul author Åsne Seierstad: "It's Not Possible to Write a Neutral Story"', *Guardian*, 31 July 2010, including corrections added on 14 August 2010.

[38] Alexandra Topping, 'The bookseller of Kabul author cleared of invading Afghan family's privacy', 13 December 2011, *http://www.guardian.co.uk/world/2011/dec/13/bookseller-of-kabul-author-cleared*, accessed 28 December 2011.

[39] Tehmina Durrani, *My Feudal Lord* (Lahore: self-published, 1991).

[40] Bee Rowlatt and May Witwit, *Talking about Jane Austen in Baghdad* (London: Penguin Books, 2010), p. 153.

[41] Ibid., p. 155.

[42] Jehan Sadat, *A Woman of Egypt* (London: Bloomsbury, 1987), p. 184.

[43] Ibid., p. 207.

[44] Christelle Hamel and Christine Delphy, 'On vous a tant aimé.e.s! Entretien avec Houria Boutelja', *Nouvelles Questions Féministes*, 25, 1 (2006), 122–35 (133).

[45] Deborah Kanafani, *Unveiled: How an American Woman Found Her Way through Politics, Love and Obedience in the Middle East* (New York: Free Press, 2008), p. 151.

[46] Pauline Cutting, *Children of the Siege* (London: Heinemann, 1988), pp. 65–6.

[47] Ahmed, *In the Land of Invisible Women*, pp. 62–3. Emphasis in the original.

[48] Mahmoody with Hoffer, *Not Without My Daughter*, p. 122.

[49] Seierstad, *The Bookseller of Kabul*, p. 88.

[50] A more or less explicit example of this can be found in Chardortt Djavann, *A mon corps défendant, l'Occident* (Paris: Flammarion, 2007).

[51] Karen Armstrong, *Islam: a Short History* (London: Phoenix, 2001), p. 157.

[52] Fatéma Hal, *Fille des frontières: récit* (Paris: Philippe Rey, 2011), p. 203.

[53] Murphy, *Tales from Two Cities*, p. 52

[54] Zaiba Malik, *We are a Muslim, Please* (London: Windmill Books, 2011), p. 171.

[55] Shappi Khorsandi, *A Beginner's Guide to Acting English* (n.p.: Ebury Press, 2009), p. 44.

[56] Rania al-Baz, *Défigurée: quand un crime passionnel devient affaire d'Etat* (Paris: Michel Lafon, 2005), pp. 83–4.

[57] Asra Q. Nomani, *Standing along in Mecca: an American Woman's Struggle for the Soul of Islam* (San Francisco: HarperSanFrancisco, 2005), p. 51.

[58] Hélé Béji, *Islam Pride: Derrière le voile* (Paris: Gallimard, 2011), p. 41. For some further thoughts on such matters, see Richard Rowson, *Working Ethics: How to be Fair in a Culturally Complex World* (London: Jessica Kingsley, 2006), and, more generally, Will Kymlicka, *Multicultural Odysseys: Navigating the New International Politics of Diversity* (Oxford: Oxford University Press, 2007).

[59] Rosemary Bechler, 'Islam and democracy: an interview with Heba Ezzat', Open Democracy, posted 11 May 2005, *http://www.opendemocracy.net*, accessed 28 October 2008.

[60] Salbi, *Between Two Worlds*, p. 144.

[61] Susan Nathan, *The Other Side of Israel: My Journey Across the Jewish-Arab Divide* (New York: Doubleday, 2005), p. 30.

[62] Saadawi, *Hidden Face of Eve*, p. 84.

[63] Fadia Basrawi, *Brownies and Kalashnikovs: a Saudi Woman's Memoir of American Arabia and Wartime Beirut* (Reading: South Street Press, 2009), p. 172

64 Azadeh Moaveni, *Lipstick Jihad: a Memoir of Growing Up Iranian in America and American in Iran* (New York: Public Affairs, 2005), p. 24.
65 Ghada Karmi, *In Search of Fatima: a Palestinian Story* (London: Verso, 2002), pp. 236–7.
66 Ibid., p. 357.
67 Marguerite van Geldermalsen, *Married to a Bedouin* (London: Virago, 2006), p. 70.
68 Nomani, *Standing Along in Mecca*, p. 23.
69 Hala Jaber, *The Flying Carpet to Baghdad: One Woman's Fight for Two Orphans of War* (London: Pan, 2010), pp. 21–2.
70 G. Willow Wilson, *The Butterfly Mosque: a Young Woman's Journey to Love and Islam* (London: Atlantic Books, 2010), p. 110.
71 Ibid., p. 112.
72 Ibid., p. 117.
73 Rodriguez, *Kabul Beauty School*, p. 121.
74 Ibid., pp. 160–1.
75 Ibid., p. 277.
76 Ibid., p. 180.
77 Ibid., p. 181.
78 Ibid., p. 281.
79 Ibid., p. 276.
80 Mai Ghoussoub, *Selected Writings*, ed. Rebecca O'Connor (London: Saqi, 2008), p. 52.
81 Janmohamed, *Love in a Headscarf*, p. 129.
82 Tawil, *My Home, My Prison*, p. 2.
83 For a relevant consideration of the experience of cross-cultural relationships in a different context, see Katherine Ellinghaus, *Taking Assimilation to Heart: Marriages of White Women and Indigeneous Men in the United States and Australia, 1887–1937* (Lincoln and London: University of Nebraska Press, 2006).
84 Annemarie Schwarzenbach, *La mort en Perse*, trans. Dominique Laure Miermont (1935; Paris: Editions Payot & Rivages, 2001).

Notes to Chapter 5

1 Shelina Zahra Janmohamed, *Love in a Headscarf: Muslim Woman Seeks the One* (London: Aurum, 2009), p. xiii.
2 Juliette de Baïracli Levy, *Summer in Galilee* (London: Faber and Faber, 1959); Sadek Hajji and Stéphanie Marteau, *Voyage dans la France musulmane* (Paris: Plon, 2005).
3 Zaiba Malik, *We are a Muslim, Please* (London: Windmill Books, 2011), p. 146.
4 Kathleen M. Kenyon, *Archaeology in the Holy Land* (1960; London: Ernest Benn, 1979), p. 11.
5 Pamela Bright, *A Poor Man's Riches* (Liverpool: MacGibbon and Kee, 1966); Martha Gellhorn, 'The Arabs of Palestine', in Martha Gellhorn (ed.), *The View from the Ground* (Cambridge: Granta Books, 1989), pp. 197–244; originally published in the *Atlantic Monthly*, October 1961.
6 Betty Mahmoody with William Hoffer, *Not Without My Daughter* (London: Corgi Books, 1988), p. 32.
7 Ibid., pp. 52, 57, 241 and 334. Emphasis in the original.
8 Nawal El Saadawi, *The Hidden Face of Eve: Women in the Arab World*, trans. Dr Sherif Hetata (London: Zed Books, 1980).

9   Oriana Fallaci, *The Rage and the Pride* (New York: Rizzoli, 2001), p. 29.
10 Ayaan Hirsi Ali, *The Caged Virgin: a Muslim Woman's Cry for Reason* (London: Simon and Schuster, 2006), p. xi.
11 Melanie Phillips, *Londonistan: How Britain is Creating a Terror State Within* (London: Gibson Square, 2006), p. 23.
12 Janmohamed, *Love in a Headscarf*, p. 154.
13 Ken Booth and Tim Dunne, 'Worlds in collision' in their edited collection *Worlds in Collision* (Houndsmill: Palgrave MacMillan, 2002), p. 5. On recent changes in Islam, see Olivier Roy, *L'Islam mondialisé* (Paris: Seuil, 2002).
14 Hélé Béji, *Islam Pride: Derrière le voile* (Paris: Gallimard, 2011), pp. 50–3.
15 Ayşe Saktander, *Living Islam: Women, Religion and the Politicization of Culture in Turkey* (London: Tauris, 2002).
16 On this point, see also the evidence uncovered in Nadia Kiwan, *Identities, Discourses and Experiences: Young People of North African Origin in France* (Manchester and New York: Manchester University Press, 2009); Faïza Guène, *Kiffe Kiffe Demain* (Paris: Hachette, 2004).
17 Hirsi Ali, *The Caged Virgin*, p. 18.
18 Joumana Haddad, *I Killed Scheherazade: Confessions of an Angry Arab Woman* (London: Saqi Books, 2010), p. 117.
19 Christelle Hamel and Christine Delphy, 'On vous a tant aimé.e.s! Entretien avec Houria Boutelja', *Nouvelles Questions Féministes*, 25, 1 (2006), 122–35 (126).
20 Malika Oufkir with Michele Fitoussi, *La Prisonnière*, trans. Ros Schwartz (London: Doubleday, 2000), p. 188.
21 G. Willow Wilson, *The Butterfly Mosque: a Young Woman's Journey to Love and Islam* (London: Atlantic Books, 2010); Na'ima B. Roberts, *From My Sisters' Lips: a Unique Celebration of Muslim Womanhood* (London: Bantam Books, 2005); Carol L. Anway, *Daughters of Another Path: Experiences of American Women Choosing Islam* (Lee's Summit, Mo.: Yawna Publications, 1996); Lady Evelyn Cobbold, *Pilgrimage to Mecca* (1934; London: Arabian Publishing, 2009), p. 89; Qanta A. Ahmed, MD, *In the Land of Invisible Women: a Female Doctor's Journey in the Saudi Kingdom* (Naperville, Ill.: Sourcebooks, 2008); Asra Q. Nomani, *Standing along in Mecca: an American Woman's Struggle for the Soul of Islam* (San Francisco: HarperSanFrancisco, 2005).
22 Chahdortt Djavann, *Comment peut-on être français?* (Paris: Flammarion, 2006). I would like to thank my colleague, Dr Timothy Jones, for his assistance with some of the ideas in this paragraph.
23 Pardis Mahdavi, *Passionate Uprisings: Iran's Sexual Revolution* (Stanford, Calif.: Stanford University Press, 2009), p. 20.
24 Wilson, *The Butterfly Mosque*, pp. 58–9. Emphasis in the original.
25 Sarah Hobson, *Through Persia in Disguise* (London: John Murray, 1973), p. 41.
26 Rona Randall, *Jordan and the Holy Land* (London: Frederick Muller, 1968), p. 110.
27 Marguerite van Geldermalsen, *Married to a Bedouin* (London: Virago, 2006), p. 74.
28 Cobbold, *Pilgrimage to Mecca*, p. 101.
29 Jehan Sadat, *A Woman of Egypt* (London: Bloomsbury, 1987), pp. 62–3.
30 Janmohamed, *Love in a Headscarf*, p. 79.
31 Wilson, *Butterfly Mosque*, p. 73.
32 Daniela Norris and Shireen Anabtawi, *Crossing Qalandiya: Exchanges across the Israeli/Palestinian Divide* (London: Reportage, 2010), pp. 76–7.

33 Phillips, *Londonistan*, pp. 34–5.
34 Dounia Bouzar and Saïda Kada, *L'une voilée, l'autre pas: le témoignage de deux musulmanes françaises* (Paris: Albin Michel, 2003), p. 15.
35 Carmen Bin Ladin, *The Veiled Kingdom* (London: Virago, 2004), p. 59.
36 Janmohamed, *Love in a Headscarf*, p. 155.
37 Zainab Salbi with Laurie Beckland, *Between Two Worlds: Escape from Tyranny; Growing Up in the Shadow of Saddam* (New York: Gotham, 2005), p. 121.
38 There is a massive volume of literature on this question. For more information and fuller discussions, see Fadwa El Guindi, *Veil: Modesty, Privacy and Resistance* (Oxford: Berg, 1999); Emma Tarlo, *Visibly Muslim: Fashion, Politics, Faith* (Oxford: Berg, 2010); Katherine Bullock, *Rethinking Muslim Women and the Veil: Challenging Historical & Modern Stereotypes* (2nd edn; Herndon: International Institute of Islamic Thought, 2002), and the useful, short introduction in Helen Watson, 'Women and the veil: personal responses to global processes', in Akbar S. Ahmed and Hastings Donnan (eds), *Islam, Globalization and Postmodernity* (London: Routledge, 1994), pp. 141–59.
39 Ahmed, *In the Land of Invisible Women*, p. 38.
40 Ibid., p. 60.
41 Anne Brunswic, *Bienvenue en Palestine: Chroniques d'une saison à Ramallah* (new edn; Arles: Actes Sud, 2004), pp. 133–4.
42 Allegra Stratton, *Muhajababes* (London: Constable, 2006), pp. 74–6.
43 Bouzar and Kada, *L'une voilée, l'autre pas*, pp. 67–8.
44 Wilson, *Butterfly Mosque*, pp. 106–7.
45 Janmohamed, *Love in a Headscarf*, p. 1.
46 Roberts, *From My Sisters' Lips*, pp. 213–27.
47 Fadia Basrawi, *Brownies and Kalashnikovs: a Saudi Woman's Memoir of American Arabia and Wartime Beirut* (Reading: South Street Press, 2009), p. 54.
48 Bin Ladin, *The Veiled Kingdom*, p. 67.
49 Cobbold, *Pilgrimage to Mecca*, p. 263.
50 Nomani, *Standing Alone in Mecca*, p. 35. Emphasis in the original.
51 Ahmed, *In the Land of Invisible Women*, p. 123.
52 Ibid., pp. 170–4.
53 Nomani, *Standing Alone in Mecca*, pp. 50, 55, 58.
54 Ahmed, *In the Land of Invisible Women*, p. 149.
55 Sadat, *A Woman of Egypt*, p. 275.
56 Nomani, *Standing Alone in Mecca*, p. 70.
57 Doris Lessing, 'Preface', *The Golden Notebook* (London: Flamingo, 1993), p. 14.
58 Cobbold, *Pilgrimage to Mecca*, p. 92.
59 Ernest Gellner, *Muslim Society* (Cambridge: Cambridge University Press, 1981), p. 7. Emphasis in the original.
60 Sayeeda Warsi, 'The 2011 University of Leicester Sir Sigmund Sternberg Lecture', 20 January 2011, http://www.sayeedawarsi.com/2011/01/university-of-leicester-sir-sigmund-sternberg-lecture/, accessed 25 January 2011.
61 For a still useful survey of relevant issues, see Akbar S. Ahmed and Hastings Donnan, 'Islam in the age of postmodernity', in their edited collection *Islam, Globalization and Postmodernity* (London: Routledge, 1994), pp. 1–20.
62 On this point, see Ira M. Lapidus, 'State and religion in Islamic societies', *Past and Present*, 151 (1996), 3–27. On Islam's relationship with global identities, see Anouar Majid, 'The politics of feminism in Islam', *Signs*, 32, 2 (1998), 321–61, and Robert A. Saunders, 'The ummah as nation: a reappraisal in the wake of

the "Cartoons Affair"', *Nations and Nationalism*, 14, 2 (2008), 303–21. Turkey is usually cited as the single example of a viable form of nationalism in a Muslim-majority society.

[63] Bouzar and Kada, *L'une voilée, l'autre pas*, p. 93. Ruba Salih, 'Shifting boundaries of self and other; Moroccan migrant women in Italy', *European Journal of Women's Studies*, 7 (2000), 321–35.

[64] Zygmunt Bauman, 'Reconnaissance wars on the planetary frontierland', *Theory, Culture and Society*, 19, 4 (2002), 81–90.

[65] Anway, *Daughters of Another Path*, p. viii.

Notes to Chapter 6

[1] Catarina Kinnvall and Paul Nesbitt-Larking, *The Political Psychology of Globalization: Muslims in the West* (Oxford: Oxford University Press, 2011), p. 80.

[2] Melanie Phillips, *Londonistan: How Britain is Creating a Terror State Within* (London: Gibson Square, 2006), p. 23.

[3] Zaiba Malik, *We are a Muslim, Please* (London: Windmill Books, 2011), p. 263.

[4] Shelina Zahra Janmohamed, *Love in a Headscarf: Muslim Woman Seeks the One* (London: Aurum, 2009), p. 144.

[5] Ibid., p. 154.

[6] Ibid., pp. 145, 151.

[7] Rowan Williams, *Writing in the Dust: Reflections on 11th September and its Aftermath* (London: Hodder and Stoughton, 2002), p. 26.

[8] Janmohamed, *Love in a Headscarf*, p. 150.

[9] Zygmunt Bauman, 'Reconnaissance wars on the planetary frontierland', *Theory, Culture and Society*, 19, 4 (2002), 81–90 (84). Similar arguments had earlier been presented in Arjun Appadurai, *Modernity at Large: Cultural Dimensions of Globalization* (Minneapolis: University of Minnesota Press, 1996).

[10] On this point, see Henrice Altink and Sharif Gemie, 'Borders: ancient, modern and postmodern; definition and debates', in Henrice Altink and Sharif Gemie (eds), *At the Border: Margins and Peripheries in Modern France* (Cardiff: University of Wales Press, 2008), pp. 1–23. For a recent defence of the frontier, see Régis Debray, *Eloge des frontières* (Paris: Gallimard, 2010).

[11] Kinnvall and Nesbitt-Larking, *Political Psychology*, p. 82.

[12] Azar Nafisi, *Reading Lolita in Tehran: a Memoir in Books* (New York: Random House, 2003); Azadeh Moaveni, *Lipstick Jihad: a Memoir of Growing Up Iranian in America and American in Iran* (New York: Public Affairs, 2005); Pardis Mahdavi, *Passionate Uprisings: Iran's Sexual Revolution* (Stanford, Calif.: Stanford University Press, 2009).

[13] Nahal Tajadod, *Passeport à l'iranienne* (Paris: JC Lattès, 2007).

[14] Nahid Rachlin, *Persian Girls: a Memoir* (New York: Penguin, 2006); Afschineh Latifi with Pablo F. Fenjives, *Even After All This Time: a Story of Love, Revolution, and Leaving Iran* (London: Fusion, 2005).

[15] *http://www.whslibrary.com/firstladyrecommends.htm*, accessed 18 August 2009.

[16] *http://www.meforum.org/542/reading-lolita-in-tehran*, *http://www.newint.org/features/2007/03/01/action/*, both accessed 25 August 2011.

[17] Betty Mahmoody with William Hoffer, *Not Without My Daughter* (London: Corgi Books, 1988).

[18] See *http://www.amazon.co.uk/product-reviews/0007178484/ref=dp_top_cm_cr_acr_txt?ie=UTF8&showViewpoints=1*, accessed on 1 September 2011.

[19] Nafisi, *Reading Lolita in Tehran*, p. 11.
[20] Ibid., p. 59.
[21] I want to signal a note of doubt here: I wonder if this reading group ever existed, or whether it is not simply Nafisi's utopian projection of what her teaching should have been.
[22] Ibid., p. 120.
[23] Hamid Dabashi, 'Native informers and the American empire', *El-Ahram Weekly Online*, 1 June 2006, http://weekly.ahram.org.eg/2006/797/special.htm, accessed 2 March 2011.
[24] Nawal El Saadawi, *The Hidden Face of Eve: Women in the Arab World*, trans. Dr Sherif Hetata (London: Zed Books, 1980).
[25] See Hamid Dabashi, *Post-orientalism: Knowledge and Power in Time of Terror* (New Brunswick: Transaction Publishers, 2009), pp. 185–207.
[26] See Mahsa Sherkarloo, 'Iranian women take on the constitution', http://www.merip.org/mero/mero072105, accessed 26 July 2005.
[27] Mahdavi, *Passionate Uprisings*, p. 122. Emphasis in the original.
[28] Ibid., p. 186. Azadeh Moaveni is more sceptical about such claims: *Lipstick Jihad*, p. 43. For a useful survey of the politics of social change in Iran, see Kaveh Basmenji, *Tehran Blues: Youth Culture in Iran* (London: Saqi, 2005).
[29] Mahdavi, *Passionate Uprisings*, p. 89.
[30] Moaveni, *Lipstick Jihad*, p. 81.
[31] Ibid., p. 209.
[32] Laura Blumenfeld, *Revenge: a Story of Hope* (London: Picador, 2002); Emma Williams, *It's Easier to Reach Heaven than the End of the Street: a Jerusalem Memoir* (London: Bloomsbury, 2006).
[33] Blumenfeld, *Revenge*, p. 308.
[34] Ibid., p. 117.
[35] I would like to thank my colleague, Dr Ali Wardak, for his advice on this point.
[36] Bee Rowlatt and May Witwit, *Talking about Jane Austen in Baghdad* (London: Penguin Books, 2010).
[37] Dounia Bouzar and Saïda Kada, *L'une voilée, l'autre pas: le témoignage de deux musulmanes françaises* (Paris: Albin Michel, 2003).
[38] Daniela Norris and Shireen Anabtawi, *Crossing Qalandiya: Exchanges across the Israeli/Palestinian Divide* (London: Reportage, 2010), p. 9.
[39] Ibid., p. 6.
[40] Ibid., p. 75.
[41] Ibid., p. 61.
[42] Ibid., p. 116.

Notes to Conclusion

[1] Anon., *Les Mille et une nuits vol I*, trans. Antoine Gallard, p. 34, downloaded from http://www.ebooksgratuits.com.
[2] Roland Robertson, *Globalization: Social Theory and Global Culture* (London: Sage, 1992), p. 59.
[3] Mary Louise Pratt, *Imperial Eyes: Travel Writing and Transculturation* (London and New York: Routledge, 1992), p. 4.
[4] Adel Iskandar, '"Whenever, Wherever!" The discourse of orientalist transnationalism in the construction of Shakira', *Ambassadors*, 6, 2 (2003), available at http://ambassadors.net.archives/issue14/selected_studies4.htm, accessed 15 November 2010.

[5] On the long-term consequences of this situation, see the uncomfortable, provocative essay by Dada Rahal-Sidhoum, 'Féministe et de culture musulmane dans la société française: une identité sans contrôle', *Confluences Méditerranée*, 59, 4 (2006), 115–24.

[6] On this point, see the thoughtful discussion in Will Kymlicka, *Multicultural Odysseys: Navigating the New International Politics of Diversity* (Oxford: Oxford University Press, 2007), and in Margaret A. Majumdar, *Postcoloniality: the French Dimension* (New York: Berghahn Books, 2007), pp. 219–21.

[7] For some thoughtful, well-argued criticisms, see Kenan Malik, *From Fatwa to Jihad: the Rushdie Affair and its Legacy* (London: Atlantic Books, 2009).

[8] On the PIR, see my *French Muslims: New Voices in Contemporary France* (Cardiff: University of Wales Press, 2010). Further information on the movement can be found at their website: *http://www.indigenes-republique.fr/pir*.

[9] On this point, see the conclusions of Peter Burke, *Cultural Hybridity* (Cambridge: Polity Press, 2009).

Bibliography

A Hundred Texts

Where there is a significant difference between the date of publication of the edition I have consulted, and the original date of publication, both dates have been recorded.

Ahmed, Qanta A., MD, *In the Land of Invisible Women: a Female Doctor's Journey in the Saudi Kingdom* (Naperville, Ill.: Sourcebooks, 2008).

al-Baz, Rania, *Défigurée: quand un crime passionnel devient affaire d'Etat* (Paris: Michel Lafon, 2005).

Al Neimi, Salwa, *La preuve par le miel*, trans. Oscar Heliani (Paris: Robert Laffont, 2008).

Ali, Nojoud with Delphine Minoui, *Moi Nojoud, 10 ans, divorcée* (Paris: France Loisirs, 2009).

Anway, Carol L., *Daughters of Another Path: Experiences of American Women Choosing Islam* (Lee's Summit, Mo.: Yawna Publications, 1996).

Asayeh, Gelareh, 'I grew up thinking I was white', in Lila Azam Zanganeh (ed.), *My Sister, Guard Your Veil; My Brother, Guard Your Eyes: Uncensored Iranian Voices* (Boston, Mass.: Beacon Press, 2006), pp. 12–19.

Basrawi, Fadia, *Brownies and Kalashnikovs: a Saudi Woman's Memoir of American Arabia and Wartime Beirut* (Reading: South Street Press, 2009).

Bechler, Rosemary, 'Islam and democracy: an interview with Heba Ezzat', Open Democracy, posted 11 May 2005, *http://www.opendemocracy.net*, accessed 28 October 2008.

Béji, Hélé, *Islam Pride: Derrière le voile* (Paris: Gallimard, 2011).

Bessis, Sophie 'Entrevista del grupo Eleuterio Quintanilla a Sophie Bessis', *http://www.equintanilla.com/web_nueva/privado/imagenes/entrevista_Bessis. pdf*, accessed 20 June 2007.

Bin Ladin, Carmen, *The Veiled Kingdom* (London: Virago, 2004).

Blumenfeld, Laura, *Revenge: a Story of Hope* (London: Picador, 2002).

Bouzar, Dounia and Saïda Kada, *L'une voilée, l'autre pas: le témoignage de deux musulmanes françaises* (Paris: Albin Michel, 2003).

Bright, Pamela, *A Poor Man's Riches* (Liverpool: MacGibbon and Kee, 1966).

Brunswic, Anne, *Bienvenue en Palestine: Chroniques d'une saison à Ramallah* (new edn; Arles: Actes Sud, 2004).

Chouder, Ismahane, Malika Latrèche and Pierre Tevanian (eds), *Les filles voilées parlent* (Floch: La Fabrique, 2008).

Cobbold, Lady Evelyn, *Pilgrimage to Mecca* (1934; London: Arabian Publishing, 2009).

Courtauld, Pari, *A Persian Childhood* (London: Rubicon Press, 1990).

Cutting, Pauline, *Children of the Siege* (London: Heinemann, 1988).

Dirie, Waris and Cathleen Miller, *Desert Flower: the Extraordinary Life of a Desert Nomad* (London: Virago, 1998).

Ditmars, Hadani, *Dancing in the No-fly Zone: a Woman's Journey through Iraq* (Adlestrop: Arris Books, 2006).

Djavann, Chahdortt, *Je viens d'ailleurs* (Paris: Autrement, 2002).

Doubleday, Veronica, *Three Women of Herat* (London: Jonathan Cape, 1988).

Durrani, Tehmina, *My Feudal Lord* (Lahore: self-published, 1991).

Ebadi, Shirin with Azadeh Moaveni, *Iran Awakening: From Prison to Peace Prize: One Woman's Struggle at the Crossroads of History* (London: Rider, 2006).

El-Cheikh, Hanan, *Toute une histoire*, trans. Stéphanie Dujois (Paris: Actes Sud, 2010).

Esfandiari, Haleh, *My Prison, My Home: One Woman's Story of Captivity in Iran* (London: Harper Collins, 2010).

Fallaci, Oriana, *The Rage and the Pride* (New York: Rizzoli, 2001).

Farmaian, Sattareh Farman, *Daughter of Persia: a Woman's Journey from her Father's Harem through the Islamic Revolution* (London: Corgi, 1992).

Filipović, Zlata, *Zlata's Diary*, trans. Christina Pribichevicj-Zorić (London: Viking, 1994).

García-Sala, Carla Fibla and Fadi N. Skaik, *Resistiendo en Gaza: Historias palestinas* (Barcelona: Península, 2010).

Geldermalsen, Marguerite van, *Married to a Bedouin* (London: Virago, 2006).

Gellhorn, Martha, 'The Arabs of Palestine', in Martha Gellhorn (ed.), *The View from the Ground* (Cambridge: Granta Books, 1989), pp. 197–244; originally published in the *Atlantic Monthly*, October 1961.

Ghoussoub, Mai, *Selected Writings*, ed. Rebecca O'Connor (London: Saqi, 2008).

Guène, Faïza, *Kiffe Kiffe Demain* (Paris: Hachette, 2004).

Haddad, Joumana, *I Killed Scheherazade: Confessions of an Angry Arab Woman* (London: Saqi Books, 2010).

Hajji, Sadek and Stéphanie Marteau, *Voyage dans la France musulmane* (Paris: Plon, 2005).

Hal, Fatéma, *Fille des frontières: récit* (Paris: Philippe Rey, 2011).

Halimi, Gisèle, *Milk for the Orange Tree*, trans. D. S. Blair (London: Quartet, 1990).

Hamel, Christelle and Christine Delphy, 'On vous a tant aimé.e.s! Entretien avec Houria Boutelja', *Nouvelles Questions Féministes*, 25, 1 (2006), 122–35.

Hamilton, Elizabeth, *Put Off Thy Shoes: a Journey to Israel and Jordan* (London: Andre Deutsch, 1957).

Hamilton, Lesley, *Where the Mountains Roar: in Search of the Sinai Desert* (London: Victor Gollancz, 1980).

Hirsi Ali, Ayaan, *The Caged Virgin: a Muslim Woman's Cry for Reason* (London: Simon and Schuster, 2006).

Hobson, Sarah, *Through Persia in Disguise* (London: John Murray, 1973).

Hoffman, Adina, *House of Windows: Portraits from a Jerusalem Neighborhood* (London: Arcadia Books, 2001).

Jaber, Hala, *The Flying Carpet to Baghdad: One Woman's Fight for Two Orphans of War* (London: Pan, 2010).

Janmohamed, Shelina Zahra, *Love in a Headscarf: Muslim Woman Seeks the One* (London: Aurum, 2009).

Kanafani, Deborah, *Unveiled: How an American Woman Found Her Way through Politics, Love and Obedience in the Middle East* (New York: Free Press, 2008).

Karmi, Ghada, *In Search of Fatima: a Palestinian Story* (London: Verso, 2002).

Kenyon, Kathleen M., *Archaeology in the Holy Land* (1960; London: Ernest Benn, 1979).

Khorsandi, Shappi, *A Beginner's Guide to Acting English* (n.p.: Ebury Press, 2009).

Khouri, Norma, *Forbidden Love: Love and Betrayal in Modern-day Jordan* (London: Doubleday, 2003).

Lamb, Christina, *The Sewing Circles of Herat: My Afghan Years* (London: HarperCollins, 2002).

Latifa, with Chékéha Hachemi, *My Forbidden Face: Growing Up under the Taliban: a Young Woman's Story*, trans. Lisa Appignanesi (London: Virago, 2002).

Latifi, Afschineh with Pablo F. Fenjives, *Even After All This Time: a Story of Love, Revolution, and Leaving Iran* (London: Fusion, 2005).

Levy, Juliette de Baïracli, *Summer in Galilee* (London: Faber and Faber, 1959).

Mahdavi, Pardis, *Passionate Uprisings: Iran's Sexual Revolution* (Stanford, Calif.: Stanford University Press, 2009).

Mahmoody, Betty with William Hoffer, *Not Without My Daughter* (London: Corgi Books, 1988).

Maillart, Ella K., *The Cruel Way* (1947; London: Virago Press, 1986).

Malik, Zaiba, *We are a Muslim, Please* (London: Windmill Books, 2011).

Matar, Dina, *What It Means to be Palestinian: Stories of Palestinian Peoplehood* (London: I. B. Tauris, 2011).

Mehdevi, Anne Sinclair, *Persia Revisited* (London: Michael Joseph, 1964).

Mernissi, Fatima, *The Harem Within* (London: Doubleday, 1994).

Moaveni, Azadeh, *Lipstick Jihad: a Memoir of Growing Up Iranian in America and American in Iran* (New York: Public Affairs, 2005).

Modiano, Colette, *Turkish Coffee and the Fertile Crescent: Wanderings through the Lebanon, Mesopotamia, Israel, Jordan and Syria* (London: Michael Joseph, 1974).

Murphy, Dervla, *Full Tilt: Ireland to India with a Bicycle* (London: Eland, 1965).

Murphy, Dervla, *Tales from Two Cities: Travel of Another Sort* (London: John Murray, 1987).

Nafisi, Azar, *Reading Lolita in Tehran: a Memoir in Books* (New York: Random House, 2003).

Nathan, Susan, *The Other Side of Israel: My Journey Across the Jewish-Arab Divide* (New York: Doubleday, 2005).

Nedjma, *L'Amande, récit intime* (Paris: Plon, 2004).

Nivat, Anne, *Lendemains de guerre en Afghanistan et en Irak* (Paris: Athème Fayard, 2004).

Nomani, Asra Q., *Standing Alone in Mecca: an American Woman's Struggle for the Soul of Islam* (San Francisco: HarperSanFrancisco, 2005).

Norris, Daniela and Shireen Anabtawi, *Crossing Qalandiya: Exchanges across the Israeli/Palestinian Divide* (London: Reportage, 2010).

Oufkir, Malika with Michele Fitoussi, *La Prisonnière*, trans. Ros Schwartz (London: Doubleday, 2000).

Phillips, Melanie, *Londonistan: How Britain is Creating a Terror State Within* (London: Gibson Square, 2006).

Puigaudeau, Odette du, *Tagent: Au coeur du pays maure, 1936–1938* (n.p.: Phébus, 1993).

Rachlin, Nahid, *Persian Girls: a Memoir* (New York: Penguin, 2006).

Randall, Rona, *Jordan and the Holy Land* (London: Frederick Muller, 1968).

Rimington, Stella, *Open Secret: the Autobiography of the Former Director-General of MI5* (London: Hutchinson, 2001).

Roberts, Na'ima B., *From My Sisters' Lips: a Unique Celebration of Muslim Womanhood* (London: Bantam Books, 2005).

Rodriguez, Deborah, *The Kabul Beauty School: the Art of Friendship and Freedom* (London: Hodder & Stoughton, 2008).

Rowlatt, Bee and May Witwit, *Talking about Jane Austen in Baghdad* (London: Penguin Books, 2010).

Saadawi, Nawal El, *The Hidden Face of Eve: Women in the Arab World*, trans. Dr Sherif Hetata (London: Zed Books, 1980).

Sackville-West, Vita, *Passenger to Teheran* (1926; London: Tauris Parke, 2007).

Sadat, Jehan, *A Woman of Egypt* (London: Bloomsbury, 1987).

Salbi, Zainab with Laurie Beckland, *Between Two Worlds: Escape into Tyranny; Growing Up in the Shadow of Saddam* (New York: Gotham, 2005).

Schwarzenbach, Annemarie, *La mort en Perse*, trans. Dominique Laure Miermont (1935; Paris: Editions Payot & Rivages, 2001).

Sebbar, Leïla, *Mes Algéries en France* (Saint-Pourçain-sur-Sioule: Bleu Autour, 2004).

Seierstad, Åsne, *The Bookseller of Kabul*, trans. Ingrid Christophersen (London: Little, Brown, 2003).

Stark, Freya, *A Winter in Arabia* (1940; London: Arrow Books, 1991).

Stratton, Allegra, *Muhajababes* (London: Constable, 2006).

Tajadod, Nahal, *Passeport à l'iranienne* (Paris: JC Lattès, 2007).

Tamzali, Wassyla, *Une femme en colère: lettre d'Alger aux Européens désabusés* (Paris: Gallimard, 2009).

Tawil, Raymonda Hawa, *My Home, My Prison* (New York: Holt, Rinehart and Winston, 1979).

Warsi, Sayeeda, 'The 2011 University of Leicester Sir Sigmund Sternberg Lecture', 20 January 2011, *http://www.sayeedawarsi.com/2011/01/university-of-leicester-sir-sigmund-sternberg-lecture/*, accessed 23 January 2011.

Wharton, Edith, *In Morocco* (1920; London: I. B. Tauris, 2006).

Wighton, Suzy, *One Day at a Time: Diaries from a Palestinian Camp* (London: Hutchinson, 1990).

Williams, Emma, *It's Easier to Reach Heaven than the End of the Street: a Jerusalem Memoir* (London: Bloomsbury, 2006).

Wilson, G. Willow, *The Butterfly Mosque: a Young Woman's Journey to Love and Islam* (London: Atlantic Books, 2010).

Woodsmall, Ruth Frances, *Women and the New East* (Washington: The Middle East Institute, 1960).

Other Published Texts

Abu-Rabi', Ibrahim M., *Contemporary Arab Thought: Studies in Post-1967 Arab Intellectual History* (London: Pluto, 2004).

Ahmed, Akbar S. and Hastings Donnan (eds), *Islam, Globalization and Postmodernity* (London: Routledge, 1994).

Ahmed, Akbar S. and Hastings Donnan, 'Islam in the age of postmodernity', in Akbar S. Ahmed and Hastings Donnan (eds), *Islam, Globalization and Postmodernity* (London: Routledge, 1994), pp. 1–20.

Al-Azmeh, Aziz, *Islams and Modernities* (2nd edn; London: Verso, 1996).

Ali, Haider Ibahim, 'The other's image: the sociology of difference', in Tahar Labib (ed.), *Imagining the Arab Other: How Arabs and Non-Arabs View Each Other* (London and New York: I. B. Tauris, 2008), pp. 17–34.

Altink, Henrice and Sharif Gemie, 'Borders: ancient, modern and postmodern; definition and debates', in Henrice Altink and Sharif Gemie (eds), *At the Border: Margins and Peripheries in Modern France* (Cardiff: University of Wales Press, 2008), pp. 1–23.

Anon., *Les Mille et une nuits vol I*, trans. Antoine Gallard, p. 34, downloaded from *http://www.ebooksgratuits.com*.

Appadurai, Arjun, *Modernity at Large: Cultural Dimensions of Globalization* (Minneapolis: University of Minnesota Press, 1996).

Armstrong, Karen, *Islam: a Short History* (London: Phoenix, 2001).

Barrell, John, 'Death on the Nile: fantasy and the literature of tourism, 1840–60', in Catherine Hall (ed.), *Cultures of Empire: Colonizers in Britain and the Empire in the Nineteenth and Twentieth Centuries* (Manchester: Manchester University Press, 2000), pp. 187–206.

Basmenji, Kaveh, *Tehran Blues: Youth Culture in Iran* (London: Saqi, 2005).

Bauman, Zygmunt, *Globalization: the Human Consequences* (Cambridge: Polity, 1998).

Bauman, Zygmunt, 'Reconnaissance wars on the planetary frontierland', *Theory, Culture and Society*, 19, 4 (2002), 81–90.

Bennett, Clinton, *Muslims and Modernity: an Introduction to the Issues and Debates* (London: Continuum, 2005).

Beverley, Jon, 'The margin at the centre', in S. Smith and J. Watson (eds), *Decolonizing the Subject* (Minneapolis: University of Minnesota Press, 1992), pp. 91–114.

Bhabha, Homi K., *The Location of Culture* (London: Routledge, 1994).

Booth, Ken and Tim Dunne, 'Worlds in collision', in Ken Booth and Tim Dunne (eds), *Worlds in Collision* (Houndsmill: Palgrave MacMillan, 2002).

Buchsenschutz, Olivier and Alain Schnapp, 'Alésia', in P. Nora (ed.), *Les Lieux de Mémoire*, III (Paris: Quarto/Gallimard, 1997), pp. 4103–40.

Bullock, Katherine, *Rethinking Muslim Women and the Veil: Challenging Historical & Modern Stereotypes* (2nd edn; Herndon: International Institute of Islamic Thought, 2002).

Burke, Peter, *Cultural Hybridity* (Cambridge: Polity Press, 2009).

Caldwell, Christopher, *Reflections on the Revolution in Europe: Immigration, Islam and the West* (London: Penguin, 2010).

Carlyle, Thomas, *Chartism* (London: James Fraser, 1840).

Chibani, Ali, 'Au miroir brouillé du petit écran', *Monde Diplomatique* (February 2009), 9.

Dabashi, Hamid, 'Native informers and the American empire', *El-Ahram Weekly Online*, 1 June 2006, *http://weekly.ahram.org.eg/2006/797/special.htm*, accessed 2 March 2011.

Dabashi, Hamid, *Post-orientalism: Knowledge and Power in Time of Terror* (New Brunswick: Transaction Publishers, 2009).

Davis, Kathleen, 'Time behind the veil: the media, the Middle Ages and orientalism now', in Jeffrey Jerome Cohen (ed.), *The Postcolonial Middle Ages* (Houndmills: MacMillan, 2000), pp. 105–22.

Debray, Régis, *Eloge des frontières* (Paris: Gallimard, 2010).

Dietler, Michael, 'A tale of three sites', *World Archaeology*, 30, 1 (1998), 72–89.

Djavann, Chahdortt, *Bas les voiles!* (Paris: Gallimard, 2003).

Djavann, Chahdortt, *Comment peut-on être français?* (Paris: Flammarion, 2006).

Djavann, Chardortt, *A mon corps défendant, l'Occident* (Paris: Flammarion, 2007).

El Alaoui, Hicham Ben Abdallah, 'Retour vers le futur dans le monde arabe', *Monde Diplomatique*, 665 (August 2009), 10–11.

El Alaoui, Hicham Ben Abdallah, 'Les intellectuels arabes entres Etats et intégrisme', *Monde diplomatique*, 677 (August 2010), 1, 20–1.

El Guindi, Fadwa, *Veil: Modesty, Privacy and Resistance* (Oxford: Berg, 1999).

Ellinghaus, Katherine, *Taking Assimilation to Heart: Marriages of White Women and Indigeneous Men in the United States and Australia, 1887–1937* (Lincoln and London: University of Nebraska Press, 2006).

Fanon, Frantz, *Peau noire, masques blancs* (1952; Paris: Seuil, 1975).

Faqir, Fadia, 'Cultural illiteracy', *The Author* (spring 2011), 18–19.

Ferraris, Zoë, *City of Veils* (London: Little, Brown, 2010).

Galilea, Carlos, 'Voces femeninas del Magreb', *El País*, 11 June 2011, 20–1.

Gellner, Ernest, *Muslim Society* (Cambridge: Cambridge University Press, 1981).

Gemie, Sharif, 'France, Orientalism and Algeria: fifty-four articles from the *Revue des Deux Mondes*, 1846–1852', *Journal of Algerian Studies*, 3 (1998), 48–70.

Gemie, Sharif, 'An extremism of the center: Jean-Pierre Chevènement, French presidential candidate, 2002', *French Politics, Culture and Society*, 22, 1 (2004), 76–97.

Gemie, Sharif, *French Muslims: New Voices in Contemporary France* (Cardiff: University of Wales Press, 2010).

Hasan, Rumy, *Multiculturalism: Some Inconvenient Truths* (London: Politico's, 2010).

Huntington, Samuel P., *The Clash of Civilizations and the Remaking of the World Order* (London: Simon and Schuster, 1997).

Iskandar, Adel, '"Whenever, Wherever!" The discourse of orientalist transnationalism in the construction of Shakira', *Ambassadors*, 6, 2 (2003), available at *http://ambassadors.net.archives/issue14/selected_studies4.htm*, accessed 15 November 2010.

Kinder, Elizabeth, 'A complex life', *FolkRoots*, 334 (April 2011), 29–31.

Kinnvall, Catarina and Paul Nesbitt-Larking, *The Political Psychology of Globalization: Muslims in the West* (Oxford: Oxford University Press, 2011).

Kivisto, Peter, *Multiculturalism in a Global Society* (Oxford: Blackwell, 2002).

Kiwan, Nadia, *Identities, Discourses and Experiences: Young People of North African Origin in France* (Manchester and New York: Manchester University Press, 2009).

Kymlicka, Will, *Multicultural Odysseys: Navigating the New International Politics of Diversity* (Oxford: Oxford University Press, 2007).

Lambert-Hurley, Siobhan, 'Afterword: Muslim women write their journeys abroad', in *A Princess's Pilgrimage: Nawab Sikander Begum's 'A Pilgrimage to Mecca'*, ed. Siobhan Lambert-Hurley (Mansfield: Kube, 2007), pp. 155–72.

Lapidus, Ira M., 'State and religion in Islamic societies', *Past and Present*, 151 (1996), 3–27.

Lessing, Doris, 'Preface', *The Golden Notebook* (London: Flamingo, 1993).

LeVine, Mark, *Heavy Metal Islam: Rock, Resistance and the Struggle for the Soul of Islam* (New York: Three Rivers Press, 2008).

Lewis, Bernard, 'The question of Orientalism', in A. L. Macfie (ed.), *Orientalism: a Reader* (Edinburgh: Edinburgh University Press, 2000), pp. 249–70.

Lewis, Reina, *Gendering Orientalism: Race and Femininity and Representation* (London: Routledge, 1996).

Macfie, A. L. (ed.), *Orientalism: a Reader* (Edinburgh: Edinburgh University Press, 2000).

MacLean, Rory, *Magic Bus: On the Hippie Trail from Istanbul to India* (Harmondsworth: Penguin, 2007).

Majid, Anouar, 'The politics of feminism in Islam', *Signs*, 32, 2 (1998), 321–61.

Majumdar, Margaret A., *Postcoloniality: the French Dimension* (New York: Berghahn Books, 2007).

Malik, Kenan, *From Fatwa to Jihad: the Rushdie Affair and its Legacy* (London: Atlantic Books, 2009).

Malti-Douglas, Fedwa, *Medicines of the Soul: Female Bodies and Sacred Geographies in a Transnational Islam* (Berkeley: University of California Press, 2001).

Martín-Muñoz, Gema, 'Islam's women under Western eyes' (2 October 2002), http://www.opendemocracy.net/faith-europe_islam/article_498.jsp, accessed 13 March 2006.

Masalha, Nur, *The Bible and Zionism: Invented Traditions, Archaeology and Post-colonialism in Palestine-Israel* (London: Zed Books, 2007).

Melman, Billie, *Women's Orients: English Women and the Middle East, 1718–1918* (2nd edn; Houndsmill: MacMillan, 1995).

Milani, Farzaneh, 'On women's captivity in the Islamic world', *Merip*, 246 (2008), http://www.merip.org/mer/mer246, accessed 4 June 2008.

Mills, Sara, *Discourses of Difference: an Analysis of Women's Travel Writing and Colonialism* (London: Routledge, 1991).

Mitchell, W. T. J., 'Translator translated (interview with cultural theorist Homi Bhabha)', prelectur.stanford.edu/lecturers/bhabha/interview.html, accessed 18 June 2007; originally published in *Artforum* 33, 7 (1995), 80–4.

Mohanty, Chandra Talpade, '"Under Western Eyes" revisited: feminist solidarity through anticapitalist struggle', *Signs*, 28, 2 (2002), 499–535.

Nafisi, Azar, *Things I've Been Silent About: Memories* (New York: Random House, 2008), p. xv.

Nair, Janaki, 'Uncovering the *zenena*: visions of Indian womanhood in Englishwomen's writings, 1813–1940', in Catherine Hall (ed.), *Cultures of Empire: Colonizers in Britain and the Empire in the Nineteenth and Twentieth Centuries* (Manchester: Manchester University Press, 2000), pp. 224–45.

Patai, Raphael, *The Arab Mind* (rev. edn; New York: Hatherleigh Press, 2002).

Paul, Kathleen, 'Communities of Britishness: migration in the last gasp of empire', in Stuart Ward (ed.), *British Culture and the End of Empire* (Manchester: Manchester University Press, 2001), pp. 180–99.

Pomian, Krystof, 'Franks et Gauls', in P. Nora (ed.), *Les Lieux de Mémoire*, II (Paris: Quarto/Gallimard, 1997), pp. 2245–300.

Prakash, Gyan, 'Orientalism now', *History and Theory*, 34, 3 (1995), pp. 199–212.

Pratt, Mary Louise, *Imperial Eyes: Travel Writing and Transculturation* (London and New York: Routledge, 1992).

Radhakrishnan, R., 'Ethnicity in an age of diaspora', in Jana Evans Braziel and Anita Mannur (eds), *Theorizing Diaspora: a Reader* (Oxford: Blackwell, 2003), pp. 119—31.

Rahal-Sidhoum, Dada, 'Féministe et de culture musulmane dans la société française: une identité sans contrôle', *Confluences Méditerranée*, 59, 4 (2006), 115–24.

Rais, Shah Muhammad, *Once Upon a Time There Was a Bookseller in Kabul* (n.p.: Shah M. Book Co., 2007).

Robertson, Roland, *Globalization: Social Theory and Global Culture* (London: Sage, 1992).

Rowson, Richard, *Working Ethics: How to be Fair in a Culturally Complex World* (London: Jessica Kingsley, 2006).

Olivier Roy, *L'Islam mondialisé* (Paris: Seuil, 2002).

Rutherford, Jonathan, 'The Third Space: interview with Homi Bhabha', in Jonathan Rutherford (ed.), *Identity: Community, Culture, Difference* (London: Lawrence and Wishart, 1990), pp. 207–21.

Said, Edward, *Orientalism* (Harmondsworth: Penguin, 1978).

Saktander, Ay_e, *Living Islam: Women, Religion and the Politicization of Culture in Turkey* (London: Tauris, 2002).

Salih, Ruba, 'Shifting boundaries of self and other; Moroccan migrant women in Italy', *European Journal of Women's Studies*, 7 (2000), 321–35.

Sand, Shlomo, *The Invention of the Jewish People*, trans. Yael Lotan (London: Verso, 2009).

Satrapi, Marjane, 'How can one be Persian?', in Lila Azam Zanganeh (ed.), *My Sister, Guard Your Veil; My Brother, Guard Your Eyes: Uncensored Iranian Voices* (Boston, Mass.: Beacon Press, 2006), pp. 20–3.

Saunders, Robert A., 'The ummah as nation: a reappraisal in the wake of the "Cartoons Affair"', *Nations and Nationalism*, 14, 2 (2008), 303–21.

Sherkarloo, Mahsa, 'Iranian women take on the constitution', *http://www.merip.org/mero/mero072105*, accessed 26 July 2005.

Soueif, Ahdaf, *The Map of Love* (London: Bloomsbury, 1999).

Spivak, Gayatri Chakravorty, 'Can the subaltern speak?', in Bill Ashcroft, Gareth Griffiths and Helen Tiffin (eds), *The Post-colonial Studies Reader* (2nd edn; London and New York: Routledge, 2006), pp. 28–37.

Sreberny, Annabelle and Gholan Khiabany, *Blogistan: the Internet and Politics in Iran* (London: I. B. Tauris, 2010).

Tarlo, Emma, *Visibly Muslim: Fashion, Politics, Faith* (Oxford: Berg, 2010).

Taylor, Charles, 'The politics of recognition', in Amy Gutmann (ed.), *Multiculturalism: Examining the Politics of Recognition* (Princeton: Princeton University Press, 1994), pp. 25–73.

Teo, Hsu-Ming, 'Wandering in the wake of empire: British travel and tourism in the post-imperial world', in Stuart Ward (ed.), *British Culture and the End of Empire* (Manchester: Manchester University Press, 2001), pp. 163–79.

Thompson, E. P., 'Time, work-discipline, and industrial capitalism', *Past and Present* 38, 1 (1967), 56–97.

Tomlinson, John, '"Watching Dallas": the imperialist text and audience research', in Frank J. Lechner and John Boli (eds), *The Globalization Reader* (London: Blackwell, 2000), pp. 307–15.

Vaughan, Alden T., 'From white man to redskin: changing Anglo-American perceptions of the American Indian', *American Historical Review*, 87, 4 (1982), 917–53.

Visram, Rozina, *Asians in Britain: 400 Years of History* (London: Pluto Press, 2002).

Voltaire, *Lettres philosophiques* (1734; Paris: Flammarion, 1964).

Ward, Stuart, '"No Nation could be broker": the satire boom and the demise of Britain's world role', in Stuart Ward (ed.), *British Culture and the End of Empire* (Manchester: Manchester University Press, 2001), pp. 91–110.

Watson, Helen, 'Women and the veil: personal responses to global processes', in Akbar S. Ahmed and Hastings Donnan (eds), *Islam, Globalization and Postmodernity* (London: Routledge, 1994), pp. 141–59.

West, Patrick, *The Poverty of Multiculturalism* (London: Civitas, 2005).

Williams, Rowan, *Writing in the Dust: Reflections on 11th September and its Aftermath* (London: Hodder and Stoughton, 2002).

Woolf, Virginia, *Collected Essays*, vol. II (London: Hogarth Press, 1966).

Periodicals

El-Ahram Weekly
Guardian
The Irish Times
New York Times

Websites

http://www.indigenes-republique.fr/pir

Index